THE COURT OF FRANCE

IN THE SIXTEENTH CENTURY

VOLUME I.

The Court of France *IN THE SIX-
TEENTH CENTURY. BY CATH-
ERINE CHARLOTTE, LADY
JACKSON*

*IN TWO VOLUMES
VOLUME I.*

WILDSIDE PRESS

Large Paper Edition

This edition is limited to one thousand copies, of which this is Number 139

CONTENTS OF VOL. I.

CHAPTER I.
                                                    PAGE

Funeral of Anne of Brittany. — The Arrival in Paris. — The Royal Funeral Litter. — The Assembled Mourners. — The Royal Mourning. — The Funeral Oration. — The Queen's Benevolence. — "Perdam Babylonis Nomen!"— The Herald King-at-arms. — The Queen's Livre d'Heures. — Jean and Clément Marot. — The Maids of Honour. — Royal Sports and Banquets. — The Ladies Invited to Court. — A Startling Innovation. — A Change in the Social *Régime*. — Reproving the Bretonne Queen. — The Duchy of Brittany 1

CHAPTER II.

Consolation Offered. — Thirty-two, or Sixteen? — Le Bon Roi Louis Douze. — Betrothal of Claude and Francis. — The Royal Nuptials. — Gloomy Splendour. — His Highness of England. — The Battle of the Spurs. — The Royal Bride. — The Bride's Entry into Paris. — Bridal Festivities. — Maternal Anxiety. — Departing Guests. — Death of Louis XII. — Les Enfants sans Souci. — Cardinal Georges d'Amboise. — Louis' Severity in Italy . . . 19

CHAPTER III.

The Type of a New Generation. — Seeking Fortune's Favours. — Reward of Loyal Devotion. — Francis of Angoulême. — The New Court. — The Special Embassy. — Loving Inquiries. — The King's Public Entry. — The Hero of the Fête. — The Great Officers of the Crown. — The Widowed Queen. — The Ladies, Litters, and Mules. — The Loves of Mary and Brandon. — Francis Discomfited. — Mary's Letter to Her Brother. — The

Devil's "Puissance."— Marriage of Mary and Brandon. — The Crown Jewels 36

CHAPTER IV.

An Idolising Mother. — The King's Governor. — The Chevalier King. — The Chancellor Duprat. — Charles de Bourbon. — Admiral Bonnivet. — La Belle Françoise de Foix. — The Duke of Milan. — Schemes for Raising Money. — A Matrimonial Alliance. — Diplomacy of Sixteenth Century. — The Treaty of Dijon. — Pedro Navarro. — Guillaume Budé. — Madame Louise of Savoy. — Shedding a Joy on Duty. — Heart-breaking Leave-takings. — The Chivalry of the Period. — The Fascinations of Lyons. — A New Route over the Alps. — Perseverance and Success. — The Modern Hannibal. — Battle of Marignan. — An Advantageous Loss. — Knighting the King . . 53

CHAPTER V.

Pontiff and King. — Leo X. — The Court of the Vatican. — Francis Fascinated. — The Bologna Conference. — Francis in Italy. — The Hero's Return. — Te Deums and Dirges. — What a Falling-off is Here! — Madame Louise Alarmed. — Sainte Claude. — Death of Ferdinand of Spain. — Henry VIII. of England. — Maximilian Alarmed. — Bourbon Recalled. — Queen Joanna of Spain. — The Archduke King. — A Rival in Glory 76

CHAPTER VI.

The News on the Crossroads. — Thanksgiving for Victory. — Nocturnal Amusements. — Triboulet the Court Jester. — The Regency of Madame Louise. — The Clerks of the Basoche. — The Concordat. — A Refractory Parliament. — One Who Had Played Many Parts. — Propitiating the Pope. — Rapid Promotion. — Menacing the Judges. — Decease of the Pragmatique. — Depravity of the Clergy. — High Mass in the Ste. Chapelle. — Coronation of Queen Claude. — Chivalric Exploits. — Decorous Recreation . 9e

CHAPTER VII.

Splendour of the Papal Court. — Art, Literature, and Chivalry. — Leonardo da Vinci. — Pencil and Palette Laid

Aside. — A Death-bed Confession. — Movable Pictures. — Unveiling Raphael's Works. — Jean Goujon. — A Hopeless Passion. — The Château de Moulins. — Park and Grounds of Moulins. — O'ershadowed by a Cloud. — A Royal Dish of Windsor Beans. — A Dish to Set Before a King. — Salads and Fruits. — More Regal than the King. — Blessings on the New-born Babe . . . 108

CHAPTER VIII.

An Auspicious Event. — Matrimonial Contracts. — Betrothal of Princess Mary. — Supping with My Lord of York. — Grand and Singular. — The Youthful Fiancée. — The Daily Bill of Fare. — England and Bluff King Hal. — Right Good Wine and Supper. — Receiving the Embassy. — Embracing the Embassy. — Receiving the King's Letters. — A Ball at the Bastille. — The State Dinner. — A Puzzling Costume. — A Supposed Spurious Dauphin. — Restitution of Tournay. — The Port of Havre Founded. — A Penitential Procession. — A Check to His Holiness. — An Honourable Arrangement 124

CHAPTER IX.

A Coffin in Case of Need. — The Imperial Crown. — Reviving the Augustan Age. — The Royal College of France. — The Crowing of the Cock. — Full of Thorns and Vipers. — Erasmus and Voltaire. — Brother Martin Luther. — The Sale of Indulgences. — Under the Ban of the Church. — The Germanic Diet. — He Stands Erect! — Sensation! — A Learned Dominican. — Retract, My Friend, Retract. — Luther Escapes from Augsburg. — Saved for the Present. — Conciliating the Elector . . 143

CHAPTER X.

The Emperor Maximilian. — Maximilian's Poverty. — Rival Claims for Empire. — The Infidel Turk. — The Bankers Fugger. — Too Late in the Field. — Frederick of Saxony. — A Stripling of Limited Capacity. — Emerging from Obscurity. — The Spaniards Dissatisfied. — The Title of Majesty 159

CHAPTER XI.

A Dream of Glory and Grandeur. — Constantinople, or Death! — Sickness and Famine. — Free Gifts to the

King. — The Most Learned Prince. — A Good Calf to
His Leg. — England's True King. — Young, Gay, and
Gallant. — The Rival Monarchs. — Mutual Courtesies. —
Journeying Toward the Sea. — A Halt in the Preparations. — Europe Astounded. — The Feast of Pentecost. —
Europe's Mightiest Prince. — The Old Spanish Doubloons.
— Espials and Counter-espials. — The Cardinal Visits the
King. — The Signal to Advance. — The Royal Retinue.
— The Chevalier King Approaches. — An Embrace on
Horseback. — Dwelling in Tents. — Henry's Visit to
Queen Claude. — Incurring a Risk. — The Royal Wrestlers. — French and English Fashions. — A More Businesslike Meeting 169

CHAPTER XII.

A Round of Flying Visits. — Check to the King of France.
— The Crown of Charlemagne. — Compensating Ferdinand.— Ignacio da Loyola.— Dona Maria Pacheco.— The
Romance of War. — The Monk of Wittemberg. — Burning the Papal Bull. — A Revolution. — Just and Generous. — Cropped Hair and Flowing Beard. — A Mark of
Noble Birth. — More Red Hats than Helmets. — "The
Hundred and One Grievances." — The Promise Given
Must Be Kept. — " The Lord is My Defence." — " If I Am
Wrong, Prove it to Me." — A Fearless Spirit. — Captured by Armed Horsemen. — A Transformation. — Mind
and Body Benefited. — The Defence of the Faith . . 195

CHAPTER XIII.

Rigid Ideas of Morality. — As Insensible as Ever. — Bent on
Wearing the Papal Crown. — War Begins in Earnest. —
Humiliating the Constable. — A Victory Missed. — An
Anxious Mother's Fears. — The Mother and the Mistress.
— Tardy Repentance. — Promises and Assurances. — Despotic Measures. — Dying of Laughter. — A Sudden Holy
Inspiration. — Driven Out of Lombardy. — The Proceeds
of Her Savings. — Stormy Family Scenes. — Vengeance
Accomplished 216

CHAPTER XIV.

A New Complication. — A Shock for the Cardinals. — Full
of Good Intentions. — The Inquisition. — The Imperial
Guest. — The Italian Emigrants. — The Rebuilding of

CONTENTS xi

PAGE

Chambord. — The Ambassador's Report. — Duprat at His Wits' End. — Colonel of the Scotch Guards. — The Insignia of Royal Justice.— Such Was His Good Pleasure. — Louise and Her Chancellor. — A Contribution to the Treasury. — Avenging a Private Pique. — A Strange Infatuation. — Madame Renée's Reply. — Advice of Anne de Beaujeu.— Was He Legitimate? — Mother and Son. — — Charles and Suzanne de Bourbon. — Too Absurd to Believe 231

CHAPTER XV.

The Great Bourbon *Procès*. — Bourbon and Charles V. — A Wealthy Bride Offered. — Ill-deserved Treatment.— The Lieutenant-General. — Not Such a Simpleton. — Under the Seal of Confession. — An Importunate Spy. — An Insolent Subject. — The Bourbon Plot.— The Capital in Danger. — A Horrifying Announcement. — A Too Lenient Parliament. — Stratagem of Madame Louise. — Mental Agony. — A Gloomy Procession. — A Message of Mercy. — Letters of Remission 251

CHAPTER XVI.

Sufferings of the Troops. — Bonnivet Wounded. — The Chevalier Bayard. — Death of the Chevalier. — A True Knight — Great and Good. — Driven Out of Italy. — Marseilles Besieged. — Three Needy Monarchs. — A March into Picardy and Back.—The Spoils of Mexico and Peru. — War Resumed in Italy. — Death of Queen Claude. — A Compliment to the Queen.— Funeral of Queen Claude. — " Plague-stricken Milan! " — Antonio da Leyva. — The Sentiment of Honour. — Georges Freundsberg. — Honour to Whom Honour is Due.— The Battle of Pavia. — A Delicate Sense of Honour. — Francis a Prisoner . 267

CHAPTER XVII.

Tout est perdu fors l'honneur. — Honour but Partly Satisfied. — Appeal to Charles's Generosity. — Meeting of Bourbon and Francis. — Bribing the Guard. — Escape of Henry d'Albret. — Alas! What a Hypocrite He Was! — Edifying Remarks. — To Arms! to Arms! — Embarrassing Requests. — An Alliance with Portugal. — The Spirit of Moderation. — A Cry of Indignation. — The Chevalier King Wavers.— Counter-propositions.— A Pledge of Reconciliation. — The Holy Italian League. — An Ungenerous Proceeding. — The Interesting Captive. — Meeting of Charles and Francis. — Marguerite's Diplomacy. — An Heroic Sacrifice. — Burgundy Ceded; Honour Saved. — The Armies of the Empire. — The Monarch's Return. — Not Long in Suspense 287

CHAPTER XVIII.

His Native Air Prescribed. — More Betrothals Proposed. — Increased Dissipation. — Mademoiselle d'Heilly. — A Numerous Family. — A Wayward Girl of Many Moods. — The Jewels Returned. — The Countess's Revenge. — The New *Maîtresse-en-titre*. — The Peasants' War. — A Cure for Lutheranism. — A Gallican Holy Office. — The Bishop and His Disciple. — The Hermit of Vitry. — Louis de Berquin. — Marriage of Marguerite. — A Restraint on Court Gaiety 310

CHAPTER XIX.

Anne Boleyn. — Vexing Her Liege Lord. — Amusing the Ambassadors. — Let Him Return to Captivity. — The Modern Regulus. — Great Services Recompensed. — Bourbon's Band of Adventurers. — Vivas for Bourbon. — The Grand Imperial Army. — In Pursuit of Bourbon. — The Doomed City. — Death of Charles de Bourbon. — Fruitless Prayers. — The Sack of Rome . . . 325

CHAPTER XX.

Relieved from a Difficulty. — Clement VII. a Prisoner. — War for the Release of the Pope. — The Pope's Ransom. — Clement Escapes in Disguise. — The Divorce and Absolution. — Burgundy or Captivity. — Royal Condescension! — A Bold and Startling Opinion. — Magnanimous Frenchmen! — The Challenge and the Reply. — The Chevalier King Holds Back. — Marriage of Madame Renée. — Madame Renée's Bridal Dress. — Edifying and Effective. — An Accomplished Pupil. — The French Fleet in the Levant. — Loss of a Faithful Ally. — Heretics and Infidels. — Two Wily Female Diplomatists. — The Ladies' Peace. — New Coinage for the Ransom. — Mutual Precautions. — The Spanish Bride. — Fall of Florence . 338

LIST OF ILLUSTRATIONS

Vol. I.

	PAGE
DIANE OF POITIERS	*Frontispiece*
ANNE OF BRITTANY	16
LOUIS XII.	34
ST. GERMAIN	106
CHARLES VIII.	160
HENRY VIII.	194
CASTLE OF BLOIS	278
LOUISE OF SAVOY, DUCHESSE D' ANGOULÊME	334

THE COURT OF FRANCE

IN THE SIXTEENTH CENTURY

1514—1559

CHAPTER I.

INTRODUCTORY.

N the morning of the 27th of January, 1514, a grand and solemn funeral pageant issued from the Château de Blois, accompanying to Paris, and thence to the royal sepulchre of St. Denis, the body of Anne of Brittany — the twice-crowned Queen of France — widow of Charles VIII., and wife of his successor, the then reigning monarch, Louis XII.

The lying in state of the deceased royal lady, in the superb apartment recently added to the Château de Blois, has been described as a scene of surpassing magnificence and solemnity, rendered more especially impressive by the youthful appearance of the queen and her singular beauty in death.

No royal funeral had been hitherto witnessed in France approaching in splendour that of this much-loved consort of Louis XII., whose premature death, on the 9th of January, in her thirty-seventh year, had plunged the king into deepest grief. Nor did the "Father of the people" mourn alone. For Anne of Brittany — the most distinguished of the queens of France — was much and sincerely regretted, not only by the Bretons, who adored her and were inconsolable for her loss, but by the French nation generally, who evinced much sympathy with the sorrow of the king.*

Owing to the inclemency of the season, and the wretched condition of the roads in those days, the last of the many stations, or appointed resting-places, on the journey from Blois to the Church of Notre-Dame des Champs, was not reached till the 14th of February. The funeral *cortége* was there joined by the chief members of the University, a numerous company of priests, and the superior clergy of the various churches of the capital, headed by the Archbishop of Paris, all wearing their richest vestments and carrying their distinctive banners and crosses.

Preceding the royal bier, they entered Paris by the Porte St. Jacques. There, a vast concourse of the people had assembled, anxiously expectant, yet of most reverent demeanour; for, when the

---
* Garnier, "*Histoire de France.*"

low, distant, wailing tones of the priests chanting the *Miserere* first reached the ear, all piously fell on their knees, and remained in that humble posture, bareheaded and with clasped hands, as if in prayer, until the whole procession had passed through the gate.

The mists of evening were o'erspreading the city, and, already, the mounted attendants had lighted their torches, thus adding much picturesque effect to the *cortége* of death, as the flickering rays, that relieved the gathering gloom of night, flashed on the gold and jewels adorning the sable garments of the cavalcade of mourners, and the trappings of their richly caparisoned horses. Black draperies covered the fronts of the houses in those streets through which the procession passed, and lighted torches were placed at the windows and doors of every dwelling.

Early on the morrow, the body of the late queen was removed from its temporary resting-place of the previous night, in the Cathedral of Notre-Dame de Paris, and borne to its final one in the Abbey of St. Denis. The bier was drawn by six black horses, their richly embroidered, gold-fringed housings reaching to the ground, covering them entirely. The length and weight of these too ample draperies greatly impeding the animals' movements, each horse was led by a *pale-frenier*, or groom, whose dress was of black velvet, satin and gold.

A crimson velvet pall, bordered with ermine, was thrown over the coffin. Above it was a litter, lined with cloth of gold, wherein lay an effigy of the late queen, magnificently arrayed in royal robes. At her head was a cushion of cloth of gold, on which stood the two crowns of France and Brittany. Her right hand held the sceptre, her left, the "hand of justice." A canopy of crimson silk, richly fringed, and embroidered with the French and Breton arms, surmounted the litter, around which the priests were grouped, praying or chanting the appointed canticles.

The princesses and ladies of the court, with the late queen's maids of honour, followed in litters,* closely covered — the cold being very severe — and curtained with velvet fringed with gold. On arriving at St. Denis, the body of the queen was placed in a splendid catafalque prepared for its temporary reception in the nave of the abbey, which was draped with elaborately embroidered velvet hangings, of crimson and black alternately. What little daylight yet remained was carefully excluded, and a dim religious light diffused through the sacred edifice by means of lamps concealed in partially darkened niches.

The sombre grandeur of the scene at the moment of commencing the service for the dead must have been strikingly impressive. The priests and the dignitaries of the Church, in their rich

* Carriages were not in use until several years later.

and varied vestments, were assembled around the catafalque. The princes of the blood, the princesses, and other ladies and gentlemen of the court, with the royal pages, having taken the places assigned them, the fifty gentlemen of the king's guards, and the same number of the queen's, who had formed the escort, ranged themselves in their rear, while behind these, filling up the nave, stood the numerous train of attendants.

The ladies wore magnificent robes of rich, black damask interwoven with gold, with sweeping trains and hanging Venetian sleeves lined with fur. A long, black veil of Italian tissue was attached by a diamond clasp, or brooch, to a small, round, velvet hat with a turned-up brim, edged with gold and pearls,—a head-dress that had been introduced by Anne herself, at her first coronation.*

Doublet, vest, trunk-hose, and mantle, all of sable hue, but enriched with gold, were worn by the princes and courtiers who accompanied the *cortége*,— a velvet hat with small black plume, the brim looped up at the side with diamond or pearl, completing their mourning costume. The royal guards and the rest of the retinue were also habited in black, material and embroidery being more or less rich according to the rank of the

---

* Less appropriate, one would have thought, for this solemn occasion, than the veil and chaperon, or hood, she was accustomed to wear at a later period.

wearer. Thus, of violet, the former court mourning, not a trace appeared, except in the vestments of the clergy; for, in deference to the wishes of the late queen, Louis had strictly prohibited it.

When Charles VIII. died, Anne had decreed that black should be worn, — "its unchangeable colour," she said, "being more suited to the outward expression of lasting grief on so melancholy an occasion than the quickly fading violet, which seemed to denote a like transientness in the sorrow of the wearer." She herself wore black, rejecting the usual white robes of the *reines blanches* — a term then applied to the widowed queens of France, because of their colourless mourning.*

---

* Yet within nine months of Charles's death Anne exchanged her black robes — symbol of the constancy of grief — for the rich and elegant ones of blue and gold damask, in which for the second time she became a king's bride. True, she was interdicted by her first marriage contract from marrying a second time, in the event of the king dying without male heirs, except to Charles's successor, or to that successor's heir. For it was imperative that Anne's noble dowry — the Duchy of Brittany with its hundred leagues of coast-line and hardy population — should not be alienated from France, but become an integral part of it by the marriage above indicated. There, however, existed, independently of this, a strong mutual inclination for the matrimonial alliance; and Anne, in her grief for the faithless Charles, was soon consoled by Charles's successor. According to Sismondi, she was betrothed to Louis XII. in the second month of her widowhood. Another historian (Henri Martin) says the fourth. At all events, before their marriage could take place Louis's divorce from poor deformed Jeanne de France, to whom Louis XI. had married him when a boy, had to be obtained

When the funeral service was ended, the archbishop began his oration.

Those were not the days of great pulpit orators, though mass, followed by a very plain-spoken sermon, often drew large congregations. But no Bossuets, or Bourdaloues, Fléchiers or Massillons, had yet appeared to thrill the hearts of their hearers and call forth vivid emotion as, with eloquent exaggeration, they extolled the virtue, the heroism, or other great qualities attributed to the noble or royal deceased. Anne, however, had merits sufficiently conspicuous to inspire a less gifted orator with a warm and deserved eulogism.

Though sometimes accused of loving her native Brittany far more than she ever loved France, and of possessing a very full share of the self-will and overbearing temper supposed to be characteristic of the Breton race, none have denied her great benevolence, and much thoughtful care for the aged poor, for whom she built an asylum.

The large revenue derived from her duchy — nearly the whole of which was assigned to her separate use — she employed to a considerable extent in recompensing services rendered to the

---

from the Pope. Louis was then thirty-six; Anne was twenty-two, a charmingly piquante brunette, full of *esprit* and intelligence, as described by the Venetian ambassador, Contarini. "She had naturally," he says, "an air of dignity, and very gracious manners, though rather haughty when displeased. A slight limp in her walk she very skilfully concealed by a difference of height in the heels of her shoes."

state; in rewarding those who had distinguished themselves in the wars by brilliant achievements or acts of bravery; in assuring an honourable retirement to officers and men disabled by wounds from further service, and generally, as the archbishop forcibly urged, in befriending the poor and the unfortunate — whether of Brittany or France.*

Anne, who was sincerely pious, had been greatly grieved by the discord and enmity so long subsisting between Louis XII. and the warlike, implacable Pope, Julian II. To such extremes had hostile feeling been carried that Louis, after convoking a council of the clergy at Tours, declared the Pope deprived of the exercise of his papal functions, and also struck a medal with the bold inscription, "*Perdam Babylonis nomen!*"

Julian retaliated by proclaiming Louis dethroned, and offering his kingdom to any other power that chose to take possession of it. Vain words, of course. At the same time he transferred the French monarch's title of "Most Christian King" to Henry VIII. of England. Henry, then but in his twenty-first year, evinced the greatest horror at the prospect of schism, with which the Church at that time was menaced; and Julian, further to stimulate the piety of this apparently most devoted of its sons, sent Henry the golden rose that year.

But when the aged yet intrepid prelate was

* See Garnier, "*Histoire de France.*"

suddenly stricken by death, almost on the battle-field, and was succeeded by Leo X., then Anne, in failing health and near her end, urged the king to seek reconciliation with the Papal Court. Regarding it as her dying request, Louis consented.

Leo, secretly, was no less hostile than his predecessor to France and her king; but, unlike Julian, he had not personally insulted Louis XII. With but little difficulty, therefore, peace with Rome ensued — a peace, in accordance with the political chicanery of the time, to last as long as it suited the convenience or good pleasure of either party to maintain it. The French clergy, however, whose interests were served by the queen's intercession, declared it the most meritorious act of her life, "ensuring her a heavenly crown in exchange for her earthly one." It was lauded by the archbishop accordingly, and with it his eulogium ended.

The abbey gates were then thrown open, and on the threshold appeared the herald king-at-arms on horseback. In loud yet solemn tones he proclaimed the death of "the illustrious sovereign lady, Anne, most Christian Queen of France, Duchess of Brittany, and Comtesse d' Étampes." Advancing a pace or two, he repeated this announcement, and again a third time at the entrance of the nave.* This concluded the funeral cere-

* Brantôme, "*Dames illustres.*"

mony. The archbishop then gave his blessing, and, after a moment or two of silent prayer, the throng of mourners dispersed in the order prearranged.

The Bretonne queen was distinguished for her royally munificent patronage of art no less than for piety and good deeds. More especially she encouraged native talent, which, in the opinion of several French writers — as regarded architecture and sculpture — had no need of Italian aid.* The splendid tomb she erected to her father, Duke Francis II., in the Cathedral of Nantes, was the work of a native artist, the famous Michel Columb, and is considered one of the *chefs-d'œuvre* of French sculpture.

Her *livre d'heures,* or prayer-book (preserved in the Louvre), is also a remarkable work of art, being a finely executed manuscript on vellum, beautifully illuminated with a series of designs representing the various operations of husbandry appropriate to each month of the year, with the plants, herbs and insects peculiar to it, designed in the margin and rendered with perfect fidelity. It is a work of the end of the fifteenth century, — a magnificent specimen of the skill and taste of the artists employed on it. Most probably it was

---

* "*En Italie,*" remarks M. Léon Palustre, in his work on the "Renaissance," "*tout renaît. En France c'est un simple renouvellement.*"

the work, or chiefly so, of Paganini, who with several other artists of ability, as mentioned by Comines, crossed the Alps with Charles VIII. on his return from Italy. Paganini appears to have been clever both as painter and sculptor, but to have excelled especially in the art of illuminating, which, as Anne doubtless soon discovered, was his favourite pursuit.*

In the course of her double reign of twenty-two years, Anne initiated many changes in the social *régime* of the court. Not only was she a patroness of learning, but was herself one of the learned ladies of her day. She read the ancient Greek and Latin authors, and had a considerable acquaintance with modern languages. To eminent men of letters, who sought the honour of being presented to her, she gave a very gracious reception, and was fond of conversing with them. The poets of the period — poets certainly of no great fame, yet a pleiad of twinkling luminaries, precursor of one of brighter lights — found a patron-

---

* Paganini was employed by Charles to carry out his projects for enlarging and embellishing the Château d' Amboise. A fatal accident soon terminated Charles's career, and Paganini was then selected to design and execute the tomb of his patron. It was of black marble with bronze figures, and is said to have been a fine work of art. Unfortunately it was destroyed at the Revolution. Comines thought so highly of it that he commissioned the artist to execute his tomb in a similar style, and the work was completed under the supervision of the man whose remains it was to cover. The tomb of Comines is now in the Louvre.

ess in the queen. Amongst them was Jean Marot, father of the more famous Clément; the youthful Clément being also her *protégé*, and his earlier productions read in the queen's apartment, while she and *"ses filles"* worked at their point-lace or tapestry.

A number of young ladies of noble birth, whom at first she was accustomed to call *"ses filles,"* but afterwards gave them the title of *"filles d' honneur,"* or maids of honour, resided in the palace under the queen's protection. They were carefully trained and educated to become her and her daughters' companions. Some were orphans, but all were slenderly provided for. When opportunity offered, however, advantageously to marry her maids, she either added considerably to their own small fortunes, or, when none was forthcoming, generously gave one.

Before the time of " Madame Anne, the duchess-queen," one might have well supposed that the Salic law not only rigidly excluded woman from the succession to the throne, but was as jealously intolerant of her presence at court, — if court it could be called, where no queen presided, no ladies attended.

The king, princes, courtiers, and nobility generally, when not actually engaged in war, which was seldom, or occupied with public affairs, — which meant chiefly devising new wars and new taxes, — found the relaxation best suited to their tastes and habits in rough sports and games. There was the mimic warfare of jousts and tournaments, by which the ancient spirit of chivalry was supposed to be sustained. There were the great hunts in the forests of Chaumont, Fontainebleau, St. Germain, or Vincennes; and when the day's exciting sport was ended, there was the amply spread supper-table to repair to, where jesting, practical joking, and boisterous mirth — partly inspired by goblets of Hypocras, champagne, or the potent old wines of the Juraçon — gave a keener zest to the viands killed in the chase.

Conspicuous amongst these were the roebuck, roasted whole and served with a sauce of balm-mint and fennel (recently imported into France with many other of the vegetable products of Italy), the highly flavoured haunch, and the wild boar's head. Royal dishes all of them, and substantial ones, too, on which only the great ones of the earth might then presume to feast. Italian cookery as yet scarcely satisfied the hearty appetites of these robust cavaliers, whose pleasures and amusements were all external, and who took but two meals a day.

To the calmer enjoyments of domestic life the men of this period, and especially those of the upper ranks, were utterly strangers. But a change in manners began, and, as regards social life, the step that may be "considered as signalising the passage from the middle ages to modern times, and from ancient barbarism to civilisation," * was taken when, at the close of the fifteenth century, Anne of Brittany — the first queen-consort of France who held a separate court — desired the ministers of state and foreign ambassadors who attended, to offer their congratulations on her marriage with Louis XII., to bring their wives and daughters with them when next they paid their respects to her. To the ladies, themselves, she sent her invitation, or royal command, to leave their gloomy feudal abodes, where they were sometimes immured for years together, and repair to the court of their sovereign lady at the Palais des Tournelles or Château de Blois.

The moment was well chosen. It was a festive occasion, and the fair châtelaines were by no means reluctant to obey the summons of their queen.

* The words above quoted are used by Sismondi with reference to the accession of Francis I. But they seem to apply with more force to an earlier date: 1st, as regards social life, to that great innovation which ushered in the sixteenth century — the establishing of a court of ladies by the Bretonne queen; 2d, with reference to the revival of art in France — surely it was the Cardinal Georges d'Amboise who, in 1599, struck with admiration of the marvels he beheld in Lombardy, induced Italian sculptors, architects, and painters to visit France, and employed them to superintend the building and embellishment of his splendid palace of Gaïllon (destroyed, unfortunately, at the Revolution), as well as in the erection of churches and other public edifices of Rouen, and in otherwise beautifying that city, the seat of his archbishopric. The cost of these great works was defrayed by the cardinal, who was no vainglorious patron, but a true lover of art.

But the lords of those ladies, and especially the more elderly ones, murmured greatly at the attempted startling innovation. Hitherto they were accustomed to expend their revenues chiefly on themselves. They must have gay court dresses, picturesque hunting costumes, horses, and dogs, and all the paraphernalia of the chase. Besides these, there was the splendid panoply of war, — the burnished helmets, the polished steel armour in which they were wont to encase themselves when, attended each by a suite of four or five horsemen similarly equipped, they went forth to fight their foes. Naturally, then, they were little disposed to incur any new outlay for wives and daughters that necessitated curtailment of their own.

By the younger courtiers Louis XII. was considered rather penurious. But, in fact, he was so unwilling to burden his people with taxes, that, beyond greatly embellishing his châteaux of Amboise and Blois (for which he employed native artists, under the direction of the great architect Fra-Giocondo), he refrained from gratifying any expensive tastes. But Anne disbursed with a more liberal hand, and kept up great state at her separate court, of Blois and Des Tournelles. She also dressed with great elegance and magnificence, and required the ladies who attended her to do likewise.

"What she has it in her mind to do," writes at this time the Ambassador Contarini, "she will certainly accomplish, whether it be by tears, smiles, or entreaties." And quietly but firmly, wholly disregarding the opposition of the elderly nobles, she effected the revolution she had long desired in the social *régime* of the court. The younger nobility and the *élite* of the world of art and letters entered readily into her views, and the receptions in the queen's apartment soon became a centre of great attraction. There, following the Italian fashion,— which Charles VIII. and Louis XII., it appears, had both found much to their taste,— sorbets and iced lemonade were served. Her banquets, too — for the duchess-queen had her banquets as well as the king — were arranged with more order and with especial regard to what was due to the ladies. Each lady had now her cavalier, which had not always been the case. Each guest had also a separate plate; for Anne would not dip in another's dish, though it were even the king's. Doubtless, the forks, long in use in Italy, would soon have been introduced at her table, had the reforming queen been spared. But they had yet to wait a century before finding in France a patron in the Duc de Montausier. *En attendant,* rose-water was handed round in silver basins.

The senior nobles, however, made no scruple of strongly hinting to the king that he would do well in this and other matters to yield less readily to the queen's domination.

To this he replied, "Some indulgence should be

Anne of Brittany.
Photo-etching from engraving by Hopwood.

conceded to a woman who loves her husband and is solicitous both for his honour and her own."

Yet, sometimes he did resist her wishes, and by fables and parables — notably, his favourite one of the does which had lost their antlers because they desired to put themselves on an equality with the stags — showed her that it was not seemly that woman's will should always prevail over her husband's. This mild method of administering reproof to "his Bretonne," as he was accustomed to call his queen, seems to have often amused, if it did not always convince her. However, to the Bretonne queen the merit undoubtedly belongs of setting the ladies of her court, in an age of lax morality, a much-needed example of virtuous conduct and conjugal fidelity, as well as of the useful employment of time and the cultivation of their minds.

Unhappily, her example was not always followed, even during her lifetime, as may be inferred from Louis's reply above quoted. But it was altogether set at naught when, after her decease and the accession of Francis to the throne, Louise of Savoy, the young king's mother, assumed the chief place at court. Anne's aversion to Louise was so intense that mortified feeling at the prospect of her Duchy of Brittany passing into the hands of the son of that depraved woman is said to have accelerated her death. But the dismemberment of France —

which to avert was a national consideration that naturally outweighed every other — would have been the result of the marriage, as desired by Anne, of her daughter Claude with the Archduke Charles of Austria.

CHAPTER II.

Consolation Offered. — Thirty-two, or Sixteen ? — Le Bon Roi Louis Douze. — Betrothal of Claude and Francis. — The Royal Nuptials. — Gloomy Splendour. — His Highness of England. — The Battle of the Spurs. — The Royal Bride. — The Bride's Entry into Paris. — Bridal Festivities. — Maternal Anxiety. — Departing Guests. — Death of Louis XII. — Les Enfants sans Souci. — Cardinal Georges d'Amboise. — Louis's Severity in Italy.

WHILE Louis XII., still in the first paroxysm of his grief, was bitterly bewailing the loss of his Bretonne — lying on the floor of his darkened apartment, according to the custom of the time, sobbing and weeping, and refusing to take nourishment — the wily Ferdinand of Spain, though leagued with the great powers of Europe against France, sought to console the royal widower by the offer of a youthful bride. Notwithstanding his wailings, his torrents of tears, and the undoubted sincerity of his attachment to Anne, Louis yet turned no unfavourable ear to this offer.

The chief inducement was the prospect it opened to him of a general peace; for France was attacked by enemies on all sides, and since the battle of Ravenna had been far from successful in opposing them. He was also influenced by the possible realisation of his long-cherished hope of leaving the crown to a son of his own.

As a preliminary to the matrimonial negotiation, a truce for a year was signed on the 13th of March, 1514. Ferdinand then offered the French king, as a pledge of his sincerity and amity, the hand of the twice-widowed Margaret of Austria, Governess of the Netherlands, and then thirty-two years of age; or that of the Princess Eleanora, sister of the Archdukes Charles and Ferdinand, and who was but in her sixteenth year. The sorrowing king rather inclined to a marriage with the younger princess, though Fleuranges states* that "for many reasons, Louis had no real wish to marry either."

Louis XII. was then fifty-three, but in constitution much older. Though never robust, his life had been wild and adventurous, and he had figured in his youth as gayest of the band of gay cavaliers. He had also suffered much in the wars from wounds and contusions, owing to frequent individual headlong charges of the enemy, — a practice, though faulty and dangerous, yet not uncommon, it appears, in those days amongst the splendidly equipped and really brave, but wholly undisciplined, corps of cavalry or gendarmerie, composed of the young nobility.† Defiant and daring, he was accustomed to say, when sometimes remon-

---

* "*Mémoires du Jeune Aventureux.*"

† Servan, "*Guerres des Français en Italie.*"

strated with for his recklessness, "I am not afraid; let those who are shelter themselves behind me."

But these brave days were past; the fire of youth was burnt out, and the once brilliant Louis d'Orléans was now "*le bon roi,*" the "Father of the people," and a confirmed invalid. Twice, during his reign of sixteen years, he had so nearly approached death's door as to have received extreme unction. On each occasion he had rallied, and again had invaded Italy at the head of his army; but frequent relapses of excessive languor now rendered him wholly unable to undergo any fatigue.

In 1510 he had deeply felt and mourned the loss of his lifelong friend, his "trusty Georges," Cardinal d'Amboise, the great patron of *les beaux* arts and letters, and Louis's first minister; indeed, the first who held that important office in France. Then the death, on the 11th of April, 1512, in the moment of victory, of his sister's son, his much-loved nephew, Gaston de Foix, the young hero of Ravenna, was a great affliction to the king, soon to be followed by a still keener sorrow, — the premature death of the queen.

Scarcely had her funeral taken place when, as mentioned above, new nuptials were proposed to the royal widower; while at the same time the States General earnestly appealed to him to fulfil the promise he had given to the nation in 1506.

At the risk of a war with Austria he had then yielded to the advice of the cardinal minister, and, to gratify the wishes of his people, betrothed his daughter, Madame Claude, to Comte Francis of Angoulême, the heir-presumptive to his throne; thereby declaring — the queen's consent and signature being also required — the contract of 1500 — by which Claude, an infant of a few months' old, was affianced to the Archduke Charles, also a babe in his cradle — null and void. The marriage of Claude and Francis was to take place when the former had completed her twelfth year, — at that period considered, it would seem, a suitable age for young ladies to marry.

Madame Claude was now half-way through her fifteenth year, and still the marriage ceremony had not taken place, Anne's repugnance to giving her daughter to Francis causing the delay. She has even been accused of an intention (Louis in 1506 being supposed to be on his death-bed) of making an effort to have the Salic law abolished in favour of her daughter, and to the exclusion of Francis from the throne. It is, however, more probable that if Louis XII. could have changed the order of succession, and put Gaston de Foix in the place of Francis, he would have willingly done so. Neither he nor Anne were very hopeful that one already old in vice, though young in years, would be likely to contribute to the happiness of their daughter, or to regard the welfare of his people so much as the gratification of his own extravagant tastes and vicious pleasures. "That big fellow," (*cè gros garçon*), Louis was in the habit of exclaiming, "will corrupt everything"(*gâtera tout*) — undo all that he had been solicitous to do for the good of the people.

Freed from the influence of the queen, the expectation was general that the nuptials of Claude and Francis would be no longer deferred. The king responded to the national wish by appointing the 11th of May for their celebration.

The marriage took place at the Château of St. Germain-en-laye; and the "Young Adventurer"* describes it as "the most splendid"— he might rather have said the most singular — "that had ever been witnessed, there being present ten thousand men no less richly dressed than the king, or M. d'Angoulême, the bridegroom." Yet, for such an occasion, the splendour was of a gloomy kind, for throughout the festivities, which lasted several weeks, this numerous and goodly company all wore deep mourning, "which," continues Fleuranges, "from respect to the late queen, was not put off even for the marriage-day by either man or woman."

This mourning-wedding was, however, a popular one, even in Brittany; the Bretons, "reserving their ancient rights and privileges," preferring union with France to becoming a dependency of

---

* This sobriquet, by which Fleuranges — who was a son of the Maréchal Robert de la Marck — was most frequently named, he gave himself.

Austria. But great difficulty, only overcome by intrigue, was made by Louis XII. to assigning the immediate possession of the duchy to Francis; yet no hesitation was shown by the Bretons to taking the oath of allegiance to their new duke and duchess.

Madame Claude had not inherited her mother's beauty, *esprit*, or self-asserting character; she was more gentle, if not more amiable, equally pious, but far less dignified. Francis had no affection for her; but, as he piqued himself on his chivalrous spirit, he was courteous and respectful in manner, as naturally a true chevalier would be towards any lady, even should she be his wife.

The bridal festivities were not yet ended when the proposed marriage of Louis XII. with Eleanor of Austria, which was to be the pledge and seal of a general peace, was suddenly broken off. "His highness of England," Henry VIII., had not been consulted in the matter, and now refused to sign the truce which Quintana, the Spanish king's secretary, had, without orders, subscribed to in his name. He was exceedingly wroth at the course secretly pursued by his unscrupulous father-in-law. For, having joined the league against Louis, Henry had nearly exhausted the full treasury left by his parsimonious father, in equipping a large army, which was to be ready to take the field in the spring, and with which he buoyed himself up with the hope that he would recover what it was his good pleasure to call "his kingdom of France." What a disappointment, then! The merry jingle of French marriage-bells was to silence the roar of English cannon! His highness would not have it so.

But Leo X., aware that in the interests of Italy peace, by whatever means obtained, was desirable, secretly sent his clerical agents to pacify the irritated monarch, who at length was induced to assent to the truce. It was, however, by the successful manœuvres of diplomacy that Henry was soon to be revenged on Ferdinand for the failure of his hopes in the manœuvres of his army.

The Duc de Longueville was then in England. He and the Chevalier Bayard had been taken prisoners on the 13th of April, 1513, at the battle of Guinegate, when an aristocratic and supposed invincible squadron of French cavalry was seized with so terrible a panic by the sudden appearance of a corps of English infantry that, forgetting their swords, they put spurs to their horses and fled in the wildest disorder; hence this brilliant affair was called the "Battle of the Spurs." Bayard and the duke, disdaining to follow their terror-stricken companions, became prisoners of war.

The courteous, pleasing manners of the duke secured him the friendship and confidence of the English king, who allowed him, being a skilful player, to win, at the then favourite game of mall, the price of his ransom, fixed at 200,000 crowns. He, therefore, relying on the king's favour, ventured to propose, as the most desirable means of securing peace, a marriage between the Princess Mary, Henry's youngest sister, and Louis XII.

Wolsey, being well disposed towards a French alliance, entered readily into these views, and undertook to lay the matter before the king, who for his own part raised no objection to it, certain though it was that a union with France would not be popular in England. Yet the mortification its announcement would occasion Ferdinand made it acceptable to Henry. Mary had been betrothed to the Archduke Charles after Louis had broken his engagement with Austria, to whom another rebuff of the same kind was now offered by England. Charles wanted yet some months of being of age, so could not claim his bride himself; and his grandfather, the Emperor Maximilian, refrained from claiming her for him.

Peace being a necessity for France, a formal request for the hand of the Princess Mary was made by the Duc de Longueville in the name of the king. The old nobility, represented by the Duke of Norfolk, opposed the match; and the princess herself, as we learn from her letters to Henry after she became a widow, " had no mind to it." *   She was a girl of sixteen, and deeply in love with Charles Brandon, Duke of Suffolk. The attachment was mutual, and not unknown to Henry. Mary seems to have been induced to consent to be sacrificed to political considerations, and to become Queen of France, by a promise that *when free* she should bestow her hand where she pleased. A hint was doubtless given that her freedom would probably not be long deferred.

After some discussion between the ambassadors concerning the surrender or retention of Tournay, of which Henry in the preceding year had taken possession, the marriage contract was signed in London, August the 7th, 1514, Mary's portion being 400,000 crowns, guaranteed by Henry. On the 13th, the marriage, by proxy, was solemnized at Greenwich, the Duc de Longueville representing the king. This union was considered politically advantageous to France, as putting an end to a dangerous war with which the country was threatened. " It was also Wolsey's first great triumph in diplomacy, sealing his supremacy and the downfall of the old nobility." †

On the 15th or 16th Mary left England. She was conducted in great state to Boulogne, the king awaiting her arrival at Abbeville. He did not leave Paris to meet his young bride until the

* See "Calendar of State Papers," Foreign Series, 1514–16.; Brewer's Introduction, etc.
† Brewer's Introduction.

22d of September, while she did not reach Abbeville until the 9th of October. The journey must, therefore, have been accomplished in the most leisurely manner possible. This may have been owing to the very numerous retinue accompanying her,— thirty-six English ladies and several gentlemen, amongst whom was Brandon, and a very large number of attendants.*

The marriage ceremony again took place on the 11th, and Louis appears to have been much pleased with his English bride. But her liveliness and the freedom of her manners, it seems, were looked on as wanting in delicacy by the ladies of the staid court of the late queen, who now formed the intimate circle of the Duchesse Claude. After the marriage there was a grand supper at which Mary was present, sitting beside the king under a canopy, and wearing a velvet hat with a diamond star and plume of white feathers. It appears to have been very becoming, as she is described as looking exceedingly pretty, with her fresh, fair complexion, and her long, bright auburn hair flowing in curls over her shoulders.

On the 5th of November she was crowned at

---

* Anne Boleyn is said to have been one of these ladies. More probably, as some writers have supposed, it was her elder sister Mary; for, according to the date, 1507, most generally given as that of Anne's birth, she would have then been but six or seven years of age. She was in France some years later. Her letters to her father at that time are wonderful specimens of phonetic French.

St. Denis, the old abbey being draped and decorated in very festive style; looking almost as grand, though minus the solemnity, as when, less than nine months before, it was prepared for the obsequies of Anne of Brittany. But Anne is now temporarily forgotten by her so recently devoted Louis. It would have been better to have kept to their violet court mourning.

The coronation was followed by a banquet, and the banquet by a ball, though hitherto there had been scarcely any dancing at court. The king, inspired by the mirth and gaiety around him, did his best to forget his gout and other infirmities, and be young again. He was very gallant, and evidently much pleased, at the admiration the young queen excited. The bride's public entry into Paris — a very grand affair — took place on the 6th. Tapestry and banners were abundantly displayed, and a long procession of halberdiers, archers, Scotch and Swiss guards, preceded by heralds-at-arms, announced the approach of the royal pair and the accompanying *cortége* of cavaliers and ladies.

Even the old Palais des Tournelles had undergone a brightening up for Mary's reception, as far as regarded the interior. The open sewer running immediately under the palace windows, rendering that royal residence almost uninhabitable, was by the king's orders to have had its course turned during his absence. The civic authorities looked at it and confessed, as before they had often done, that it was a terrible nuisance. But when the bridal *cortége* arrived the sluggish, pestiferous stream still rolled on in the same direction, as it was destined to do for yet many a year, and yet many more times to generate the plague and depopulate Paris.

But this plague-spot interfered not then with the round of banquets and bridal festivities which continued uninterruptedly for the space of six weeks. The weather was exceedingly inclement; but bonfires, torches, and some attempt at an illumination, together with the wild joy of the people at "their father's" new marriage (looked on, it appears, as a new lease of life for him), served in some small degree to mitigate its rigour.

No better pastime had yet been devised for the chivalric band of cavaliers than the ever-recurring jousts and tournaments and combats *à outrance*. In these encounters Francis especially excelled. No less so Charles de Bourbon and the Chevalier Bayard, who both bore a part in them; also Brandon and other English gentlemen in Mary's suite. Francis, seemingly, was very desirous that his prowess should attract the notice of the queen, and it was commented upon as "exceedingly heroic that he evinced no displeasure at the king's marriage; no alarm at its probable results, and the consequent destruction of his hopes of succeeding his uncle."*

* Uncle after the manner of Brittany; that is, Francis was the son of Louis's first cousin.

The fêtes were, however, drawing to a close, and Mary, sometimes so gay, laughingly calling Francis "*Monsieur mon beau-fils*," was now observed to be frequently silent and sad; for nothing escaped the vigilance of Louise of Savoy. The starting tear, the ill-repressed sigh, she attributed to love for her son, and for the first time, probably, sought to restrain the ardour of that libertine youth's assiduities in his pursuit of any lady who momentarily took his fancy. The depravity of her mind made her see, in the *liaison* she suspected, her son's probable loss of the throne. She ventured, therefore, to whisper about doubts of the young queen's chastity, and urged the gentlemen of honour in attendance upon her to warn the king of the danger of the intimacy subsisting between his nephew and his bride. But Louis gave no heed to it.

He was beginning to feel the reaction consequent on a life of fatigue and exhaustion, so different from the regularity and quietude of that he had so long led with his Bretonne queen.

> "*Lever à six, dîner à dix,*
> *Souper à six, coucher à dix,*
> *Fait vivre l'homme dix fois dix,*"

had been the rule of his life for many years past. Lately, he had not dined till the now fashionable hour of noon; very often not till one. Supper had not been served till eight or nine, and midnight had sometimes found him concealing with smiles the pains that racked him while mingling with the gay throng of ladies and cavaliers in the great hall of the Palais des Tournelles.

These unseasonable hours soon began to tell rapidly on the health of so confirmed an invalid. Physicians had warned him, without much avail, that the gaieties which suited well the bride would surely prove fatal to the bridegroom. Yet much was hoped from a speedy removal to Blois.

The English guests were departing. Mary, with throbbing heart, had taken the necessary formal farewell of Brandon, and the royal retinue was on the eve of quitting the pestiferous capital, when the king, already utterly prostrated, was attacked by dysentery. The journey to Blois was deferred; but all hope that he would rally was soon at an end. A day or two he languished, quietly passing away at near midnight on the 1st of January, 1515; with his last breath requesting to be laid in the same tomb with his beloved Anne.*

Never was any king of France so deeply mourned as Louis XII. When, as was the custom of the

---

* A very splendid monument covered the remains of Louis XII. and his queen. It was the work of Florentine sculptors (the Justas or Giusti; of whom there were three, either brothers or father and sons). Four years, however, had elapsed from the death of Louis ere the tomb was begun, and it was not completed until 1532 — so many times had its progress been suspended, owing to neglect, or inability to make the stipulated payments to the artists, and to the difficulty of supplying them even with the necessary materials for their work. The cost was 400,000 *francs.*

time, the "death-bell ringers" (*clocheteurs des tré-passés*) passed through the streets of Paris, loudly ringing their bells and mournfully announcing, "The good King Louis, father of the people, is dead!" there was lamentation and weeping in every household in the city. As the doleful news spread, cries of heartfelt woe arose throughout the kingdom, and many bitter tears were shed for the loss of the people's sympathetic father and friend. He alone of their kings, since the time of the saintly Louis IX. (to whom he has been sometimes likened), had taken any interest in them, or evinced any real desire to promote their welfare.

On coming to the throne, Louis generously overlooked the conduct of those who, in the preceding reign and under the regency of Anne de Beaujeu, had shown themselves inimical to him. They had looked for banishment, imprisonment or other marks of his disfavour. But, on the contrary, he commended their fidelity to their sovereign, bade them retain their posts, and serve him with like zeal. Many much-needed judicial reforms were introduced by Louis XII., many abuses abolished, and the burdensome taxation imposed by his predecessor was reduced by nearly a third.

The king's frugal habits and thrifty management of the state's finances were attributed by the younger nobility to parsimony and avarice, and were the subject of frequent jests among them. They were even broadly alluded to in one of the satirical performances termed "*farces, soties et moralités*," of the clerks of the Basoche, who, under the title of "*Enfants sans souci*," formed themselves into a sort of dramatic company, and thus became the originators of French comedy. Louis was represented in one of their "*soties*" (or *farces*) drinking with much relish a bumper of liquid gold. When informed of their audacity, the king merely replied, "Let them jest as much as they please, so that they presume not to refer to the queen" (which once they had done) "or forget what is due to the honour of ladies."

France was very prosperous under Louis XII. All classes had improved in their circumstances. Much land was brought into cultivation, and commerce became greatly extended. The king had, therefore, the real satisfaction of seeing the result of the economy and order he had introduced into the routine of government, in the increased comfort of his people and general prosperity of his kingdom.

Les beaux arts also flourished — the impulse given to their revival in France being due to Louis XII. and his great minister, Cardinal Georges d'Amboise, "to whose ministry belongs one of the most glorious periods of French art which has too long been absorbed in the reign of Francis I." *

"Louis XII.," says M. Michelet, "was himself probably one of the people. He had not the soul

* Henri Martin, "*Histoire de France.*"

Louis XII.
Photo-etching from painting by Ad. Brune.

of a king." Whether this insinuation be well founded or not, he made, notwithstanding, a very good king. Seissel, a contemporary writer, Rœderer, and others of later date who have written of him, are of opinion that France never had a better ruler, or the French more true liberty, than during the reign of Louis XII. His chief failing seems to have been excessive severity towards the Italians, in the conduct of the war he unceasingly made on their country, for the purpose of enforcing his very vague claims on Milan and Naples, — severity strongly contrasting with his solicitude for the happiness and well-being of his own subjects, and the lenient, even indulgent, spirit he ever exhibited in all his relations towards them.

CHAPTER III.

The Type of a New Generation. — Seeking Fortune's Favours. — Reward of Loyal Devotion. — Francis of Angoulême. — The New Court. — The Special Embassy. — Loving Inquiries. — The King's Public Entry. — The Hero of the Fête. — The Great Officers of the Crown. — The Widowed Queen. — The Ladies, Litters, and Mules. — The Loves of Mary and Brandon. — Francis Discomfited. — Mary's Letter to Her Brother. — The Devil's "Puissance." — Marriage of Mary and Brandon. — The Crown Jewels.

THE nervous fears of Louise of Savoy being effectually set at rest, Francis of Angoulême was proclaimed king; and, while the *bourgeoisie* of Paris and the mass of the people were still deploring the death of "*le bon roi Louis Douze,*" the young nobles thronged to the court of Francis I., hailing his accession with exultant joy as the type of a new generation.

They were weary of Louis and his economy, of prosperity that simply meant the welfare of the nation; not, as they understood it, the lavishing of the state's finances on court favourites, or the creation of superfluous posts in the government, to enable them to lavish them themselves. It was, however, a select few only; the gay, the gallant, and especially those of the chivalric band — the young king's companions — on whom nature, with liberal hand, had bestowed personal graces, who looked hopefully forward to share in the ensuing redistribution of place, power, and wealth.

Many of the provincial nobility also would, at this crisis, have willingly sought fortune's favours at court. But the distance of their small domains from the capital, and, greater hindrance still, restricted means, forbade them to incur the great expense of living there, or even of travelling — which on such grand occasions was imperative — in a manner suited to their rank and according to the fashion of the time. This was with a numerous retinue, a train of servants, a goodly number of horses and mules, and a superabundance of litters. These last were certainly useful, as they might, covered or otherwise, be turned to account, *en route*, as sleeping-cots, when other accommodation failed.

Rarely at any greater speed than a foot-pace could such a company of travellers advance on their journey; for no roads were made in those days, except the two or three that led to the royal hunting-seats, and even they were kept up but indifferently.

Great expectations, however, were then fostered by all who claimed to be noble, whether wealthy or poor. This was owing to the young monarch's reputation for chivalrous feeling and sympathy of sentiment with them, as well as from the open-handed generosity ascribed to him, so strikingly contrasting with the niggardly penuriousness attributed by the nobility to the "Father of the people." The idea, therefore, that a display of loyal devotion towards him might be more or less substantially rewarded, is said to have led more than one needy noble, whose rank did not exact such service of him, to attend the sovereign at his coronation, arrayed with befitting splendour. Vain attempt indeed, it proved, to attract either the notice or favour of the new court — for only disappointment or, too often, ruin followed.

But from all parts of France, from one motive or another, people were making their way, as best they could, to the capital. Unwonted bustle and stir, therefore, prevailed in the good old city of Paris; its muddy, pestiferous, dark and abominably crooked ins and outs called streets being thronged with the grave and the gay, — mourners, arriving for the burying of the old king, and revellers to take part in the festive doings to follow the crowning of the young one.

The successor of Louis XII. was but in his twenty-first year, but in appearance and habits of life several years older. He was born at Cognac, on the 12th of September, 1494, and was the son of Charles d' Orléans, Comte d' Angoulême, a man of fragile, puny physique, and feeble health, very unlike his robust son; or, as some said, his reputed son, two years after whose birth he died. There was very slight prospect, indeed, at that time, that Francis would be called on to ascend the throne. A young king of twenty-four then reigned, and two sons had been born to him — the dauphin being then in his second year. If, unlikely though it seemed, there should eventually be a failure of male issue, still the first prince of the blood, Louis d' Orléans — then in the prime of manhood — stood between Francis and the throne.

Gradually the pathway to it was opened before him; first, by the death of Charles's two sons, and a few years later by the fatal accident to Charles himself. After the accession of Louis XII. and his marriage with Charles's young widow, Madame Claude came into the world instead of the much-desired heir. This was a vexation to the parents, but an immense satisfaction to Louise of Savoy, who, with her son and her daughter Marguerite (two years the senior of Francis), was residing, by order of the king — which was almost equivalent to banishment — at her château of Cognac, or that of Romorantin. The levity of her conduct was so offensive to Anne of Brittany, that she would not receive her at her court.

Some writers say that between 1499 and 1510, when Mesdames Claude and Renée were born, Anne gave birth to two sons, who died in their infancy; but whether or not, two daughters alone survived Louis and Anne. The elder, Claude, was now queen, and Renée, just entering her fifth year, was residing at her sister's court with her governess, Madame d'Aumont. This lady had formerly been one of Anne of Brittany's *filles d'honneur*, a title about to become one of great distinction, significative of the difference of conduct and sentiments that prevailed in the court of the late queen, and the tone and manners of that over which Louise of Savoy, with her *dames de deshonneur*, was about to reign supreme.

Few of the sovereigns of France have been much regretted by the people. In more than one instance, in order to avoid insult to their remains, they have been carried to their tombs almost secretly, and without any outward show of respect. But for a monarch so beloved and lamented as was Louis XII., the scanty *cortége* that accompanied the body to St. Denis fell short, it would seem, of the honour considered to be justly due to him. Perhaps the best tribute to his worth was in the regrets and tears of the voluntary procession of mourners that followed the official one. But Francis was in haste to be crowned. He was athirst for military glory; and if the funeral *cortége* of the late king was somewhat shorn of its due splendour, so was the customary pomp of the preparations for the coronation at Rheims.

Usually they occupied many months, and during that interval the court and the people mourned, outwardly, at least, for their departed ruler. But so eager was Francis to bring these ceremonies to an end, that when, in less than a month (27th of January) after Louis's death, a special embassy to compliment him on his accession arrived at Senlis from London — having "travelled," it was said, "with the speed of the wind," as it probably sped in those days — "the king," as the ambassador informed his sovereign, Henry VIII., "had gone to Rheims for his sacring;" and for his "sacring" only, it appeared.

For, contrary to all precedent, the full ceremony did not take place at Rheims. He was anointed there only; and that, probably, because the *sainte ampoule* containing the miraculous holy oil sent from heaven for the consecration of the French kings could not be removed from the Cathedral of St. Remi. Singular innovation also, which none of his successors adopted, the ceremony was performed at night, on the 25th. On the following day Francis set off for St. Denis, — where, hitherto, only the queens of France had been crowned, — to complete, apparently with little *éclat*, his own coronation. The ceremony ended, he journeyed to Noyon, having announced that he would there receive the English deputation, on Candlemas eve. Consequently, the gentlemen composing it, the Duke of Suffolk being the head, repaired to that town, and were "very graciously greeted and heartily welcomed by the king." He even listened with exemplary patience to a long Latin harangue spoken by the Bishop of Ely, but gave no direct reply to it, for which omission there was probably a sufficient reason. But his majesty "made many inquiries, most lovingly," and in French, of course, "after the health of King Henry and Queen Katharine."

With reference to the young dowager, Queen Mary, Francis remarked "he had hoped that the marriage of that princess with the late king, which he had greatly promoted, would have been of long endurance; and he trusted she would write to her brother of how lovingly he had behaved to her; of how he had done her no wrong, and would suffer her to take wrong of no other, but would be unto her as a loving son to his mother." But Brandon, already, was charged by Henry to thank Francis for "the singular comfort he had given Mary in her affliction." Having done so, he and the rest of the embassy took leave of the king and departed for Paris, to witness the public entry of Francis into his capital, which event was fixed for the 13th of February.

This public entry was a brilliant spectacle. Old Parisians remembered nothing to compare with it since the bringing home of the Bretonne bride, with its vestiges of mediæval customs, twenty-three years gone by. But even the grand pageant which celebrated that event (a truly important one for France; the *tour de force* of "La grande Madame," the daughter of Louis XI.) may have owed at this period much of its vaunted splendour to that misty veil which distance of time and space hangs over so many events and scenes of the past; leaving imagination to fill in with its own vivid colouring all that during the lapse of years has become blurred and indistinct.

Now, as then, damask and tapestry made grand and gay the mean lath and plaster houses. The king's musicians — on this occasion habited in white velvet — preceded the monarch, probably not discoursing very excellent music, yet vigorously playing on their " sambucas, hautbois, and trumpets " some inspiring equivalent to the modern " See the Conquering Hero Comes ; " a little discordantly, perhaps, for music had not yet crossed the Alps, and as an art in France was then far away in the background.

It was, however, the hero of the *fête* whom all most desired to see, — from the groups of great ladies who filled the windows of the houses and public buildings, to women and men of lower degree, even to the *canaille*. These last, like the rest of the Parisian world, appeared on the scene in full force; they crowded the doorways and entrances, and, in spite of the efforts of the provost's archers to dislodge them, took possession of every niche, every projection that afforded the most risky foothold; even hazarding life and limb from the kicks of restive, prancing, curveting horses, for but the bare chance of a glimpse of the new king and the brilliant cavaliers who formed his *cortége*.

No traces of mourning were visible. The king's dress was composed entirely of white satin and silver damask. Over it he wore a mantle of silver cloth bordered with a deep silver fringe. His toque also was of white velvet, ornamented with precious stones and a plume of white feathers. His horse's mane was interlaced with silver cord, and both bit and bridle were of silver, elaborately engraved. The damask housing was covered with silver lozenge-shaped spots, each bearing a device in low relief. Thus brilliantly arrayed, the young king of the Renaissance no doubt looked remarkably well, sitting his horse with much grace — horsemanship being an accomplishment in which all the young nobles of that day excelled. The master of the horse (*grand écuyer*) was similarly attired in white and silver.

Other great officers of the crown wore sumptuous dresses of satin damask and cloth of gold, profusely ornamented with jewels. Perhaps the most splendid of these costumes was that worn by the grand chamberlain of France, Louis d'Orléans, Duc de Longueville. It was of crimson satin interwoven with gold. On either side of the tunic, in gold embroidery, was an eagle looking at the sun and preparing to wing his flight towards it. The duke's cap, or toque, was of black velvet. In front of it were three rubies of remarkable size and fine colour, and between them was placed the great diamond of the House of Dunois, cut as a brilliant. Besides these, arranged in a square, were some smaller diamonds, and in the centre, and at each angle, a pear-shaped pearl of rare size and great price.*

When the king, with his great officers of state and the rest of the brilliant throng who made up this dazzling show, had all passed by, " Suffolk and others remained," writes Gattinara, the Venetian envoy, "to see the queen (Mary) return to the palace after she and other ladies had witnessed the king's entry from the windows of a neighbouring dwelling. It was remarked that Mary also had cast off her mourning, and that her litter was preceded by twenty of the Duke of Suffolk's servants on horseback, all clad in gray damask, with the servants of the other envoys similarly clad and mounted. Madame d' Angoulême " (Louise of Savoy) " was with her, and little Madame Renée and two other children in another litter." Francis's youthful and amiable queen, Madame Claude, seems not to have been present; no mention is made of her. She was not crowned until two years later, after Francis returned from Italy.†

" In a third litter were old Madame de Bourbon " (daughter of Louis XI.) " and young Madame

---

* This was not the Duc de Longueville to whom the idea of the marriage of Louis XII. and Mary of England had firs occurred. He appears to have died very soon after his return to France. The office of grand chamberlain being hereditary, his son or nearest relative would succeed him.

† "*Le Bourgeois de Paris,*" 1517.

d'Alençon" (Marguerite d'Angoulême.) Fifty other litters followed, each containing two ladies. Then came ambling along twenty-four *haquenées* (mules), each led by a servant and ridden by a lady. The first fourteen of these venturesome ladies were magnificently dressed in cloth of gold; the rest were attired in satin damask and various rich materials.* Of pearls and diamonds they made also a great display, and, generally, the recently introduced white Italian gloves were worn, embroidered and fringed with gold or silver. A company of the king's archers, carrying lances and doing duty as escort to this long array of ladies, litters, and mules, closed the procession, and a grand state banquet concluded the day's proceedings. Six weeks of festivity followed, with much dining, supping, and dancing, jousts (in one of which conflicts the Count of St. Aubin was killed), tiltings, tournaments, and flirtations.

During this interval devoted to pleasure, the little romantic episode of the loves of Mary and Brandon seemed menaced with a result unfavourable to the lovers. Mary had written to her brother "thanking his grace for sending Brandon to comfort her in her heaviness." It does not appear that the death of Louis XII. was any great affliction to her. Her sadness or "heaviness" arose from the young king's importunate attentions,

---

* "State Papers and Letters," Foreign Series, 1515; also Brewer's Introduction to same.

"which," as she said, "were not to her honour;" and she was further distressed by the arrival of ambassadors with proposals of marriage from several of the princes of Europe. That of the Duke of Savoy, the king's uncle, was favoured by the French court, and much urged on her by Louise of Savoy, the duke's sister, as well as formally made to King Henry.

As Francis, notwithstanding, continued to press his "singular comfort" on Mary, she determined to free herself from his importunities, "of which she was so weary, as well as so afeared that he would try to ruin her lover." As she informs Brandon, she said to the king, "Sire, I beseech you will let me alone, and speak no more to me of such matters; and if you will promise me by your faith and troth, and, as you are a true prince, that you will keep it counsel and help me, I will tell you all my own mind." Of course he promised. Mary then confessed her love for Brandon, and her engagement to him; begging also "the king's pity and help to mitigate her brother's displeasure."*

Francis, though evidently no less astonished than annoyed by a confession which showed him, what he probably never before suspected, that another might be preferred before him, nevertheless graciously promised his good offices in the matter. There would seem, however, to have been

* Foreign Series of "State Papers and Letters," 1515.

no need for them. An understanding existed between Mary and her brother that she should please herself in her second nuptials. Suffolk was one of his chief favourites. Wolsey, too, was friendly to the lovers. Mary must have feared that some political motive might induce Henry to fail in his word to her, and for this reason to give his sanction only to a royal marriage.

As for Francis, much discomfited at being so firmly repulsed, he "went immediately to his bed-chamber and sent for Brandon, to whom, on entering, he said abruptly:

"My Lord of Suffolk, there is a bruit in this realm that you have come hither to marry the queen, your master's sister."

Taken by surprise, Brandon could only reply that "his master had sent him to comfort his sister." But the king informed him that the queen had confessed to him their mutual attachment, and that he proposed, by interceding with Henry, to aid in securing the object of their wishes. But this English Queen Mary of France seems to have had as much tenacity of will as Henry himself; and to have been as determined to marry Brandon, in spite of her brother, as he, some years later, was determined to marry Anne Boleyn, in spite of the Pope.

Accordingly, Mary, not relying on Francis's intercession, writes to her brother, reminding him that, "having once sacrificed herself for his pleasure, she hopes now to be suffered to do what she list. His grace knoweth where she proposeth to marry, and further knowing there are numerous suitors for her hand, and projects to bestow it on this prince and on that, if his grace will have her married in any place but where her mind is, she will be there where his grace nor none other shall have any joy of her; for she doth promise his grace that he shall hear that she will be in some religious house, which she thinks his grace would be very sorry of, and his realm also. She knows," she continues, "that Suffolk hath many hinderers about his grace."

Suffolk's opponents are said to have made the most strenuous efforts to prevent his marriage with Mary. One of their devices was to send a priest named Langley, to alarm her by an absurd tale of "both Brandon and Wolsey having dealings with the devil; and, by the puissance of the said devil, keeping Henry VIII. subject to their will. By Suffolk's devilish arts, Langley told her, a disease in Compton's leg was caused." But Mary was stanch, and the result of the story of Brandon and the devil's "puissance," together with a renewal of the king's offensive attentions, was her secret marriage with Brandon.

Fleuranges — with whom Francis was on more familiar terms than with many of his favourites — says, in his memoirs, that "the king was very indignant and much vexed on hearing of this secret marriage; Brandon having given him his word that he would do nothing dishonourable. But Brandon pleaded the ardour of his love for Mary." Whether this in any way appeased the anger of the indignant monarch, Fleuranges does not inform us; yet neither he nor Francis appears to have seen any dishonour attaching to the latter in his persistent persecution of the young widowed queen, to induce her to become his mistress.

It is singular, however, that the testimony of Fleuranges, which might well be supposed trustworthy, as regards the king's indignation with Brandon on account of the secret marriage, is not confirmed by the documents relating to it contained in the series of "State Papers." So far from it, it would appear that ten persons were present at this *secret* marriage, and that Francis was one of them. Yet it is possible that he was not; but that it was expedient it should be so represented, in order to conciliate Henry, who, though he seems to have been little adverse to the match, might have greatly resented Brandon's presumption in marrying his sister without his consent.

The presumed presence of Francis would give a sort of sanction to the dowager French queen to dispose of her hand "where she had a mind," as she had warned her brother she would do. Yet, that it was none the less a very serious matter for Brandon may be inferred from Wolsey's reproachful words, that "he had saved his head from the block," when years after Brandon showed himself less mindful than he should have been of his former obligations to the fallen minister. Wolsey's friendly efforts on behalf of the romantic pair enabled them fearlessly to leave Paris for London on the 15th of April (ten days after the treaty between Louis XII. and Henry VIII. had been ratified by Francis I.), Mary being a second time a bride within six months.

On the 13th of May they were publicly married at Greenwich in the presence of Henry and Queen Katharine, Mary taking the title of the duchess-queen.

Unlike most love marriages, this was a happy one. But Henry made the lovers pay for their happiness by the very hard bargains he drove with them respecting their property. They appear to have very readily complied with his exactions, though Brandon was far from being rich. He indeed complained some years after of straitened means from the alienation of so large a portion of their income. Henry acted in this instance with the niggardliness characteristic of his father, seeking to recover from France the expense he had incurred for Mary's marriage to Louis XII., and exacting from his sister a large part of her dowry.

A lively correspondence ensued respecting the jewels given by Louis XII. to Mary. Those of greatest value the Duchesse d'Angoulême seems to have taken a fancy to. They therefore were claimed as part of the crown jewels of France. Henry contended that they were the French queen's private property. But only a very few of Louis's valuable gifts to his bride were allowed to be retained by her.*

Death rather prematurely parted Mary and Brandon. She died in 1532, in her thirty-fourth or thirty-fifth year.

* See "Letters," etc., Foreign Series of "State Papers," 1514 and 1515. Also Brewer's Introduction to same.

CHAPTER IV.

An Idolising Mother. — The King's Governor. — The Chevalier King. — The Chancellor Duprat. — Charles de Bourbon. — Admiral Bonnivet. — La Belle Françoise de Foix. — The Duke of Milan. — Schemes for Raising Money. — A Matrimonial Alliance. — Diplomacy of Sixteenth Century. — The Treaty of Dijon. — Pedro Navarro. — Guillaume Budé. — Madame Louise of Savoy. — Shedding a Joy on Duty. — Heart-breaking Leave-takings. — The Chivalry of the Period. — The Fascinations of Lyons. — A New Route over the Alps. — Perseverance and Success. — The Modern Hannibal. — Battle of Marignan. — An Advantageous Loss. — Knighting the King.

FRANCIS'S first act of kingly power was one full of sinister foreboding, both for himself and the nation. Louise of Savoy, his "idolising mother," yet his evil genius, was created by him Duchesse d'Angoulême and d'Anjou; to which new dignity were added extensive estates in Berry. Besides this, such was the filial piety of the son towards the indulgent parent who so sedulously pandered to his vices, that he allowed her to share with him several of the prerogatives of royalty, thus admitting her at once to participation in the government of the country, — a privilege of which she was not slow to avail herself.

The pernicious influence of this ambitious, astute, and most corrupt woman was further exhibited in the young monarch's choice of ministers. Perhaps that of Artus de Gouffier Boissy, who had been his governor, and whom — with Florimond Robertet, Louis XII.'s minister of finance, as intendant — he promoted to the high office of grand master of the household, may have been dictated by feelings of personal attachment. For it was Boissy who fostered in him all those heroic sentiments attributed to the paladins of French chivalry; and in Boissy's accomplished pupil were supposed to be united the high-bred courtesy, the love of glory, the valour and generosity characteristic of the redoubtable Roland of Roncevaux, and that type of constant lovers and bravest of knights errant, the Knight of the Lion — Amadis of Gaul.

Of business of state, of the political situation of France with reference to the other powers of Europe, of the internal condition of the country, or of aught that was conducive to its prosperity or the well-being of the people, Francis knew nothing. Boissy, it seems, had never contemplated the probability of the Comte d'Angoulême being some day called upon to govern France. He was, indeed, from his own inexperience but little qualified — though a man of letters with a decided taste for *les beaux arts* — profitably to direct his pupil's education to that end. But Francis had read with avidity the old chivalric romances, and from them had imbibed certain notions of the relative duties, as he conceived them, of a chevalier king and the people whose fortunate lot it was to be born his subjects.

In all athletic sports and exercises Francis of Angoulême had borne off the palm. He was distinguished by his skill in the tournament; he excelled in the race, and his horsemanship was regarded as the perfection of grace and daring. As a wrestler few could compete with him, and he was a dexterous swordsman. Nor did his accomplishments end here. He was also the glass of fashion, dressing sumptuously, and regulating, as *arbiter elegantiarum*, the form and colour of court costume — always, of course, with an eye to the especial setting off of his own stalwart form, or the concealment of its defects.

The *élite* of the young nobility — an Olympian throng of whom he was the chief — took him for their model, and were delighted with the prospect which the new reign, with its extravagance and its court of gallantry and beauty, opened before them. Very eagerly, therefore, they sought to bask in the sunlight of the accomplished royal hero's favour.

The plebeian part of the nation, at first a little dazzled also, rashly expected to find in this brilliant apparition, this elegant creature, the like of whom had never before been seen, and never was likely to reappear among the race of French king's,— in stature a demigod * or knight of the Round Table, — that a great man had arisen to govern France. But, alas! like all who looked to him for anything great, they were doomed to disappointment.†

The seals of the important post of chancellor were confided to Antoine Duprat, the first president of the Parliament of Paris. Duprat was the intimate friend and adviser of Madame Louise, and was a man of considerable ability, but utterly unprincipled, and of dissolute life.

For twenty-seven years the sword of state of the Constable of France had been rusting in its scabbard. Both Charles VIII. and Louis XII. had shrunk from bestowing on a subject, and especially on a prince of the blood, a dignity second in influence only to the monarch's, and

---

* A man of five feet ten inches, or eleven, at most, which the armour of Francis I. in the Louvre shows the height of that monarch to have been, was regarded, apparently, as gigantic in that age of humpbacked, stunted growth, and deformed royalty. Deformity was then very general in France. Infants and young children were so tightly swathed and bound up that their muscles became contracted, their limbs crooked, and rarely did any grow up without some bodily defect more or less developed. Francis may, therefore, have well been looked on as a wonder. He was moderately tall and straight, broad chested, but high shouldered, and, on the whole, by no means so symmetrical in form, or handsome in feature, as his flatterers have represented him.

† See Henri Martin, "*Histoire de France.*"

which, once conferred, could not be withdrawn. So absolute, indeed, was his power, that the monarch himself could give no orders during a campaign, respecting his army, but through the agency of the constable. Duc Jean de Bourbon, who died in 1488, was the last who held the post. But the constable's office was now revived, and the sword presented to the haughtiest, wealthiest, and most powerful subject in the realm, — the second prince of the blood, the young, handsome, ambitious, and austere Duc Charles de Bourbon.

He was but four years older than Francis, with whom he was certainly no favourite, — his manners being grave and dignified, and his aversion to join in the frivolous pastimes and dissipations of the court openly avowed. He had very early displayed great military talent, and distinguished himself by his bravery in the recent Italian wars of Louis XII.; who is said, in one of the many versions French historians have given of Bourbon's early career, to have promised him the constableship when, after a few more years, he should have acquired that experience and maturity of judgment considered essential qualifications for this responsible post.

Francis was by no means anxious to carry out so hurriedly, if at all, in this instance, the intentions of his predecessor. But his mother had long been the slave of an absorbing passion for this young duke, who treated her advances with coldest disdain. She, however, yet hoped to bring him to her feet, by using the influence she now possessed for the furtherance of his ambitious views. To her suggestions, then, in this as in other matters, Francis dutifully yielded, and together with the constable's sword conferred on Bourbon the governorship of Languedoc. Francis was, in fact, of too indolent a character to offer much opposition except where his pleasures were concerned.

Another nomination, more agreeable to Francis and his courtiers, but due to good looks and lively manners rather than to ability, was that of Gouffier Boissy's young brother, Bonnivet, to the post of admiral. Bonnivet was considered the handsomest man, and most accomplished gentleman, according to the notions of that time, of the court of Francis I., — the king, of course, excepted. What mortal could compare with a demigod! And very rapidly the admiral rose in his sovereign's good graces, and acquired a princely fortune. For Francis was lavish towards his favourites, and often not only overlooked their fatal mistakes in their conduct of his wars, but, as in the case of Bonnivet, — who, if not deficient in bravery, was certainly not an able commander, — even rewarded acts that would have entailed disgrace on others.

The number of the marshals of France was increased at this time from three to four, and the appointment raised in dignity. Henceforth, the marshals ranked as great officers of the crown, holding their commissions for life, with the further honour of being addressed by the king as "*mon cousin.*" But it was the young Maréchal de Foix (Lautrec) whom Francis, on this occasion, most especially distinguished, appointing him governor of Guyenne, and conferring on him other marks of confidence and good-will.

The marshal was the eldest of the three brothers (Lautrec, Lescun, and Lesparre) of Françoise de Foix, the young Comtesse de Châteaubriand, whose beauty had already attracted the notice of the king, even while bestowing his "singular comfort," on Queen Mary. It was to find favour, then, in the eyes of the fair countess that Lautrec, so brave and daring, but so cruel in war, was promoted to greater honour than the rest of the marshals.

But affairs of gallantry did not at this moment so exclusively occupy the young king's attention as to abate the ardour of his desire to signalise his accession to power by some brilliant achievement that should add to his other perfections a halo of military glory. From the 20th of January an army had been assembling at Lyons, which, from its continually increasing number, promised to be the largest, as well as best equipped, that France had yet in her Italian wars brought into the field. Its destination was the invasion of Italy and the reconquest of Milan, of which, at his coronation, Francis had taken the title of duke, — an announcement to the Italian states that they were not yet free from the ravages of "*les barbares,*" otherwise the French.

His claim to the duchy was but the extremely vague one acquired by his marriage with Madame Claude, and inherited by her from her father. But Francis, not satisfied to act in the name of his wife, required of that young and docile lady the cession to him, personally, of all the rights of the House of Orléans to the Milanais.

If Louis XII., notwithstanding his expensive wars, had incurred no debts, he had also hoarded no money, and unexpected emptiness of the treasury at his death proved a great check to the young king's martial views. His vast preparations for recovering "his heritage" were therefore somewhat delayed, by the necessity of devising expedients for obtaining the large sums he needed, as well for his pleasure as for the equipment of his troops.

His chancellor, Duprat, was fertile in schemes for raising money. But, as Francis was not indifferent to popularity, he shrank from the convenient course of beginning his reign by a large increase of taxation, which would have exhibited so striking a contrast to that pursued on his accession, by the people's lamented "good king, Louis." He, therefore, contented himself for the present with some trifling augmentation of the taxes called "*les tailles*" and "*les aides;*" the contracting of large loans and the introduction of the practice of creating and selling appointments in the royal household and places in the judicature, in order to obtain funds.

Meanwhile, not to awaken the jealousy of neighbouring states, or by a premature declaration of his views to put them on their guard, he affected to be anxious only to maintain friendly relations with the European powers, and to give stability to the new reign.* Consequently, he had readily confirmed Louis's treaty of peace with Henry VIII., and in the previous month (March) entered into one with the Archduke Charles of Austria. This politic youth, Francis's future rival, but then only Count of Flanders, having attained his majority (fifteenth year), and with it the sole government of the Netherlands, sent his ambassador, Count Henry of Nassau, to propose a treaty of peace and amity with France, and to make a formal demand for the hand of the queen's sister, Madame Renée; the marriage to be solemnized when Madame, who was not yet five years old, should have completed her twelfth year.

Many concessions and promises of a political nature were eventually agreed to, and every possible guarantee given for securing in due time the celebration of the marriage; a large pecuniary forfeiture being stipulated should either party to the

* J. Servan, "*Guerres des Français en Italie.*"

treaty fail to carry out his engagements. The *"Bourgeois de Paris"* (1515) informs us that this auspicious event was proclaimed throughout the capital, and celebrated by *Te Deums* and sermons, bonfires, processions, and ringing of bells; also jubilee pardons and indulgences from the Pope. Charles was so well pleased with his ambassador's conduct of the negotiation that he rewarded him with a wealthy wife, — Madame Claude de Chalon, heiress of Philibert, Prince of Orange.

This treaty was at that moment favourable to the French king's designs on Italy; but with reference to the future, most contrary to the interests of France. This was quite in accordance with the system of diplomacy generally adopted in Europe in those unstable and turbulent times. Chicanery and deceit were its chief characteristics. If success in immediate objects could be achieved by onerous treaty engagements, there was no hesitation in entering into them, and none in setting them aside when they had served their purpose, or in trusting to the chapter of accidents to nullify all it might hereafter be inconvenient to carry into effect.

Francis, then, did but follow the example of contemporary sovereigns when, solely with a view to the success of his own secret plans, he sent ambassadors to negotiate alliances with the Venetians, the Emperor Maximilian, the Pope, and Ferdinand of Spain. He would have included the

Swiss cantons — whose inhabitants then fought the battles of Europe — in this universal bond of amity he was apparently so desirous of effecting. But, at the instigation of Cardinal Sion, the representative of the cantons in Italy, and the irreconcilable enemy of France, passports were refused to the French envoy, and the king informed by the Diet, that, if the unfulfilled treaty made with the Swiss at Dijon, in 1513, by Maréchal de La Trémoille, in the name of Louis XII., was not fully executed, an armed force would enter Burgundy.

The conditions of this treaty were extremely onerous. It had been made at a critical moment for France, without authority from the king, who was expected to repudiate it, which he did, expressing much dissatisfaction with La Trémoille. But when better informed of the state of affairs that led to it, he perceived and acknowledged that what he had thought a harsh and unjustifiable act had really been one of necessity, and had saved his kingdom.

The demands of the Swiss Diet, which Francis bitterly inveighed against and made known to all Europe, served him, however, as a pretext he was glad to avail himself of for raising more money as well as troops in Burgundy and Dauphiny, and still further increasing his army for the defence, as he now gave out, of his frontiers. At this crisis it was suggested to him to offer liberty and the command of a detachment to the Biscayan general, Pedro Navarro, who, from his great military renown, would in himself be almost worth an army.

This experienced officer, who was skilled in all the science of war of that epoch, had been taken prisoner at Ravenna. In that famous battle Navarro had played a distinguished part; but Cardona, the Viceroy of Naples, who fled with all speed when victory seemed to declare for the French, accused him of being the cause of the Spanish defeat. Consequently, Ferdinand refused to pay the captive's ransom, and for nearly three years Navarro had languished, a prisoner of war in France. The offers of the king were accepted by him, after renouncing the fiefs he held of Ferdinand; the allegiance of a Biscayan to Spain being so weak a tie that soon after, with nearly 10,000 of his countrymen, Navarro joined the army of Lyons, now numbering 60,000 strong.

It consisted of men of all nations, even cavalry from Albania; but what was remarkable on this occasion was the absence of the Swiss, who usually formed the strength of all armies, even of states opposed to each other. The French troops were always few in number. Louis XII. had been so anxious to spare his own people the hardships and perils of warfare, that the boasted martial spirit of the nation was believed to be much subdued, and it was scarcely expected that they should fight their own battles.

The old monarch of Spain was far too astute to be lulled into security by the peaceful professions of the young King of France, and declined his proposal to prolong the truce, then drawing to a close, which he had concluded with Louis XII. Having urged the Pope to open his eyes to what his enemy was doing, Ferdinand, together with the Emperor Maximilian and the Duke of Milan, Maximilian Sforza, formed a league with the Swiss, who were to furnish a large army in support of it, for the defence of Italy.

Francis, being desirous of securing the alliance of the Pope, Leo X., by way of showing his appreciation of the character of his prelate, as an enlightened and munificent patron of art and letters, despatched to Rome, as his negotiator, a *savant* of high repute in the Parisian world of letters. This was the learned Guillaume Budé, the head of the literary movement of the Renaissance in France. A most flattering welcome, both from Leo and the illustrious men of his *entourage*, awaited Budé at the Papal Court. But, though treated with great distinction, the only result of his mission was a secret promise from the Pope of neutrality, he having, with the same secrecy, already promised the Swiss envoys to cooperate with the league. Leo, who cherished ambitious designs of his own—having reference rather to the establishment of his family and his own personal power than to the upholding of the greatness of the Church and the independence of Italy — had hoped thus to be enabled without compromising himself to await the issue of the first movements of the armies, and to fulfil his promise to either or neither as circumstances should suggest. For that Francis's object was the reconquest of Milan could no longer be doubted, since Genoa had openly declared for the French,— an intrigue of the doge, Ottavio Fregosa, having restored that state, under certain conditions, to France.

The army of invasion being fully equipped and ready to march, Francis, on the 15th of July, confided the administration and regency of the kingdom, with unlimited powers, to his mother, Madame Louise of Savoy.

The grand military spectacle of the assembling and departure of the troops had attracted Queen Claude and Madame Louise, with the ladies of their respective courts, to Lyons. The army consisted of three divisions composed of various corps, each bearing some distinctive mark of its nationality. The constable, in virtue of his office, commanded the vanguard, with 3,000 pioneers and artillerymen to clear the passage of the Alps. Francis reserved for himself the *corps de bataille*. The command of the rear-guard devolved on the Duc d'Alençon.

There was a first attempt, it seems, as regarded

the French army, to "shed a joy on duty," by adopting the fifes, with the accompaniment of "timbales" or small Saracenic kettle-drums, which had been introduced by the Swiss. Francis also made some changes in the accoutrements of his troops. To the *corps d'élite*, or perhaps one may venture to say the crack regiments, was allotted a small plume in their hats, and the standards of the cavalry were altered in form. But, except that some improvement was made, or supposed to be made, in the weapons of war then in use, with the view of superseding the longbow and the crossbow, which were, however, employed with great effect in this war, the changes were rather ornamental than useful. The 2,500 gentlemen volunteers, each with his suit of four or five horsemen, vied with each other in the richness and elaborate and expensive workmanship of their armour. But common to all of them was the very long single feather attached to the helmet, and thence trailing down and falling on the horse's back.*

Poor horses! they had a burdensome part to play in these wars, what with the weight of the heavy steel-clad heroes they carried, and the restraint of their own ponderous trappings. Of the 30,000 chargers which, in spite of their fetters, are said to have set out from Lyons full of the war-horse's fire and animation, a frightful

* Paul Lacroix, "*Le Seizéme Siécle*."

proportion succumbed to the terrible fatigue and the many casualties of the passage of the Alps.

But one must not sympathise only with the horses. Openly or secretly, heart-breaking leave-takings are going on around us; and the longing for military glory that flames in many a chivalric breast is quenched, at least for the moment, by the tears of beauty. While the softer emotions prevail, the steel-encased lover, as he gazes into the sad, imploring, uplifted eyes of his "ladye fayre," is sorely tempted to throw off the odious panoply of war and, bound by the silken cords of love, retreat to his lady's bower.

But honour forbids it! It must not be! His lady is the first to say so. Bidding her knight "be of good courage," she regains her own, smiles through her tears, and, detaching the silken scarf that engirdles her, hands it to him. He presses it to his lips, and with it the white hand that gives it, then, mounting his charger — which, impatiently pawing the ground, seems more anxious to be gone than he — rides off with great speed, lest courage again should fail him; the white scarf waving in the breeze. Oh, may he return safe and sound, and find his lady true! But the chivalry of this period was a mere affectation, and the constancy of either knight or lady not greatly to be depended on.

Doubtless there were many distressing forebodings, many painful partings, at this renewal of the Italian wars. But the memoirs of the period, being chiefly military, do not enter much into domestic matters. Now and then — as in the memoirs of Tavennes — great indignation is expressed at the influence of women in affairs of state, and the evils resulting therefrom to France, and especially from the regency of Louise of Savoy and the depravity of the band of women who composed the court of this voluptuous woman.

Sentimental scenes between the constable, Charles de Bourbon, and Marguerite, Duchesse d' Alençon, have been suggested by more modern writers, but on very slight grounds. The constable was married, and so was Marguerite, whom all have agreed to praise, and many to prove that her almost licentious writings were the productions of a mind of perfect purity. She may, therefore, well be supposed to have had her thoughts more anxiously occupied with the probable dangers about to be incurred by both brother and husband, but especially the former, than by a romantic passion in which she was the favoured rival of her mother.

However, two divisions of the invading army have arrived at the foot of the Alps. Francis, with the division he commands, still lingers at Lyons. Like Charles VIII., when bound on a similar expedition, he finds fascinations in that city from which he cannot easily tear himself.

The wiles of fair women detain him. But soon he is roused from his pleasures by messengers from the army. The Swiss have been beforehand with the French. They occupy the mountain passes with an army 20,000 strong, and await in full force the advance of their enemy at Susa.

The French officers, to whom mountain warfare is utterly unknown, are in great perplexity; when, by a fortunate chance, they are relieved by the offer of an aged man — who for many years past had traversed the mountains in all directions, in search of game — to point out to them a new route. It is a difficult and most perilous one; but after as much inspection as is possible by the dauntless Lautrec and the more prudent and skilful Navarro, the latter undertakes to make it practicable, even for the artillery. This is a sort of reprieve for Francis.

The work begins. The Durance is forded, and the army ascends the mountains; first by narrow and tortuous defiles that present obstacles to their progress at every step. The soldiers aid the pioneers, the officers aid the soldiers — all, without distinction, working with pickaxe and hatchet. Navarro, with his sappers and miners, overthrows all accessible rocks that frowningly seem to confront and oppose the onward march of the troops. The wide rents and chasms which then appear in these rough, rude mountain roads are filled up with the branches of trees, and the *débris* of the paths the men clear for themselves as they advance. Mounting still higher, temporary bridges — frail constructions of planks, or fallen trees, supported by ropes or any available material at hand — are thrown across the yawning abysses, over which those dauntless men, braving death, essay to pass; sometimes succeeding, by sheer force of arm and the strength of indomitable will, in what would appear to be a superhuman effort, — the dragging up of their cannon in safety to these rocky heights never before trodden by foot of man.

Sometimes, too, on those rough, craggy roads, made slippery by melted snow, — which, with deafening noise, rushes in foaming cascades from the mountain tops, — a false step or a fall occurs. Then a whole line of men and beasts of burden, whom one frail cord unites, is precipitated into the fathomless gulf beneath; while the roar of the Alpine torrents, the cries of the wounded and dying, the shriekings and neighing of the weary and terrified horses, are echoed and re-echoed with frightful reality by surrounding rocks and mountains; adding fresh horror to this weird scene of terror, tumult, and calamity.

Towards the end of their terrible journey, and after so many dangers and difficulties overcome, one vast flinty rock, precipitously steep on all sides, long defies all such means for blasting as Navarro can bring to bear on it. The spirits of the men droop, for they fancy they perceive that even he begins to despair. But the industry, audacity and perseverance, which he has hitherto shown, fail him not yet, and his minute search for a favourable spot for renewed operations is rewarded with success.

On the eighth day from that on which their perilous attempt to traverse the Alps by an unknown route was begun, the French army enters the Marquisate of Saluzzo; the troops for the most part shoeless and footsore, their fine feathers bedraggled or lost, and their smart new uniform tattered and soiled, but all proudly rejoicing in the great feat now accomplished. It is the exploit of Hannibal renewed — the modern Hannibal being Pedro Navarro, not he on whom the fame of it is to rest, and who is still at Lyons, a prisoner in silken fetters.

Great is the consternation of the Swiss and their confederates. Scarcely can they believe their eyes as they behold the approach of their enemy. A panic seizes them; their first impulse is flight or dispersion, and the frenzied harangues and reproaches of Cardinal Sion restrain but a part of them, and offend the rest, who demand their pay. Bayard and Bourbon are of opinion that to begin the attack while confusion and discord are rife among them will ensure an easy defeat of the Swiss.* Messengers are despatched

* Serven, "*Guerres des Français.*"

with all haste to Lyons, to communicate this idea to the king. He, however, thinks it more prudent that active means should be delayed until he appears on the scene at the head of his *corps d'armée*.

He must, of course, take his share of the hardships of this glorious war, which is to bring him European renown. So, hastily he dons his armour, receives from the fair countess a riband of the same heavenly hue as her own beautiful eyes, and half a dozen, at least, of other tokens from ladies no less fair. Meanwhile, the drums are beating to arms; the merry fifes, too, are heard. The king tenderly embraces Madame Louise, kisses Marguerite's hand, presses it to his heart, then, from the tips of his fingers, gracefully wafts his adieux to the tearful Claude. Quickly he mounts his charger; his brilliant staff surround him, and soon he is on his way to where duty and glory call him.

Safely and without obstacle he passes the Alps, then, crossing his uncle's territory of Piedmont, with his troops joins the rest of the army at Marignan (Melegnano).

The details of the battle of Marignan, which would be out of place here, are given at length by several French historians.* The battle did not

* See Servan, "*Guerres des Français;*" Gaillard, "*Histoire de François I.;*" Sismondi, "*Histoire des Français;*" the historians Varillas, Mézéray, Garnier, Michelet, Henri Martin, Dareste, and others; also, Guicciardini, Du Bellay, and other contemporary writers.

take place, owing to the king seeking to negotiate with the Swiss, until the 13th of September. It lasted part of two days, and 15,000 Swiss and 10,000 men of the French army are said to have been slain in it. It was a sort of murderous hand-to-hand fight, stimulated by hatred, and less distinguished in military annals for valour or generalship than for the rage of the combatants, their desire for vengeance, and mutual thirst for blood. It terminated in a victory, such as it was, for the French.

But the chief objects of the war were gained by bribery and concessions rather than successful fighting, — the Swiss evacuating the fortress of the capital only on the king undertaking to pay them a million crowns, and to restore and augment several pensions suppressed by Louis XII.; while the Duke of Milan, who had retired to the fortress, was induced to resign his claims to the duchy by the grant of a pension of 30,000 ducats, a residence in France, and a recommendation for a cardinal's hat — some writers say the hand of a French princess in marriage. It was, however, an arrangement by which, as he acknowledged, his gain was greater than his loss; as "it freed him from the tyranny of the Swiss, the rapine of the emperor, and the trickery of the Spaniards."

The undisciplined valour of the king and his heavy-armed cavaliers rather prolonged the carnage than gained the battle. But what his generals accomplished for him spread the renown of

Francis I. throughout Europe, as the conqueror of the Swiss, the "invincible destroyers of the power of Charles the Bold."

After the battle the king insisted on being knighted by Bayard, — the "Chevalier without fear and without reproach;" then proceeded to confer that distinction himself on Fleuranges, Lautrec, and other favourites. To the constable, who lost a brother in this sanguinary contest, the government of Milan was confided, in acknowledgment of the valour he had displayed in its conquest, as also to relieve the king of the uncongenial presence of that very austere personage.

A letter was despatched to the regent mother informing her of the laurels won by "her lord, her love, her Cæsar," and Francis, having made his public entry into Milan with as much military pomp as the terrible condition of the shattered French army permitted, then set off for Viterbo; prepared to make many concessions, and to subscribe to almost any proposals, in order to secure the alliance of the Pope, and the amity of the Medici family, in support, as he flattered himself, of his views on Naples and the rest of "his heritage in Italy." The negotiation was conducted by representatives of the Pope and king; but, as it appeared to be advisable that they should discuss in person the secret objects of the treaty, an interview between Leo X. and Francis I. was arranged to take place at Bologna.

CHAPTER V.

Pontiff and King. — Leo X. — The Court of the Vatican. — Francis Fascinated. — The Bologna Conference. — Francis in Italy. — The Hero's Return. — Te Deums and Dirges. — What a Falling-off is Here! — Madame Louise Alarmed. — Sainte Claude.— Death of Ferdinand of Spain. — Henry VIII. of England. — Maximilian Alarmed. — Bourbon Recalled. — Queen Joanna of Spain. — The Archduke King. — A Rival in Glory.

ON the 10th of December Francis I. and Leo X. met in great state at Bologna, and a very grand spectacle it was; as might well be inferred from the known habits and tastes of both pontiff and king. The royal chevalier, with his valiant knights and most distinguished captains, was attended by an escort brilliantly arrayed, and displaying much more of the pomp and circumstance of war than after a conflict so desperate and so recent could have been expected. If the ragged, shoeless, half-naked remnant of the Swiss army had succeeded in triumphantly carrying off their great guns, and slowly and defiantly, in face of the French, retreating in good order, it was evident that the victor, so nearly vanquished, had contrived to secure his own and his knights' military finery. Doubtless, this made its due impression.

In striking and effective contrast with the martial pomp of the king's retinue, the Pope arrived in all the solemn splendour of pontifical surroundings, and accompanied by several of those unequalled and world-famed artists whom it was his pride to attach to his court. Leo X. (Jean de' Medici), the son of Lorenzo "the Magnificent," was a man of high intelligence, affable in conversation, and with manners that gave the idea of sincerity, goodness and gentleness. He possessed all the agreeable qualities that distinguished his father, and *prestige* even more brilliant than his. He was still in the prime of life — thirty-seven — remarkably young for a Pope, being, in fact, the youngest man that had ever sat on the throne of Saint Peter.

To this celebrated pontiff belongs the appellation, "Apostle of the Renaissance," far more than to his predecessor, the warlike Julian II. — a man, however, of nobler nature than Leo X., and of more patriotic views — to whom it has been sometimes given. But Leo was especially the patron of letters, science, and art, and his boundless liberality, together with the high degree of development and perfection attained by the arts under his pontificate, has effectually associated his name with this most brilliant period of their history. Though many of the qualities of a great prince are attributed to him, they were sadly marred by the extreme impurity of his life, of which his countenance bore the traces. But the Cardinal Pallavicini, while acknowledging, what could scarcely be denied, that Leo in that respect was not quite blameless, declared that he yet was far less profligate than many of the prelates and others who composed his court. His high-bred courtesy and distinguished manners veiled, it appears, in some degree, the grossness of his vices. Nevertheless, the Papal Court, if the most learned and magnificent in Europe, was also the most recklessly extravagant and dissolute.

Leo was passionately fond of music, and daily, echoing through his palace, was heard the sound of instruments in tone and construction the most perfect known at that period; and often, while pacing to and fro, he would hum the lively airs that had been played before him. In his presence the first Italian comedies were represented, and few were produced in his time that he had not seen performed. No expense was spared by him to render the *fêtes*, sports, and theatricals given at his court both splendid and effective. He was also prodigally munificent in offering presents and conferring rewards, while it was his daily custom to scatter a purseful of gold amongst the people.

Thus, in magnificence, expenditure, pleasure, and gaiety, the sovereign pontiff's court surpassed all others. When, however, it was known that Giulio de' Medici, Leo's nephew, thought of bringing his young bride to Rome, and fixing his residence there, "Heaven be praised!" exclaimed Cardinal Bibliena — the most influential of Leo's admirers — "for all we wanted here, as a necessary complement to the Papal Court, was a court of ladies." As to any religious sentiment, it was not only disregarded but wholly unknown there.*

Francis I. was greatly fascinated by the engaging manners of Leo X. — the powerful head of the Church, who employed the pontifical treasure in the patronage of the men who produced those miracles of art his eye now met at every turn. The pontiff was quick to perceive the impression he had made, and well knew how to turn to his own advantage the sympathy and the vivid imagination of the young king, whose heart his amiability and his artistic tastes had so readily won.

The three principal subjects for discussion at the Conference were — first, the invasion of Naples, which, as part of "his heritage," Francis was desirous of reconquering, and hoped for the Pope's assistance in doing so; secondly, the interests of the feudatories of the Holy See; and thirdly, the ecclesiastical question of the abolition of the Pragmatic Sanction, and substitution of the new order of things known afterwards as the Concordat.

Francis had intended to march on Naples as soon as the Bologna Conference was ended. The Pope, however, not caring to pledge himself to aid

* See Merle d'Aubigné, "*Histoire de la Réformation.*"

in any such scheme (being really more desirous of expelling the French from Italy than of aiding to establish them in it), recommended delay; the views and aims of other states rendered, he said, any hostile measures unadvisable at that moment. Thus Francis was dissuaded from then carrying out his design.

The second question was soon satisfactorily disposed of. The third and most important one was left for further discussion and settlement to the chancellor, Duprat, and two cardinals named by the Pope. The cession of Parma and Placentia was once more promised to France; and the king, who believed that he had secured some advantages by his diplomacy, took the House of Medici and the government of Florence — then tending towards monarchy — under his especial protection. But Leo is said to have entered into his engagements with the king fully determined to elude their fulfilment.*

The charms of the Italian climate, the attractions of the too facile Italian beauties, purposely thrown in his way, and the seductive *dolce far niente* sort of life Francis so readily fell into, were fatal to his military ardour. Casting aside all restraints, he plunged into a round of vicious and degrading pleasures.

Early in January, however, messengers from his

---

* J. Servan, "*Guerres des Français;*" Henri Martin, "*Histoire de France.*"

generals, who were anxiously awaiting his arrival at Milan to head his army, as he had purposed, and to lead it to the conquest of Naples, compelled him to tear himself, though cruel was the pang, from the delights of the congenial life he was leading at Bologna.

On arriving in his Italian capital, to the astonishment of his generals and the great disappointment of the troops — who, not doubting of victory, were looking forward to the pillaging of Naples — Francis announced his change of plans; dismissed a large part of his army, confirmed Bourbon in his government, and despatched Lautrec and Navarro with the "Black bands" (German lansquenets) and the Gascon archers to assist the Venetians, as he had promised, in retaking Brescia and Verona.

Accompanied by the Duc d'Alençon, Fleuranges, Bonnivet, and other valiant knights and favourites, and escorted by a regiment of his guards, the "chevalier king" set out on his return to France. The Alps were crossed towards the end of January; after which Francis and his military *cortége* halted at Blois, where, on making a public entry into that city, he was received with enthusiasm. At Amboise, Bourges, Moulins, and other cities on his route, a like ovation awaited him; but his greatest triumph was at Lyons. There laurel crowns were preparing to grace the conqueror's brow. There his timid young queen with an infant daughter, born during his absence; his adoring mother, frantic with exuberant joy, yet with a pang at her heart when she learns that Charles de Bourbon remains at Milan; and his fondly attached but less demonstrative sister, Marguerite, assembled to welcome their victorious warrior home. There, too, are the supposed rather staid ladies of the court of Queen Claude, and the very free and fair ones who accompanied Madame Louise, as well as the far from prudish *belles* whom Madame d'Alençon has gathered around her. *Fêtes*, processions, ecclesiastical and military, *Te Deums*, bonfires, and general rejoicings, rough and uproarious as any similar demonstrations of the present day, celebrate the monarch's return to the second capital of his kingdom.

Yet lamentation, mourning, and woe mingle with the songs of triumph, and bitter tears are shed for many a gallant youth, husband, or son, slain in an unworthy cause on the gory field of Marignan; for all who fought, and many of those who fought most recklessly, were not the hired mercenaries, but scions of the most illustrious families of France, who, as volunteers, had eagerly joined the gendarmerie, and, full of enthusiasm for their "chevalier king," followed him joyfully to the battle. Therefore, while the multitude sing loud pæans in honour of the triumphs of their monarch, the clergy alternate the chanting of *Te Deums* for victory with solemn dirges and masses for the dead.

Meanwhile the heroic Francis solaces himself after the fatigues of war in the society of that galaxy of youth and beauty his tenderly solicitous mother has brought with her to Lyons. Under the skies of Italy other *belles* had enthralled him, and it is quite probable that since he left France he had thought as little of the fair Comtesse de Châteaubriand as he had of Madame Claude. But now he recognizes her amongst the ladies of honour who accompany his queen. In her presence he speaks with warm praise of the valour and daring of Lautrec; and the pride and pleasure which naturally animate her countenance, as she listens to the king's commendations of her brother, so heighten her beauty in his eyes, that while admiringly gazing on her the libertine monarch becomes a captive at her feet.

Françoise de Foix did not spurn the husband of the young and amiable queen with whom she had been brought up. Ah! what a falling off is here! For Françoise was one of the virtuous Anne of Brittany's piously trained maids of honour, and the wife of Jean de Laval, Comte de Châteaubriand — an alliance formed for her by the late queen. Was it, then, the love of power that led her astray, or the desire to use it in elevating her three ambitious brothers to the posts of honour they coveted? More probably it was the immoral influence of the new court that occasioned this sudden fall from virtue to vice.*

The power of the new favourite soon rivalled that of Madame Louise, who, alarmed to find that her sway over her son was becoming less absolute, took every opportunity of depreciating the countess, of thrusting ladies fair as she into notice, in order to supplant her, and, by unfounded suggestions, striving to bring disgrace on her brothers. But the countess maintained her empire over the king for several years, and her influence is said to have been less prejudicial to the interests of the state than that of Madame Louise, with her unlimited powers as regent, her propensity for hoarding money, and unscrupulousness as to the means of obtaining it.†

The sovereign's young, neglected wife, much attached to her faithless husband, must have been

---

* The story told by Brantôme of a stratagem employed by Francis to bring this lady to his court, despite the desire of her husband to prevent it — namely, by having a facsimile made and forwarded to her of a ring which the count had arranged to send to his wife should he wish her to join him — is no more worthy of credit than many other gossiping tales related by the famous *chroniqueur scandaleux*. He was not born until 1540, therefore he personally knew nothing of the reign of Francis I., and very little of that of Henry II. His grandfather was page to Anne of Brittany, and from him and his father the court scandal was obtained which Brantôme gives, adding thereto the suggestions of his own depraved fancy. Some incidental remarks in the "State Papers" of 1532 quite disprove the sequel also to Brantôme's story.

† Henri Martin.

deeply wounded by this flagrant disregard of her feelings, and no less so by the perfidy of the countess, hitherto her companion and friend. But, though Francis is acknowledged to have had no love for Claude, he is represented as having so high a respect for her as to have refrained, during her lifetime, from offering her the indignity of publicly recognising even the most influential and favoured of his numerous mistresses by the honourable appellation of *maîtresse-en-titre*. This is, of course, to be considered a convincing proof of his nobility of mind, and of the chivalric sentiments which animated the breast and guided the conduct of the "chevalier king" and first gentleman of France. The people, however, adored his young queen — "Sainte Claude," as they called her, the daughter of the good King Louis.

At about the time that Francis was returning from Italy — January the 23d, 1516 — there died, somewhat suddenly, his most powerful and persistent enemy, Ferdinand the Catholic. The news soon after reached Lyons; and Francis, who seemed to have abandoned the government of his kingdom to his mother and her council of regency, giving his own attention exclusively to external politics, during those brief intervals he could spare from his pleasures, thought the moment favourable for attacking Naples.

Influenced by the famous Cardinal Ximenes,

Archbishop of Toledo, Ferdinand, a few hours only before his death, had altered his will in favour of the Archduke Charles, Count of Flanders, whom he had intended to deprive of his right to the regency of the Spains (kingdoms of Castile and Aragon), to transfer it to his younger grandson, Ferdinand. The latter had been born and brought up in Spain; Charles in the Netherlands, where, under the care of his aunt, Margaret of Austria — who during his minority so ably governed his heritage — he had constantly resided. The Spanish king, having never seen him, regarded his daughter's eldest son, from his birthplace and bringing up, as a foreigner, therefore unacceptable to Spain.

Believing that civil war and hatred between the brothers would be the result of Ferdinand's arrangement, the cardinal remonstrated with him, pointing out, also, its injustice. To the admonitions of the severe and powerful prelate the dying king readily yielded, and Charles was named regent — the queen, his mother, Joanna "the Demented," being incapable of governing. Ferdinand, however, determined that his enmity to France should not end with his death, left 200,000 crowns to the Emperor Maximilian for the purpose of raising an army to attack the French in Italy.

Henry VIII. of England had heard with exceeding jealousy of the victory and exploits of the youthful conqueror whom he had vainly counselled to refrain from making war on Milan, and in his irritation, which Ferdinand encouraged, had allied himself more closely with Spain. He now followed his father-in-law's example, and despatched a contribution of 200,000 crowns towards increasing the army the emperor was hurriedly getting together.

An order was sent off to Bourbon to march at once on Naples, Francis expecting that the papal troops would join him in attacking it. But instead of conquering Naples, it was necessary to defend Milan against an army 30,000 strong, with which Maximilian early in March appeared in the Tyrol. No troops, however, were despatched by Leo to assist the French either in attack or defence; but as a part of the Swiss cantons were still favourable to France, they consented to furnish a reinforcement of 17,000 men. A still larger number from the dissatisfied cantons had joined the imperial forces. Hostilities were about to commence, and the two armies to face each other in the field, when messengers arrived with orders from the Helvetian Diet forbidding the Swiss soldiers to slay each other in the interest of foreigners, and commanding them to return home.

The Swiss of the imperial army immediately demanded their pay. As usual, Maximilian had no money. The clamour that ensued, together with the contents of a letter from General Trivulzio to the Swiss commandant, written to be intercepted, and from which it was made to appear that a plot existed to deliver the emperor into the hands of the French, so alarmed Maximilian, who remembered the fate of Ludovico Sforza, that he fled with all haste and secrecy to Bergamo, leaving word that he had gone thither to obtain the requisite funds. No one looked for his return; and, as their chief had forsaken them, the troops disbanded themselves, and, by way of indemnity for the loss of their pay, they pillaged Lodi and other towns on their route homeward. The issue of this enterprise, announced so formidable, and at first believed to be so, was that the terror-stricken emperor became the laughing-stock of all the courts of Europe.

Soon after this event the constable was recalled, Lautrec superseding him in the governorship of Milan. This was at the instigation of Louise of Savoy, who thus procured herself the double pleasure of annoying Bourbon and of seeing him again. She suggested to the king the extreme danger of leaving a prince so wealthy, so ambitious, and with troops devoted to him as a brave and able leader, in uncontrolled power at Milan, insinuating that he had designs on the duchy. Francis took alarm, and Bourbon, much chagrined, returned to France. The promotion of Lautrec is attributed to the influence — then rivalling that of the king's mother — of the Comtesse de Châteaubriand. The prize of valour was thus awarded to beauty, the charms of the sister being a more powerful incentive than the acknowledged services of the brother.

The death of Ferdinand greatly changed the relative positions in which, by their treaty of March, 1515, Francis and the Archduke Charles stood towards each other. Naples, which Francis so anxiously desired to reconquer, was now possessed by Charles, to whom Ferdinand, together with his kingdoms, had transmitted the war he so long had carried on against France. Both princes, however, then wished for peace. Consequently Gouffier Boissy, on the part of Francis, and Guillaume de Croy Chièvres, Charles's minister — who, like Boissy, had formerly been his master's governor — met at Noyon to negotiate a new treaty.

The claims of Francis on Naples were now transferred to his daughter Louise, an infant of scarce a year old, whom, instead of Madame Renée, Charles engaged to marry on her completing her twelfth year. It was agreed that in the interval Charles should retain Naples, but pay annually 100,000 gold crowns to Francis, who was absolved by the Pope from fulfilling the promise of the former treaty to give Renée in marriage to the archduke, now Charles I. of Spain.

Charles, though actually only regent, had immediately, on the death of Ferdinand, assumed the title and honours of king, acting on the advice of Chièvres and other Flemish nobles. Both Castile and Aragon resented this sort of usurpation of the prerogatives of their queen; and when, after a long delay, he made up his mind — being greatly urged by Ximenes, who governed so ably as regent — to visit the Spains, it was with great difficulty that the Cortes were prevailed on to consent to his bearing the title of king conjointly with his mother, whose name in all public acts was to appear with, and precede, his.

The Spaniards thought his conduct as a son unnatural, and strangely wanting in that delicacy of sentiment with which Joanna's subjects regarded her malady; the Cortes having declined — Joanna being unwilling to resign her rights — to declare her incompetent to govern. Among the grandees there were, in fact, some who detected, as they imagined, signs of the same mental infirmity in Charles as that which afflicted his mother. This arose chiefly from his inability at that time to speak Spanish with any fluency; for scarcely did he open his mouth except to utter a few incoherent, disconnected words in reply to the addresses and harangues of both nobles and people; and even these were suggested to him by Chièvres, who, apparently, still exercised the full powers of his governor.

Of the vast ambition which was his ruling passion no indications were perceived in Charles in his sixteenth year. Doubtless he already knew from Chièvres — a man of very different character from Boissy, who had influenced the youth of Francis

— how vainglorious were the sentiments that actuated and guided the young French monarch; his indifference to affairs of state, his eagerness in pursuit of pleasure. For Charles flattered the vanity of Francis, and, as the betrothed of the baby Madame Louise, addressed him in his letters as his "good father." Nothing, therefore, yet revealed to the conqueror of Marignan that in this youth, so grave, so frigid, and, as it seemed to him, so dull and spiritless, he was to find a rival in glory.

The treaty concluded by the two ambassadors at Noyon, and ratified some months later by Charles and Francis, was followed by the "perpetual peace" with the Swiss, leaving the French for a while in undisturbed possession of Lombardy, and Europe in the enjoyment of an interval of repose. But, too soon, it is destined again to be devastated, and blood must flow in torrents; the rivalry and ambition of Charles V. and Francis I. spreading discord and misery throughout their dominions during the remaining years of their reigns.

CHAPTER VI.

The News on the Crossroads.— Thanksgiving for Victory.— Nocturnal Amusements.— Triboulet the Court Jester.— The Regency of Madame Louise.— The Clerks of the Basoche.— The Concordat.— A Refractory Parliament.— One who Had Played Many Parts.— Propitiating the Pope. — Rapid Promotion.— Menacing the Judges.— Decease of the Pragmatique.— Depravity of the Clergy.— High Mass in the Ste. Chapelle.— Coronation of Queen Claude.— Chivalric Exploits.— Decorous Recreation.

THE political complications resulting from Ferdinand's death and the emperor's expedition against the French in Italy had delayed the king's triumphal entry into Paris. But now, crowned with fresh laurels (Maximilian's fight being regarded as a new victory), peace with Spain and the Swiss proclaimed, and a general peace negotiating, Francis leaves Blois for his capital.

As then was customary, the heralds had made these great events known to the people by sound of trumpet, on the crossroads and public places of the city. An enthusiastic reception therefore awaits him — a little less warm and spontaneous perhaps than it might have been. This is owing to the great unpopularity of the regent, in which

Francis already is beginning to share, because of the tendency he evinces of it being too frequently his "good pleasure" to levy new taxes.*

He arrived with his court at the Palais des Tournelles on the 4th of October, the royal pageant attracting crowds of sightseers into the narrow streets of Paris. The next day, Sunday, he went to the Abbey of St. Denis in great state and with much military pomp, "to return thanks to God and the glorious saints for the great victory gained in Italy. The bodies of the saints which, in order to ensure on high their intercession on his behalf, had been exposed during his absence, were then restored to their places behind the altar." †

The "Bourgeois" adds that while Francis remained in Paris he and his favourite companions "went about every day in disguise, besides mumming in masks at night." These royal and noble roysterers, it seems had not the fear of the provost-marshal before their eyes. That high civic authority, with his lieutenant, the recorder, and his archers, rode all armed every night through the streets of Paris, "punishing the misdeeds of noisy revellers, arresting thieves and other evil-doers." But he is said not to have shown, or rather not dared to show, the same rigour towards all classes;

---

* Francis I. was the author of the formula, " *Tel est notre bon plaisir.*"

† "*Journal d'un Bourgeois de Paris,*" *1516*.

otherwise the streets of old Paris after dark would have been more orderly and quiet. The noble youths, whose amusement it was to roam the tortuous lanes and streets of the capital at such unseemly hours, had their passes ("*lettres de passe,*") which enabled them to set the patrol at defiance, to frequent the gambling-houses, and to mingle in midnight brawls with impunity.

But that the dignity of the law and that of the officers deputed to enforce it might not thus be compromised, the provost and his aide-de-camp fell into the convenient habit of closing both eyes and ears when the clashing of swords and voices loud, yet perhaps less fierce than bantering, with shouts of laughter mingled with piteous cries for mercy, plainly indicated that the chivalric gentlemen armed with passes — Francis too often being of the party — were abroad that night, and for fun and frolic were attacking peaceable belated citizens.

The good people of Paris, long accustomed to a quiet, sedate life under the reign of the orderly Louis XII. and the pious Anne of Britanny, were exceedingly scandalised by these riotous revels, and loudly complained of the negligence of the patrol. All honest citizens, when compelled to be out after dark, carried with them, as decreed by the law, small hand-lanterns. Generally the first efforts of their assailants were to possess themselves of the lanterns and extinguish the light. In the scuffle that ensued hard blows were often given and received, while a falling mask or two would reveal to the affrighted *bourgeois* some well-known faces amongst the brawling party of aristocratic and royal practical jokers.

The king was readily recognised, from his large oval face and very bold features. He is said to have had a larger nose than any other man in France, except Triboulet, the court jester, which would seem rather to impugn his claim to that large share of manly beauty with which his flatterers have credited him. The royal nose was, of course, a more shapely one than poor Triboulet could boast of. He, who said so many wise and witty things, and to whom so many more he did not say are attributed, was a sad object to look upon; his appearance being that of a sort of deformed man-monkey.

The clerks of the Basoche, who so often had raised a laugh by satirising the thrift and economy of the late king,—mirth in which Louis himself had sometimes joined,—now ventured to introduce the new monarch into their farces, and, under a very thin disguise, to hold up in a farcical fashion his and his courtiers' unseemly revels, and low *amours*, to public contempt and ridicule. Nor did they scruple to express after the same manner their and the people's indignant censure of the government of the kingdom by Madame Louise, the regent mother, whom they represented, under the name of "Mère Sotte," as pillaging the public treasury, plundering on all sides, and of being the main cause of the troubles of the state.

Great was the rage of both king and regent, and a stormy scene ensued; for Francis had inherited his mother's unbridled temper, her ill-organised mind, and violent, absolute character. When in a passion he would break and destroy furniture, and throw glasses, dishes — anything, indeed, that came in his way — at his attendants or at any of the people about him. The offending players soon discovered that the times were changed, and that to satirise royalty was a crime of *lèse majesté*. Three of their number were immediately seized, bound hand and foot, and sent to Amboise in irons.*

The court, a few days after, left Paris. A long sojourn in the pestiferous Palais des Tournelles was next to impossible. The foul, open ditch still ran sluggishly on under the windows of the grand *salon*.†

---

* "*Journal d'un Bourgeois de Paris*," 1516.

† The king's urgent commands to the civil authorities to turn its course were as ineffectual as those of his predecessor. The reports of experts as to the best method of abating or abolishing the nuisance were forwarded to him, but the money needed to carry them out was not forthcoming. This was the real obstacle so difficult to overcome, — neither king nor municipality being willing to incur the cost of freeing the city from a plague-spot that annually counted its victims by thousands.

Arrived at Blois, Francis sent twelve archers to bring thither other presumptuous players from Paris, and to imprison them in one of the cells of the château. There they were kept for some months closely confined. One night, however, they contrived to make their escape, and sought refuge in the Church of the Cordeliers at Blois, where they remained until the coronation of Queen Claude, when, at her intercession, Francis graciously and unreservedly (*à pur et à plein*) pardoned the culprits.* Henceforth, the *farceurs* of the Basoche, if they did not altogether refrain from satirising royalty, at least did so more guardedly, and with less freedom of speech than hitherto.

However, an affair of far greater importance, agitating the people and bringing the king into further disfavour with the nation, occurred while he and his court were amusing themselves at Blois. This was the return of Duprat from Bologna, bringing with him the Concordat, and announcing the repeal of the Pragmatic Sanction, considered for nearly a century past the bulwark of the rights of the Gallican Church. The Concordat was, therefore, received, both by the clergy and the members of the judicature, with unanimous indignation. The priesthood and the magistracy being the two most influential classes of the community in the olden time, as regarded the *bourgeoisie*, their excitement soon spread to the people, causing a general fer-

* "*Journal d'un Bourgeois de Paris*," 1517.

ment, not only in Paris, but in all the large towns of the kingdom.

The Concordat abrogated the right guaranteed to the clergy in 1438, at Bourges, by the decree called the Pragmatic Sanction, of the free election of their bishops, abbots, and priors, and transferred their nomination to the king. On the other hand, it revived the "Annates," or claim of the Pope to the first year's revenue of every benefice conferred — a claim regarded by the assembly of Bourges as the most exorbitant of the papal exactions, and henceforth to be abolished.

To Leo X., who disbursed with so liberal a hand, whose revenue, vast as it was, still fell short of his needs, an increase of income from any source was welcome. But with the restitution of the "Annates" there was the further gratification of having won back a right of which the papacy had been so long, and so ignominiously, as it considered, deprived. "As to the barren privilege," writes Mézéray, "of nominating the French prelates, though rightly belonging to the spiritual power, Leo was willing to cede the exercise to the temporal prince, so that the profits were ceded to him. A singular exchange, indeed!"

Francis was greatly amazed at the presumption of the clergy and Parliament in expressing disapprobation of any measure it pleased him to introduce and require the formality of their assent to. Immediately he summoned the refractory Parliament, with several prelates, the Chapter of Notre Dame, and the chief doctors and professors of the university, to the Palace of Justice; where he went in person on the 5th of February, accompanied by the chancellor, whom he directed to explain to the assembly the objects of the great measure he had concluded with the Pope, and to order its registration. The Concordat being mainly the work of the chancellor, he, of course, could best explain it. He was a man who had played many parts in his time, from that of a humble attorney in Paris, until, after a variety of ups and downs, he was raised, through the favour of Madame Louise, to the highest judicial post in the realm. She, however, had not further enriched him. Her own grasping fondness for money, and her habit of hoarding it, made her chary of conferring pensions, or of dipping into the coffers of the state, except to increase her own concealed treasure; not a crown of which would she part with, even for the "idolised son — her Cæsar, her lord, her love " — when, some few years later, without applying to the state, she could have paid his children's ransom.

Duprat had recently become a widower, and, having a numerous family growing up, desired to secure a large increase of income to establish them in the world with the *éclat* befitting the sons and daughters of the great chancellor of France. The king, being then anxious at any sacrifice to secure friendly relations with the Pope — notwithstanding his recent failure in his promise to aid him — afforded the chancellor the opportunity he sought. To enter the Church with the hope of obtaining some rich benefice had before occurred to him; but while the system of election was in force, he knew that the hope was a vain one.

It had been customary with the popes to urge the kings of France to abolish the Pragmatique. Leo X. had greatly pressed it both on Louis XII. and Francis I. The latter, still hoping to secure Leo's concurrence in his views on Naples, consented to Duprat's suggestion that the question should be discussed at Bologna, and some new arrangement more satisfactory to his holiness entered into. The result was the Concordat, and a cardinal's hat for Duprat, as an acknowledgment from the Pope of the ability with which he had conducted the negotiation.

"To propitiate the Pope, Duprat induced the king servilely to submit to attend on his holiness, to walk before him, and hand him a basin of water to wash his holy hands in" — of all responsibilities, probably. But with this famous Concordat, he told his royal master — the Pope receiving only one year's revenue, and leaving the nominations to him — he would have six archbishoprics, eighty-three bishoprics, and a large number of abbeys and priories to dispose of. "A fine civil list, indeed," says Michelet, "for one who knew how most advantageously to dispose of it."

Francis, indeed, profited little by the Concordat, in the way of putting money in his purse. But, as his purse had rarely any money in it, the Concordat furnished him with an excellent substitute for it. Instead of his newly acquired power opening a way, as was expected, to preferment in the Church to the younger nobility,— then confined solely to the profession of arms,— he made archbishops and bishops of his favourites, abbots and priors of architects, painters and sculptors, — exempted, of course, from any ecclesiastical duties. "Nothing, therefore, was left for the *noblesse*, whose irritation exceeded even that of the people."*

But Duprat, besides attaining, at one bound, to the dignity of cardinal, was nominated, under the new *régime*, Archbishop of Sens, Bishop of Meaux, Albi, Coutances, Diez, and Gap, also Abbot of Fleury, or Saint-Benoît-sur-Loire. Duprat, should, therefore, have been an eloquent advocate of the advantages of the Concordat. Yet his advocacy of it did not convince the assembly convoked by the king. The Parliament demanded time for its due examination, the prellates and doctors suggested the summoning of a national council, to decide on its adoption or rejection, they being unable to give an opinion upon it.

"You are not able!" exclaimed the king, rising,

* Michelet.

in a passion. "I will compel you to be able, or I will send you all to Rome to give your reasons to the Pope."

Nevertheless, the opposition to the Concordat continued, and the king, losing all patience, signed, on the 15th of May, letters patent ordering the Parliament and other tribunals henceforth to take the Concordat as the basis of their decrees, or judgments in ecclesiastical matters. The tribunals boldly replied by a demand for the restoration of the Pragmatic Sanction, to which the king responded by menacing the judges with imprisonment.

These persistent opposers of the royal will were the magistrates who had bought their places, and could not be removed at his majesty's good pleasure. Little did Francis and his chancellor suspect, when they introduced this venal practice, in order to supply the king's needs, that they were creating an independent body of judges, who generally would care more for their reputation with the public, as impartial administrators of the laws, than to conform to the views and wishes of the sovereign when not in accordance with justice.

Not until the following year was the Concordat registered, and then under protest only, and with all sort of reservations, "by the express order of the king." Street disturbances occurred, for the priests from their pulpits raved incessantly against "the unworthy abandonment of the liberties of the Gallican Church," a phrase that excited the people almost as much as the revolutionary cry of *"La patrie en danger."*

But the Concordat, though registered, was treated by the Parliament of Paris — the provinces following their example — as a mere dead letter, and nearly ten years had elapsed — 1527 — when the king, unable to conquer the resistance of the judges, transferred from the Parliament to the Grand Council the right of giving judgment in any proceedings relative to the ecclesiastical elections. Then the Concordat was observed, but it never found favour, and, from generation to generation, was protested against;* while the virtues of the deceased and universally lamented Pragmatique were lauded, even by every successor of the great Cardinal Duprat, as long as the French monarchy existed.

Francis I., besides his arbitrary edict concerning the chase, had made two long strides towards despotism. First, he usurped the rights of the States General by levying taxes without their sanction; secondly, he usurped the right of the Church to elect its own chiefs. To resist this gradual invasion of national rights — not to show sympathy with the dissolute priesthood — was the object of the Parliament's strenuous opposition to the Concordat.

* Henri Martin.

The prelates elected by the suffrages of monks and canons were men of the most licentious lives; jovial companions and epicures, who could be confidently counted upon to offer no obstacle to the infamous state of things existing, as a rule, in every monastery and convent in the kingdom. The example of the wearer of the triple crown was duly followed by bishops, abbots and priors, in all its revolting depravity. What startling horrors are revealed by some writers of that period of clerical impurity, as scenes of monastic life of ordinary occurrence! The mind turns from them with a shudder. Morals, then, suffered not by the establishing of the Concordat, nor did they in any way gain by it. "The only change was that the revenues of the king's lay prelates were squandered at court instead of in their dioceses and abbeys." *

During the earlier period of this agitation of Church and state, popular indignation was often soothed, excitement kept down, and the love of the Parisians for gay pageants frequently gratified, by grand displays of royal pomp and splendour. Early in 1517, an embassy arrived in Paris from the young King of Spain, accompanied by two or three grandees, in order to ratify the treaty of peace Charles and Francis had agreed on, and to attend the ceremony of the betrothal of the former to the infant daughter of the latter.

* Henri Martin.

One can readily imagine that the celebration of high mass, which followed the betrothal, and took place in the Ste. Chapelle, was of unusual impressiveness — the marvellous beauty of the edifice; the magnificently decorated altar; the rich vestments of the officiating priests; the splendid and picturesque Spanish costumes worn by the grandee representing Charles, and the nobles of his suite, who occupied one side of the chapel, must have formed a spectacle of imposing grandeur. On the opposite side, worthily completing the picture, stood Francis and his queen, his mother and sister, splendidly arrayed; with them were the princes of the blood, the great officers of state, and the nobles and ladies composing the French court.

In compliment to the Spaniards, Francis wore on this occasion "an ample mantle of crimson velvet, similar to the ambassador's, very long and trailing on the ground; with a large chaperon, or hood, of the same thrown over his shoulder, in Spanish fashion. He wore also the Archduke King's Order of the Golden Fleece." After mass there was a banquet, both being repeated on the following day, with the additional and concluding ceremony of touching for the king's-evil — when many sufferers are said to have been cured of their malady.*

Having betrothed his daughter, Francis be-

* "*Journal d'un Bourgeois de Paris.*"

thought him of the long deferred coronation of his queen. It had greatly disappointed the people, whose sentiments towards the daughter of Louis XII. were those of love and reverence, that she was not crowned at St. Denis with the king; many believing that he derived his right to the crown from his marriage with Claude. But disappointment was deepening into resentment, as gradually they were learning to estimate their king at his proper value.

The coronation of Claude was therefore a politic act at this time of general discontent; discontent arising not merely out of the affair of the Concordat, and the famine which then prevailed in France — for which no better remedy could be devised for the relief of the suffering people than carrying the shrine of "Madame Ste. Geneviève" in procession through the city. But complaints to the civic authorities, often accompanied by threats, had been more numerous of late of the gross outrages nightly committed in Paris. These flagrant acts, it was observed, always occurred when it was the good pleasure of the king with his dissolute favourites to sojourn a short time in his capital, or, for the enjoyment of the chase, at the hunting-seat of St. Germain.

This chivalric band, emboldened by their immunity from arrest or imprisonment, no longer confined themselves to attacking inoffensive people in the streets. They now forced their way into

Palace of St. Germain.
Photo-etching from an old print.

houses, to the great terror of the inmates, wherever they could effect an entrance; ill-treating masters and servants, insulting wives and daughters, upsetting furniture and "playing pranks which the people took very complainingly." *

But the coronation of Queen Claude is announced, and for the moment diverts attention from all besides. Again St. Denis is the scene of a very grand show, and Claude's public entry into Paris is a perfect triumph. It is graced by all the great nobles and ladies of Brittany, while the enthusiasm of the people is boundless. Forty-two ladies arrayed in rich velvet robes, and wearing gold hats in the form of a crown, ride in the queen's procession, mounted on mules with housings of cloth of gold. Trumpets and clarions precede them, "sounding together very melodiously, as a sort of decorous recreation (*récréation honnête*) according well with *Te Deums* and praises to God and the Virgin Mary." †

The usual *fêtes*, tournaments, bonfires, etc., followed — amusing the people in spite of their many privations, and inspiring a hope that the crowning of "Madame Sainte Claude" would lead to that change for the better which "Madame Sainte Geneviève" had not deigned to grant to their prayers.

* "*Journal d'un Bourgeois de Paris*," *1517*.
† "*Journal d'un Bourgeois de Paris*."

CHAPTER VII.

Splendour of the Papal Court. — Art, Literature, and Chivalry. — Leonardo da Vinci. — Pencil and Palette Laid Aside. — A Death-bed Confession. — Movable Pictures. — Unveiling Raphael's Works. — Jean Goujon. — A Hopeless Passion. — The Château de Moulins. — Park and Grounds of Moulins. — O'ershadowed by a Cloud. — A Royal Dish of Windsor Beans. — A Dish to Set Before a King. — Salads and Fruits. — More Regal than the King. — Blessings on the New-born Babe.

DURING his sojourn in Italy, brief though it had been, Francis was vividly impressed by the great superiority of the Italians, compared with the French, in all that concerned art and literature. The splendour of the Papal Court, so lavishly displayed by Leo X., with its luxury and voluptuousness, its varnish of exceeding refinement combined with and concealing its excessive depravity — forming a sort of pagan elysium — was also in a high degree fascinating and seductive to a mind like that of the young French king's, which had never known any moral training, or been subjected to any wholesome restraints whatever.

Henceforth, then, the Papal Court was to be rivalled by the Court of France; and in prodigality and licentiousness doubtless it was. But the "chevalier king" had determined that under his patronage art and letters also should receive further development, and flourish in France as in Italy. He had, indeed, little true feeling for either, and rather proposed to invite eminent Italians to reside in France than to cultivate native talent.

Like Leo, to surround himself with great artists, with men of genius and of eminent scholarship, would be enhancing the *prestige* of a reign destined, as he fancied, to be distinguished by the revival of ancient chivalry (instead, as it really was, of its decay and extinction), and, in short, placing on his already laurel-wreathed brow an aureola of literary and artistic glory.

Francis, while in Italy, is said to have seduced Leonardo da Vinci from the service of the Pope; and it is true that this celebrated master did visit France towards the end of 1516 or early in 1517. He was of course well received by the king, who gave him an apartment in the Château de Clous, near to that of Amboise. He had bought in Italy, for 4,000 gold crowns, this painter's portrait of the beautiful "Mona Lisa." He now commissioned him to paint a cartoon ("Santa Anna") and to decorate several palaces. These, as yet, had either no existence, or at best were but hunting-seats destined to become royal châteaux when, by and by, Blois and Amboise did not offer variety enough to a court always *en voyage*.

Leonardo had for some time been in failing health, and was suffering from partial paralysis of the limbs; for the dissipations of the Italian courts told on the lives of those sons of genius who were their glory. His determination to leave Florence for France was, however, induced by Michael Angelo's departure from that city, and the mortification he felt on learning that he had left because Leo X. had sent for the great architect and painter — between whom and Leonardo da Vinci rivalry and consequent discord had long subsisted — to design the façade of the Church of St. Lorenzo, at Rome. Seventeen years earlier, when at the height of his fame, Leonardo had declined to visit France, though urged by a patron more enlightened and enthusiastic, and even more liberal, than Francis I. in his payments for the *chefs-d'œuvre* of sculpture and painting executed for him. This was Cardinal Georges d'Amboise.

The climate of France was supposed by the Italians to have a depressing effect on genius. Besides, life was not so pleasant at Des Tournelles as at the Vatican, or even at Blois and Amboise as at Florence, Pisa, Umbria, and other Italian courts. But as Francis continued for years to come to ravage Italy, Italian artists at times sought refuge in the dominions of their oppressor from the ruin he had heaped on their country. Many of the industrial arts and manufactures for which France has since become famed were in like manner introduced by Italian refugees.

Leonardo, however, had not visited France to paint pictures and decorate palaces, but only to die there. He had thrown pencil and palette aside, and taken up the Catholic mass-book, being anxiously desirous of acquainting himself with the Roman ritual and the Christian faith, in order to secure the salvation of his soul, which hitherto he seems to have neglected. He died at the Château de Clous, in 1519, aged sixty-six, not, as has been sometimes related, "in the arms of the king, his head resting on the royal shoulder," but with his friend Melzi at his bedside; his death being announced to Francis at the same time as Melzi sent the intelligence to the painter's relatives in Florence. He was buried at Amboise, in the Church of St. Florentin.

Leonardo da Vinci was one of the most dilatory and indolent of the great painters,—delaying for a most unconscionable time the execution of the many commissions he received. Patrons would sometimes grow weary of this long waiting. Leonardo would then rouse himself from his dreamy mood, and dispel any possible latent feelings of dissatisfaction by the beauty of his work, which may indeed have owed something to that meditative habit ascribed to indolence, or too great a love of the *dolce far niente*. He confessed this failing as a sin, on his death-bed, regretting that he had neglected to employ the great talents God had given him as extensively and usefully as he might have done.

Vasari speaks of the countenance of Leonardo da Vinci as of so perfect a type of manly beauty, that no portrait or description had ever done justice to it; or, to use his own words, it had "never been adequately extolled."

No other Italian painter of eminence was then in France, or probably was inclined to displease Leo X. by responding to the king's invitation to accompany or follow him thither. Raphael was then at the zenith of his fame, and to have borne him off to France would, in some sense, have been a conquest greater than the conquest of Milan. But the Pope — to whom any discomfiture inflicted on France or her king gave such hearty enjoyment, whether by his own or another's hand — had very effectual means at command for preventing the stars of the Italian courts from shedding lustre on the court of the "barbarians." Leo was no less prone than Julian II., his predecessor, to apply that epithet to the French, and to exclaim with that warlike prelate, "Drive out the barbarians from Italy!"

If, however, Francis could not carry off the artist, he at least succeeded in obtaining several of his works. Raphael was accounted a wonderfully prolific painter; though of the numerous productions attributed to him, many, doubtless, are either wholly the work of some one of his band of fifty pupils, or, at most, received but a few finishing touches from the master's hand.

At about this time only, movable pictures, to be hung on walls as ornaments, began to be in frequent demand. It is considered doubtful whether before the sixteenth century any such existed. For what would now be termed the easel pictures of the older masters have been detached from some articles of civil or ecclesiastical furniture. Altar-pieces, portraits of saints, Madonnas, etc., were not then suspended, put up, or taken down, as adventitious adornments, but formed part of the solid structure, included in the general conception of the building, as the necessary adjuncts of architecture.*

When Raphael's "Saint Michael," in 1517, and "Holy Family," in 1518 (now, or not long since, at Fontainebleau), arrived in France, Francis gave each of them a no less solemn reception than that which the early Christian kings were wont to accord to the most holy *reliques* brought from the East. It was a mark of the highest favour to be permitted to take a furtive glance of the great artist's *chef-d'œuvre* before the day when, in the principal gallery of the palace and to the sound of trumpets, the curtain was drawn aside

---

* See *Quarterly Review*, 1840, Passavant's "Life of Raphael."

and revealed it to the eager gaze of the Court.* Raphael's last great work, "The Transfiguration," appears to have been intended for France; but the painter's death, in 1520, gave it another destination.

The remarkable talent of Jean Goujon, afterwards so famous as a sculptor and architect, had already begun to develop itself in his painting on glass, † to be followed by painting in oil. Yet Francis gave no encouragement to this rising young artist, though the talent, so evident in the early efforts of Jean Goujon, might have been thought worthy of royal protection. But it was not the youthful aspirations of native genius that awakened interest in the self-absorbed mind of the "chevalier king" (title little deserved). His patronage was reserved for men already renowned for their genius and learning, and who, by their presence at his court, were able to add something to the refulgence of his own glory.

But other interests than those of art now forced themselves on the king's attention.

The usually smooth course of his vicious pleasures had been constantly ruffled ever since — acting on the advice of Louise of Savoy — he recalled Charles de Bourbon from Milan. His

---

* Henri Martin.

† Some specimens of his glass-painting still exist in the Cathedral of Sens, and in the chapel of the Château de Vincennes.

presence at court gave rise to continual annoyance and perplexity, as well to the king as to Louise and their favourites. Cold, haughty, and of severely moral life (surprising rarity in the age in which he lived), it was yet the constable's melancholy fate to inspire the *belles* of the court with love that he sought not. His grave demeanour should indeed have had a contrary effect on ladies of such gay humour. Yet if his dark Italian eyes (his mother was a princess of Gonzaga) rested but a moment on the fair face of Françoise de Foix, as it appears they sometimes did, perhaps in pity, the lynx-eyed Louise, who watched his every look and movement, failed not to see it, as well as the deepened colour, fancied or real, that suffused the cheek of the countess.

Urged by jealousy and the ardour of her hopeless passion, that could not wrest from the duke even a glance of pity, she sought consolation in raising suspicions in the king's mind of the fidelity of his mistress, whom, as her rival also in influence over her son, she hated and endeavoured to ruin. Further, by thus inflaming his already resentful feeling towards the constable, whom she believed she loved, she hoped to effect his downfall, too, for so persistently slighting that love.

An event, tending to increase the estrangement already subsisting between the king and his cousin of Bourbon, occurred soon after Claude's coronation. It was the christening of the Comte de Clermont, the constable's newly born son and heir. The king having acceded to the wish of the parents that he and his queen should become the child's sponsors, he and Queen Claude, with the Duchesse Louise, Marguerite of Angoulême, and other ladies and gentlemen of the court, left Blois for the Château de Moulins, for the celebration of the ceremony.

Moulins was a princely residence, — Charles de Bourbon, no less than Francis, being a lover of magnificence, also a patron of the beaux-arts, and, perhaps, a more enlightened, but at all events a more munificent one. Not that Francis was inclined to be sordid in his awards to great artists. He was liberally, lavishly, prodigally disposed. But other expensive tastes, together with his wars, made heavy demands on an exchequer which, notwithstanding all the expedients of Duprat's fertile brain for raising money, was more frequently empty than full.

Francis seems to have been startled by the unexpected grandeur of the Château de Moulins, and the regal state in which the constable lived in the chief town of his duchy of Bourbon. This grand old ducal palace — as described by Navagero,* who visited it — was a magnificent edifice, in the style of a fortress, standing on an eminence in a park of great extent.

* The Venetian ambassador, in his interesting account to the Senate of his journey to Paris.

This was unusual; the royal châteaux and those of the nobility of the fifteenth and sixteenth centuries being all, or nearly so, built in low positions, because of the suitableness of the adjacent forests for the enjoyment of the chase. The chase alone was thought of — the landscape was of utter indifference, as indeed were the beauties of nature generally. Moulins was at this time surrounded by fine gardens recently laid out after the Italian manner, with terraces and fountains, and many trees and plants newly introduced into France, where gardening, though its progress was slow, was then becoming an art, and one believed to be greatly favoured by Francis himself.

But his interest in it, apparently, had been less keen than that of the constable; for no royal residence had yet any gardens that could compare with those of Moulins — the work of skilled horticulturists who had accompanied Bourbon to France, when recalled from Milan. In the park was a large number of animals and birds, and in the more distant part of the domain, left wild for the chase, "partridges, pheasants, francolins (a species of partridge, but of larger size), and other game abounded; as well as turkeys and parrots of different kinds" (Navagero).

When the royal cavalcade (all journeys being then made on horseback), followed by the long train of litters and escort of archers, had passed the castle gates, the vista, as they advanced, gradually opening before them, and a reminiscence of Italian palaces meeting the eager gaze of the cavaliers, no gleam of pleasure o'erspread the young monarch's countenance. Rather, we are told, it was o'ershadowed by a cloud as his magnificent host, attended by a large number of the gentlemen of his household, stood ready to receive him with a cordial but dignified greeting.

But if being forestalled in the laying out of an Italian garden was a cause of displeasure (Francis desiring to take to himself the credit or glory, as it might be, of initiating all changes or improvements), still more so was Bourbon's presumption in founding a convent at Moulins to commemorate *his* and the king's victory of Marignan — that great victory which deprived the Swiss of their boasted title of "Chastisers of kings."

But the greatest of mortifications to the much-tried monarch was the interior splendour of the ducal residence and the pomp with which its owner had surrounded himself and his young duchess. No royal palace then equalled the Château de Moulins, or even approached it, in the magnificence of its decorations and furniture. "It was," says the Venetian, "in every respect a sumptuous and suitable abode for a prince." A further advantage being, that its furniture was intended to remain permanently there — not merely for temporary use.

The royal palaces at that period were furnished only when inhabited. "The court, like an itinerant company of comedians, carried their wardrobes, scenery, and properties with them." * The tapestries, hangings, ornamental and other furniture travelled with the royal party, and were hastily arranged on arrival, and packed up at short notice on departure, by the numerous train of servants. †

But to return to Moulins. The christening took place in the chapel of the château, draped for the occasion with velvet and gold brocade from Genoa and Venice — the ceremony being performed with all possible pomp, ecclesiastical and civil. The banquet that followed, one may be sure, was worthy of both host and guests. Italy, Lorraine, Flanders, Normandy, contributing to it their special delicacies; even England furnishing a dish of fine Windsor beans, Milan supplying the parsley, and Vanvres the melted butter.

Médoc oysters in those days, as still the custom,

---

* Paul Lacroix (Bibliophile Jacob), "XVIème Siècle."

† "This practice continued for upwards of a century later, even until Louis XIV. became of age. For at the time of the Fronde — 1648 to 1653 — when Anne of Austria fled from Paris with her two sons, and in such haste that she could carry nothing with her, all they found at St. Germain was the shelter of its roof. There was not a bed for either the queen or her children, or even a chair to rest on."—"Mémoires de Mdme. de Motteville."

preceded a light *potage;* and at a banquet of so much importance, the guests being persons of high distinction, the royal sturgeon would then appear, accompanied by the turbot, the swordfish (*dorado*), and lampreys from Nantes. Chief of the feathered tribe would next enter — the heron, covered with powdered sugar and spice, moistened with orange-juice or rose-water — "a dish," as Liébout, the great *chef* of that time, declared "fit to set before a king." But the bittern divided honours with the regal heron, though the savour of its flesh could hardly be termed savoury. Yet it was one of the chiefest of French delicacies. The swan and peacock were also esteemed most exquisite eating, with olives, capers, and acid fruits.

Pheasants, red-legged partridges, and the little wild gélinotte — more esteemed than the pheasant itself, which it somewhat resembled — surrounded the larger birds; dishes of Genoa artichokes, fresh peas, and Barbary cucumbers, intermingling with them. But that favourite dish, roast sucking-pig, must not be forgotten. Like other roast meats, it was parboiled before being put to the fire, then stuffed with chopped meats, aromatic herbs, dried raisins and damson plums.

Several kinds of salad would be served. That recommended by the king's physician was composed of oranges, lemons, sugar, and sweet herbs; another, of parsley and mint, pepper, cinnamon, and vinegar; a sort of seasoning to the chopped livers and heads of boiled poultry, varied at times with marsh-mallow and lettuce.

The desserts, except where Italian confectionery, ices, sorbets, etc., formed part of them, were not famous; the indigenous fruits being small and flavourless — wild fruits, in fact — with the exception of the Corbeil peaches and pears of Lorraine — fruit-culture having been hitherto wholly neglected. The plum named la Reine Claude, because of the queen's fondness for it, had been but a few years previously brought from Italy.*

As it was the season for late summer and early autumn fruits, the queen's favourite plums would of course not be wanting at this grand banquet. Many others, not here enumerated, would also have a place there, as well as poultry, game, fish, and meat, new in their mode of preparation, and recently introduced from Italy to the tables of the noble and wealthy of France.

Such a repast, with its appropriate wines and other beverages, such as Clairette-au-miel (the white wine of the south flavoured with honey or made golden with saffron), Hypocras-au-vin d'Espagne, gooseberry and plum wines, iced lemonade and champagne, should have cleared the clouds from the young monarch's brow. For he was fond of good cheer, and with his favourite companions could throw off the king, return jest

* Paul Lacroix, " *Vie Privée des Français XVIeme Siècle.*"

for jest, take part in the practical jokes, then a source of so much amusement, and enjoy himself heartily.

But now he is ill at ease, deeply mortified by the splendour displayed to do him honour, revealing, as it does, the unwelcome fact which before he seems not to have realised, that the surroundings of this great feudal prince are more regal than those of his sovereign. His household consists of five hundred gentlemen, who wear rich velvet dresses, with massive gold chains passing three times round the neck and depending low in front.* Succeeding each other, in divisions of one hundred each, they attend on the royal guests in the noble banqueting hall of the château; where youth and beauty, splendid attire, gold and jewels, royalty and high rank, make up a grand and effective scene.

But the hour of departure has arrived — a relief no doubt to many. The breaking up of an entertainment is often, as it was on this occasion, its most cheery moment. The health of the heir of the House of Bourbon had been pledged at the banquet with much solemnity. Now blessings on him flow glibly from every tongue. Even good wishes are uttered by Louise of Savoy; though it was perhaps at this moment she first coveted, and conceived the design of claiming, the vast wealth and extensive possessions the baby Comte

* Brantôme, Varillas, Michelet.

de Clermont then seemed destined to inherit.*
But with what feelings did Francis take leave of
his cousin? Resentful ones, certainly. Yet, from
the natural indolence of his character, and his
occasional good impulses, they would probably
have been evanescent, had not the promptings
and suggestions of his unprincipled mother raised
suspicions in his mind of the constable's loyalty,
and urged him on to a course of persecution, of
which the result was nearly fatal to France.

* This child, whose birth caused so much joy to his parents, died in less than a month after his christening.

CHAPTER VIII.

An Auspicious Event.—Matrimonial Contracts.—Betrothal of Princess Mary.—Supping with My Lord of York.—Grand and Singular.—The Youthful *Fiancée*.—The Daily Bill of Fare.—England and Bluff King Hal.—Right Good Wine and Supper.—Receiving the Embassy.—Embracing the Embassy.—Receiving the King's Letters.—A Ball at the Bastille.—The State Dinner.—A Puzzling Costume.—A Supposed Spurious Dauphin.—Restitution of Tournay.—The Port of Havre Founded.—A Penitential Procession.—A Check to His Holiness.—An Honourable Arrangement.

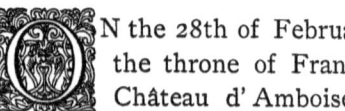N the 28th of February, 1518, an heir to the throne of France was born at the Château d'Amboise. This auspicious event was celebrated throughout the kingdom by great rejoicings and *Te Deums* innumerable. Before the year was ended general festivity was again the order of the day; Monsieur le Dauphin being betrothed to Mary of England — born in 1515 — the daughter of Henry VIII. and Katharine of Aragon.

It is remarkable how frequent at that period were the betrothals of infant children of the royal houses of Europe, and the treaties of marriage entered into as pledges of peace and amity, when, exhausted by war, breathing-time was needed to prepare for fresh encounters. Rarely indeed did those matrimonial contracts result in marriage. When they had served the object in view, the treaties were torn up and war was renewed, until the failure of resources, reverses in the field, or other disasters incidental to a state of continual warfare, again made betrothals and nuptial arrangements necessary.

The young King of Spain, just entering his eighteenth year, had already been several times betrothed. Once more he was free; absolved from his vows by the death of his *fiancée*, the infant Princesse Louise of France. Released also from the further observance of that air of respectful and filial obedience he had chosen to assume towards Francis — the prudent youth thus veiling from his young father-in-law his already vast ambition. Efforts were then secretly making to secure his election to the imperial crown, to which Francis himself, as secretly, also aspired.

The hand of his cousin Mary, who had attained her second birthday but two or three months before, was promised to Charles; but the political situation of the moment made the baby dauphin a more eligible *parti* — consequently preference was given to him. However, Charles had not long to wait for his turn, other turns also succeeding it and passing away with a like result, until, seven years after, his marriage really followed his betrothal to a princess with an immense dowry — Donna Isabella, daughter of Portugal's great king, Emanuel "the Fortunate." But the little Princess Mary, in spite of the double betrothal and the treaties to amity that bound her to the young dauphin, and afterwards to Charles himself (frail bonds, indeed, at which Fate seemed to laugh, just as Love — though in a somewhat different sense — is said to laugh at locksmiths), was destined to wait for the marriage tie some thirty-five years, or more, when she became the wife of Philip of Spain, Charles's son.

A numerous embassy, of which Admiral Bonnivet was the head, as the representative of the dauphin, was sent by Francis I. to England, and was received by Henry VIII. with "exceeding courtesy, and entertained with great sumptuousness."

As a preliminary to the ceremony of the betrothal and the gaieties that were to succeed it, Henry, attended by a retinue of a thousand mounted gentlemen, all richly dressed, went in procession, on Sunday, the 3d of October, from Durham House, in the Strand, to St. Paul's. There, mass was sung by Wolsey, bishops, and mitred abbots; after which the king took his oath, in the presence of the legates and foreign ambassadors. The embassy, with a large company of distinguished guests, dined that day at Greenwich;

but the king appears to have spent at least the Sabbath morning in more retirement than the Frenchmen, and to have dined in privacy with the Bishop of London.

After the Greenwich dinner the whole of the company followed my Lord of York to his own house at Westminster, where a sumptuous supper awaited them. It is to be hoped their journey to town had created an appetite, and that no less justice was done to the various delicacies of the evening repast than to the substantial viands and other dishes of the midday meal. The Venetian envoy, Giustiniani, who was present, says of this second banquet: "The like of it was never given by Cleopatra or Caligula — the whole banqueting-hall being so decorated with huge vases of gold and silver, that I fancied myself in the tower of the Persian king, Chosroes the Great, where that monarch caused divine honours to be paid to him."

However, referring generally to the whole day's proceedings, from the procession to St. Paul's, the dinner at Greenwich, the evening banquet at Westminster, to the grand and singular entertainment that unexpectedly followed it (masking, mumming, music and dancing, gambling with dice — bowls full of ducats being provided for the gamblers to dip into — playing at mumchance, procession of torchbearers, etc., etc., all the performers being dressed in fine green or crimson satin and cloth of gold), "it was altogether," says Bonnivet, "too magnificent for description." *

When each set of mummers, minstrels, or dancers took off their visors, the king and his sister Mary, the dowager Queen of France, were always found to have taken part in the performance, and to have enjoyed themselves immensely. Queen Katharine, if present, shared not in the diversions of the court. She was averse to the French alliance, preferring that which offered the remote possibility of her daughter becoming Queen of Spain, rather than of France, Spain's enemy.

The 4th of October seems to have been devoted to the signing and sealing of treaties. On the 5th the betrothal took place at Greenwich.

Mass having been sung, "the king took up his station in front of the throne. On one side stood Queen Katharine and Mary, the duchess-queen; on the other, the two legates — Wolsey and Campeggio. The princess," a much interested and wondering spectator of the proceedings generally, "was placed in front of her mother. Her bridal

---

* All that relates to the festivities and ceremonies in connection with this famous embassy has been very minutely described both in French and English State Papers, as well as ably summarized in Mr. Brewer's most interesting Introduction to the Calendar of the Foreign Series of Letters and Papers of that period. He mentions that the details of the entertainment following Wolsey's supper may have suggested to Shakespeare the scene of the masked ball in "Romeo and Juliet."

dress was of cloth of gold, with a cap of black velvet on her head, blazing with jewels. The king having been duly harangued, his little daughter was lifted up, and his and the queen's consent to her marriage with François, the Dauphin of France, requested and granted. Wolsey then presented the Lord Admiral Bonnivet with a small gold ring, of suitable size, and having in it a large and valuable diamond. As proxy for the bridegroom, the admiral placed the ring on the young bride's finger, and pressed it over the second joint. Prayer and a blessing followed; the ceremony concluding with mass in the royal chapel, Wolsey officiating, and the king and queen, with the whole of the court, attending."

During the rest of the stay of the embassy in England the court was engaged in a continual round of costly entertainments, mirth, and feasting. The daily bill of fare is simply marvellous — numberless courses of "beeves and muttons, porkers, fat hogs, and pigs, fat capons and Kentish capons, chicks and pullets, swans, cranes, peacocks, peachicks, pigeons, larks, and geese. Three thousand loaves of bread (size not named), with tuns and pipes of wine, and hogsheads of ale." Vegetables, too, there must have been, if only the famous Windsor beans that already had found their way to the royal banquets of France; but the vegetables are not mentioned; neither is fish. The dessert consisted of prunes, small raisins, dates, and almonds, green ginger, pears, apples, and quinces; long comfits and small ones; no end of gallons of cream, milk, curd, furmenty, and dishes of butter.

This was, truly, an unstinted and a substantial banquet; perhaps not very refined in its cookery, yet looking grand on gold and silver dishes. It also suited the gastronomic taste of the day, and, as is recorded, was heartily enjoyed by the gentlemen who had been "wrestling and tilting" all the morning, and by the delighted ladies who had been looking on at these games, and dispensing smiles as rewards to the most skilful.

At the balls and masques which followed the evening banquets, Henry and Mary, in "high glee," led off all the dances, and were the most joyous of the throng of "mummers,"— in short, "the oldest inhabitant," tax his memory as he would, according to his usual custom, could remember nothing like these general rejoicings having ever before happened in England.

But these gay doings having lasted a week, the Frenchmen were compelled to bid merry England and its "bluff King Hal" farewell, carrying away with them the most favourable impressions of both. A valuable present was made by Henry to each member of the embassy, for which mark of his "royal favour and good-will Admiral Bonnivet and the lords of France did heartily thank the king, also for the disport with which it had pleased him to visit them." Henry, in replying, expressed the "anxious pleasure with which he looked forward to a meeting with Francis I."

Queen Katharine alone seems to have taken no interest in the festivities into which her husband and sister-in-law entered with so much zest. She was by no means the dignified personage generally imagined and poets have depicted her. On the contrary, she was of low stature, and very thin. Her complexion was swarthy, and her features plain — as described by one of those diligent Venetian ambassadors who kept the "potent, grave, and reverend seigniors" of the Senate of Venice so well informed of the characters, the personal appearance, and doings of the chief personages of the courts to which they were accredited.

In the month following the departure of the French (November) an English embassy, headed by the Earl of Worcester, was despatched by Henry VIII. to France. The earl was accompanied by the Bishop of Ely, the Prior of St. John's, Sir Nicholas Vaux, and a numerous retinue of attendants.

In acknowledgment of the splendid reception the French had met with in England, "Lord Worcester's embassy, on landing at Boulogne, after a stormy passage, was received with shooting of guns, and lodged in the castle, whence M. de La Fayette attended my lord and his gentlemen to Abbeville, where three puncheons of wine and a right good supper were offered them." The same courteous attention was repeated at every town on the route to Paris — an unfailing supply of "right good wine" accompanying the "right good feasts." As Mr. Brewer remarks, "their new continental friends seem to have been fully aware of the national infirmity."

A league from Paris, a hundred gentlemen of the king's household, accompanied by a bishop, received the embassy. The provosts and merchants of Paris awaited them in the faubourg. "On their way to the capital they were met by divers gentlemen in masks, amongst whom the king was surely supposed to be." The first audience took place on the 12th of November, at the Palais des Tournelles. There, "in a very great chamber, appointed with blue hangings full of *fleur-de-lys*, the floor covered with the same in blue tiles, and seats prepared round for the noblemen, closed round about with rails, the king himself sate, in a chair raised four steps from the ground, under a rich cloth of estate, with a pall of cloth of gold, and a curtain of the same under his feet."

Francis wore a robe of cloth of silver embroidered with flowers and lined with heron's feathers. His doublet was of cloth of gold; but his cap was only his ordinary one of cloth with feather-edging. Under a satin and gold canopy, on his right, were seated the Roman legate, the King of Navarre, and the Ducs d' Alençon and de Bourbon. On his left were four cardinals, the papal nuncio, the Chancellor Duprat, and several bishops.

All the assistants in this grand scene having taken their seats, "two hundred gentlemen carrying battle-axes conducted the English envoys into the royal presence." They, too, were arrayed with due splendour for the occasion. "The earl wore a robe of crimson satin lined with sables; Sir Nicholas wore cloth of gold similarly lined. Ely appeared in his rochet; the lord of St. John's in black satin. Twenty English gentlemen followed, in cloth of gold and sables, jewelled pendants in their bonnets, and massive gold chains, studded with jewels, round their necks and waists."

"On their reaching the centre of the daïs, the king rose, descended the steps, embraced the earl and members of the embassy, and bade them be seated. Then West (Bishop of Ely) rose to deliver his Latin oration, which was much commended for good emphasis and discretion, also for boldness of spirit and audacity."

The oration ended, the king again left his seat and "embraced the English gentlemen," in return for a similar compliment paid by Henry VIII. to the French gentlemen accompanying the embassy. Francis, with the Earl of Worcester, then withdrew. Closeted with the ambassador, he assured him of his great satisfaction at the peace just concluded, adding that "henceforth he would repute himself and his subjects Englishmen, and the king's grace and his subjects Frenchmen; and that it might so appear he would endeavour to learn the English language."

The ambassador then presented Henry's letters. Francis received them as though he imagined the earl had brought him a lady's perfumed *billet-doux*. He raised them to his lips, read them with a sort of eager pleasure, then placed them in his bosom, saying that "all the letters that ever his grace had sent him he had in his own custody and keeping, and in like manner he would keep these present ones." The great courtesy of the "chevalier king," "the best bred gentleman in Europe," "pleased the English envoys mightily."

As in England at St. Paul's, so in Paris at Notre Dame, the king, after a grand mass, made a solemn oath at the high altar — a cardinal holding the book, and the legate standing before the king while he signed it. The legate's blessing, "with pleasing indulgence," followed; the legate then saying to the king, "Sire, ye have done a noble act to-day." "By my faith," he replied, "I have done it with a right good heart and good will." Thus concluded the religious ceremony; the envoys and the English gentlemen, on leaving the church, repairing to the archiepiscopal palace to dine with the archbishop, who gave them "a stately banquet served solely on gold plate."

The entertainment of the evening was a no less stately supper, given by a stately host, yet courteous and genial as "the best bred gentleman" himself, and in many qualities of mind and person far surpassing him — the constable Charles de Bourbon.

Twelve days of unceasing amusement and "right good feasting" were brought to a close by a brilliant ball at the Bastille — probably the only one that ever took place there, until the people, in 1789, joyously held their public dances on the ruins of that gloomy stronghold of sinister renown. The inner courtyard was chosen for the occasion, and "covered in with blue canvas, powdered over with gilt stars to represent the heavens." Over the canvas smooth timber was laid to keep out cold and rain. The royal colours, white and tawney, were festooned along the galleries erected round the ball-room, which were provided with benches covered with cloth of gold. The floor was also of laid boards, carpeted. "An immense chandelier hung from the centre, throwing such a marvellous blaze of light on the starry ceiling as to rival the sun. Over-arching a daïs or platform was a latticed bower of box, ivy, and other evergreens, with roses and various kinds of flowers trailing over it."

"The ball was preceded by a dinner. A flourish of trumpets having announced that it was time to wash hands and a second flourish that dinner was served, the king entered, and took his seat on the platform, having on his left his sister, the Duchesse d' Alençon, and next her the Bishop of Ely "— probably because she was able to converse a little with him in Latin. "On the king's right was the legate with the beautiful Comtesse Bissonne, and next her the Earl of Worcester, then ladies and gentlemen of the court alternately; the gentlemen of the embassy dining at tables on the floor below the platform."

Doubtless the hospitable board of the sovereign of France was as amply spread as that of Henry VIII. of England, but posterity has not been favoured with the bill of fare. It is, however, highly probable that, besides the more substantial viands, many productions of the Italian *cuisine* were served at the royal table, prepared from the same recipes as those choice dishes that figured with *éclat* at the luxurious repasts of which Francis had partaken with Leo X. The "Bourgeois de Paris" says that "such an expenditure in eating and drinking and fine clothing had hardly ever been known in France."

The "heraldic dishes," one may feel sure, would not be wanting, it being the general custom in the sixteenth and seventeenth centuries, when entertaining distinguished guests, to arrange the principal dishes of the dessert, pastry or fruit, so as to form the coats-of-arms of those it was desired to honour. Apricots represented the *or*, or gold of heraldry; damask plums, *azure;* cherries and raspberries, *gules,* or red; the Reine Claude plum, *vert,* and so on for the rest of the colours and metals.*

After dinner, dancing began, to the sound of trumpets and fifes, and continued until nine o'clock, when the guests were invited to leave the mazy dance for a while to partake of a grand supper served on gold and silver dishes. Having refreshed themselves, the entertainment was varied by the entrance of "several companies of maskers in quaint costumes, last of whom came the king in a long, close-fitting dress of white satin (intended to represent Christ's robe), embroidered in gold, with compasses and dials, the meaning of which much puzzled the spectators." Dancing was resumed when the masquerading ended, and the whole concluded long after midnight, by ladies handing round to all the company confectionery and bonbons in silver dishes.†

Neither Madame Louise of Savoy nor the queen appears to have been present at these bridal ceremonies and festivities. The young dauphin also bore no part in them. They were regarded as sealing the ceremony of betrothal that had taken place at Greenwich. The dauphin was at Blois, and it was announced that he was in good health.

* Louis Loiseleur, "*Châteaux royaux de France.*"
† This grand entertainment is said to have cost the king more than 450,000 gold crowns — £160,000.

But an idea prevailed, or, as the "State Papers" express it, "the fame went, that the king at this time had no son." The Bishop of Ely and other members of the embassy accepted the invitation to visit him at Cognac, "where they were shewn a fair young child, and when they had seen him they departed; but this was believed to be but a colour of the French king." ("State Papers.")

On the same day — 4th of October, 1518 — that the marriage contract of the Princess Mary to the dauphin — pledge and seal of the reconciliation of the two countries — was signed at Greenwich, another contract, far more important to France, was also signed. By it, Tournay, taken by the English in 1513, was restored to the French on payment of an indemnity of 600,000 gold crowns (£88,000) for the sums expended on its fortifications.

Since the battle of Marignan, England and France had not been on good terms, Henry VIII. being extremely jealous of the successes of Francis I. in Italy. The more so as he had strongly urged him against undertaking a war which, while he was looking, and no doubt hoping, for its failure, had ended in victory. Henry then joined the league against him; but after the general peace, Francis I. having made frequent friendly advances towards the English king — through Wolsey, of course, whose good offices, by presents and promises, it is said, he succeeded in gaining — the acrimony of Henry's feelings towards France abated.

Wolsey convinced his highness that Tournay was a possession of no value to England, yet involving vast expenditure to retain. This, together with Francis I.'s timely recall of the Duke of Albany from Scotland, whereby preponderance of French influence in that country was withdrawn, brought the affair of Tournay to a successful issue. The real motive, however, of Francis I.'s courteous advances to Henry VIII., and his liberality and complaisance towards his all-powerful minister, was to obtain the restitution of Calais. But of this no question could for a moment be entertained. Calais was not to be given up, but reconquered, and the glory of that conquest was not destined for Francis I.

Yet, so diligently did he then visit and inspect the northern seaports of France, that it would almost seem that a fresh invasion of the kingdom was expected, notwithstanding the renewal of friendly relations with England, the betrothal, and the sumptuous *fêtes*. It was then that the port of Havre was founded, and orders given for fortifying the adjacent village of Havre-de-Grâce. Probably it was then the king's intention to build ships of war, as Seyssel and others strongly urged him; for, although there was a grand admiral of France, there was really no navy to command. If ships were wanted, merchantmen were hired; a few small vessels, scarcely larger than fishing-boats, forming the only fleet which that spacious harbour in course of construction was likely for years to come to give shelter.

The navy of England at that time was hardly more formidable than that of France. Warlike demonstrations by sea could, therefore, only be looming in the far-distant future; besides, war, or the prospect of it, in another direction then occupied the attention of Europe.

At the solicitation of the Pope, the four great Western Powers — Austria, Spain, England and France — had recently bound themselves by treaty to unite their forces, in order to oppose the advance of the sultan, Selim I., who threatened to ravage Italy. That powerful Ottoman ruler had usurped the throne of his father after murdering him and his brothers. His ferocious disposition and religious fanaticism increased the terror he already inspired by his genius for war and his numerous conquests. Persian provinces had yielded to him; Syria and Egypt were conquered, and a band of Turkish pirates at Algiers now menaced the Spanish settlements on the African coast with speedy ruin. The Italian States were in great alarm; and Venice, whose commerce, the source of her great prosperity, was drawing to an end, made then some vain attempts, in order to avert that calamity, to check the progress of the Portuguese, whose flag now waved along all the coast of Hindostan.

Violently indeed, both mentally and bodily, must Italy generally have been agitated by Selim's terror-exciting name, when consternation so prevailed in the Vatican that a voluptuary, such as was Leo X., was induced to put aside for even a brief space the licentious pleasures for which alone he seemed to live, and at the head of a penitential procession to walk through Rome barefoot.

Its object was, first, to implore in this dilemma the protection and aid of the Mother of God, and the holy saints; secondly, by the moving spectacle of the holy pontiff's self-abasement, to inspire languid Christendom with pious zeal liberally to contribute towards the expenses of a contemplated crusade against the unbelievers. The clergy were asked for a tithe of their income, and the traffic in Indulgences — against which the great reformer was already loudly lifting up his voice — was pushed forward with great vigour. The Germanic Diet of Augsburg were required by the Pope to furnish a large subsidy for the same pious purpose. Soon after, it became known that a raid on Italy formed no part, at least for the present, of Selim's military programme, and the idea of a crusade consequently was abandoned. The subsidy was still demanded, but for offensive warfare. It was, however, refused, with many complaints of the papal rapacity, — a check to his holiness from an unexpected quarter.

Of the large sum of money then extorted from the inferior clergy and the people, the greater part found its way into the coffers of the Pope. The sovereigns who had promised to aid his holiness had their share, but Francis was most benefited by it — Leo ceding to him the tithe imposed on the French clergy, in consideration of the suppression of certain articles of the treaty of Bologna. This honourable arrangement in no way affected the interests of the "chevalier king," but merely was prejudicial to those of his friend and ally, the Duke of Ferrara, who lost by it his cities of Reggio and Modena, which the Pope had bound himself by the above-named treaty to restore to him.

CHAPTER IX.

A Coffin in Case of Need. — The Imperial Crown. — Reviving the Augustan Age. — The Royal College of France. — The Crowing of the Cock. — Full of Thorns and Vipers. — Erasmus and Voltaire. — Brother Martin Luther. — The Sale of Indulgences. — Under the Ban of the Church. — The Germanic Diet. — He Stands Erect! — Sensation! — A Learned Dominican. — Retract, My Friend, Retract. — Luther Escapes from Augsburg. — Saved for the Present. — Conciliating the Elector.

FROM the end of 1516 to the close of 1518, France and the other European Powers had been free from actual war, if not wholly from war's alarms. This interval of peace had been diligently employed both by Francis I. and the young King of Spain in secret intrigues to secure each his own election to the imperial throne, and to thwart that of his rival. The Emperor Maximilian, then in failing health, and carrying his coffin about with him in case he should want it when on a journey, yet was sufficiently well to devote himself, with energy unusual to him, to the furtherance of his grandson's interests. But in this, as in all other projects the emperor had ever taken part in, his first demand was for money, and an unstinted supply of it.

Charles himself was then but scantily supplied with money, both his Dutch and Spanish subjects refusing to furnish the sums he needed. Maximilian, in this dilemma, turned towards Henry VIII., holding up the imperial crown as a lure. But Henry, whose treasury was far from being so empty as were the coffers of the young monarchs of France and Spain, yet declined — though he, too, had aspirations in the same direction — to confide his gold crowns and angels to the spendthrift Maximilian.

Charles, meanwhile, promised and forwarded to him 100,000 gold ducats for bribing, where necessary, desiring his grandfather to dispose of it with economy. Maximilian then gave his sole attention to the promoting of Charles's candidature, for which, however, a further remittance of ducats was soon requested.

While these intrigues and counter intrigues were still going on — the balance sometimes inclining towards France, at others towards Spain, according to the amount of cash each actually expended, and the value of pensions promised — Francis was aiming also at other honours.

The *savants* who at that period enjoyed the highest distinction were the philologists. The study of the classic languages and literature was making great progress in France; so much so that even the court, whose latest literary affectation was the expression of their feelings and sentiments in verse — more frequently puerile than felicitious — now seemed fired with the noble ambition of making Latin the language of the court; thus, in their avidity for literary celebrity, in some sort reviving the Augustan age in the reign of Francis I.

Chivalric courtiers and (quoting Brantôme) "elegant courtesans" proposed to vary their licentious amusements by the study of the Latin language. Probably Greek would have followed, had the scheme been fully carried out. But the studious fit was of short duration. Yet while it lasted the *naïve* and *piquant*, though rather libertine, love-ditties of the poet *par excellence* of that depraved court, Clément Marot, did indeed suffer a partial eclipse.

Francis, too, put aside his rhymes and his sonnets to ladies' eyes; and, aspiring to the glory he saw redounded on those princes who favoured the study of the ancient languages and literature, determined to adopt the suggestion of the distinguished philologist, Guillaume Budé, to found a college in Paris for the study of Hebrew, Greek, and Latin, on the plan of that recently organised at Louvain by Erasmus.*

---

* To this barren project — barren so far as he was concerned — Francis mainly owed the epithet applied to him of the

It was to be called the "Royal College of France," or "College of the Three Languages," and was to be built on the site then occupied by the Hôtel de Nesle. Accommodation was to be provided for six hundred students, and the endowment was to be a yearly *rente* of 50,000 crowns. For nearly two years Francis I. continued persistently to renew the offer of the presidency, or direction, of this projected college to the distinguished *savant* Erasmus, though the Parisian Budé, esteemed the most profoundly erudite of the learned men of his day, might be considered to have had a prior claim to it. Budé, however, added his solicitations to those of the king; but Erasmus, after long hesitation, finally declined the proffered honour.

Years went on, but no steps were taken for commencing the building of the projected college. The professors of the three languages were not even appointed until 1530, and then no residence was either ready or in course of construction for them. No hall or room, temporarily or otherwise, was assigned to them for lectures or lessons, and no salary assured to the professors.

"Father of letters;" while the choice he made of illustrious *savants* for his diplomatists, if it did not always further his political interests, contributed to spread his reputation as a protector or patron of learning. It was thus, at that moment of ardour for the revival of learning, that the princes, great and small, of Italy, Germany, and France, hoped to immortalise themselves.

The first Greek professor was Pierre Danés, of the College of Navarre, whose learned writings in Hebrew and Greek obtained him less celebrity than a happy *mot* when ambassador at the Council of Trent. A French orator was declaiming against the lax morality of the Court of Rome, when the Bishop of Orvieto exclaimed contemptuously, "*Gallus cantat*" — It is but a cock that's crowing. Danés immediately replied, "*Utinam ad galli cantum Petrus resipisceret*" — Would to heaven that at this crowing of this cock Peter might repent! — *gallus* signifying both "cock," and "Frenchman." Two or three years later, three other professorial chairs (mathematics, philosophy, and medicine) were added; conditions as to dwelling, students' hall, and salary, remaining the same.

In 1539 Francis approved the arrangements then made for the erection of the college — all that was wanting being the issue of his order to begin. Eight years after, 1547, when Francis died, the order had not been given; and the first stone of "the noble institution," about which the "Father of letters" had once seemed so eager, and continued, though with abated interest, to talk through the whole of his reign, was not laid until 1610, sixty-three years after his death, by Louis XIII.

One cause of the delay has been suggested as probable — the opposition of the priests to the introduction of the study of the dead languages and the sacred books into the schools. It was denounced by them as verging on sacrilege, and from the pulpit "the newly-discovered language, called Greek," was declared to be one to be "carefully guarded against, as giving birth to all the heresies;" while the book written in that language, and called the "New Testament," which the enlighted priest, to whom this warning to his flock is attributed, "saw with pain in the hands of many persons," was described, with picturesque eloquence, as "a book full of thorns and vipers." As to Hebrew, all who learned it, he informed his terror-stricken (as one may imagine) congregation, "immediately became Jews." *

Bitter warfare had recently broken out between learned laymen and the monks. Portions of the Hebrew and Greek Scriptures had been translated and freely commented upon. Reuchlin, the celebrated legist and Hebrew scholar, after correcting the Latin Vulgate, had published a Hebrew grammar and dictionary; thus "opening," as Merle d'Aubigné says, "the long-closed books of the Ancient Alliance." †

Other writers had also begun closely to scrutinise the origin of all authority, whether ecclesiastical or laic; while "the great Erasmus, with liveliness and sparkling fancy, had already nearly

* Sismondi, "*Histoire des Français.*"
† "*Histoire de la Réformation.*"

exhausted every form of ridicule on the frock and the cowl, and the superstitions of the age," in his "Dialogues," his "Éloge de la Folie," and numerous pamphlets and sketches — his raillery and oblique censures preparing the way for Luther's more violent invectives and more direct attacks. "One cannot help being struck by the analogy this period of the Renaissance offers with the eighteenth century," writes M. Henri Martin; "Erasmus is its Voltaire."

But Truth, in the person of Luther, had at last raised her head in the very centre of Christendom, and, victorious over the inferior agents of the papacy, was about to enter the lists with Rome's pontiff himself. When Luther's theses were first published, Leo X., overlooking the severe truths they contained, found them very diverting, and, judging them rather as the friend of letters than as Pope, pronounced Brother Martin Luther a man of fine genius, and all that was said against him but the suggestions of monkish jealousy. Frequently, when urged to take cognisance of the heretical preaching and teaching of "the monk of Wittemberg," he would merely, with a shrug of the shoulders, reply, "Monkish quarrels."

The priesthood generally, notwithstanding the indifference of the Pope, were greatly alarmed at the rapid spread of Luther's opinions, and by means of that art whose invention was ascribed by monks to the devil — the art of printing. The progress of religious reform would certainly have been long retarded, but for the timely invention, or rather perfecting, of printing. The power of the press was then for the first time made known. Not only were the Scriptures quickly disseminated amongst the people, but, with speed that seemed marvellous in that age, heretical pamphlets, catechisms, ballads, and caricatures — such as wolves in sheep's clothing confessing, and granting absolution — followed each other, and spoke to the unlettered in another form.*

But the great source of revenue, the sale of Indulgences, which hitherto had produced in Germany a larger sum than elsewhere, was sensibly diminishing, and the power of the Pope to forgive the living their sins — past, present and future — as well as to release souls in purgatory, beginning to be called in question. The cardinals, therefore, and others composing the Papal Court, thought it high time that his holiness, hitherto so singularly lenient or apathetic in this matter, should be urged to put to silence the presumptuous monk who was troubling Christendom with his heretical teaching — agitating the minds of the faithful, and even calumniating the Holy Father.

* "To some of Luther's contemporaries, the rapidity with which his opinions spread appeared so unaccountable that they imputed it to a certain uncommon and malignant position of the stars, which scattered the spirit of giddiness and innovation over the world." — Robertson, "Reign of Charles V."

Leo is said to have felt a sort of admiration for the humble monk who had the courage to stand up, alone and unsupported, to proclaim in the face of the papacy the utter worthlessness of those Indulgences, employed to beguile money from the pockets of the credulous poor, the ignorant, and the superstitious. But his admiration continued only so long as he believed that the blow now aimed at the power of the Pope would prove as harmless in its results as many others which from time to time had feebly fallen on it.

The monk, however, continues his attacks, and, taking the Bible for his guide, condemns, as erroneous, some vital doctrines of the Roman Catholic Church. From the approval his teaching meets with from eminent men within the Church itself, it is evident that what he boldly proclaims is but the expression of the long pent-up thought of many minds too timid to openly avow it. The heresy spreads, and Luther is at last cited by the Pope to appear at Rome within sixty days to retract his errors, repent, and seek pardon.

If he did this readily he was to be again received as a son in the tender embrace of Holy Mother Church. If he obstinately persisted in his errors, all the vengeance of that same holy mother was to fall on him and all who were in any way attached to or interested in him. He was to be cursed, banished, and all true Christians were to drive him from their presence. Failure to do so would bring the offender also under the ban of the Church.

Friends were alarmed, but Luther was unmoved. He complained only of being declared a heretic before he had been granted a hearing. However, the Elector Frederick of Saxony — notwithstanding a flattering epistle accompanying the present of the golden rose of that year from Leo, to his dear son in Christ — refused to send Doctor Martin Luther to Rome. Ultimately he was ordered to repair to Augsburg, where the legate to the Germanic Diet, Cardinal da Vio (known as Cajetan, or Gaëtano, from his native place Gaëta), was appointed to receive his retraction, and bless or curse (as it was full or partial) in the name of the Holy Father.

Resisting all attempts to dissuade him, Luther set out from Wittemberg, on foot. The Germanic Diet, convoked by the Emperor Maximilian at Augsburg, ostensibly for considering the proposed crusade, but really for the purpose of obtaining his grandson's election as King of the Romans, in which he was unsuccessful, had just concluded its sittings. Augsburg was, in consequence, full of great personages, princes of the empire, ambassadors — French, English, Italian, and Spanish — clerical and lay, accompanied by their respective suites.

But none among them compared in interest with the poor, weary-footed, travel-soiled monk, whose arrival anxious crowds were awaiting, eager to obtain but a glimpse of him. Many tried friends were among those who crowded about him, vying with each other in their offers of an asylum and the repose he was so much in need of.

The cardinal legate believes that an easy victory lies before him, whether to ensure it he employs his "flowing tongue," or that the awe-inspiring presence of a prince of the Church alone should suffice to bring the monk to his knees. Yet his eminence sends his secretary to prepare the monk for the terrible ordeal that awaits him, and to inform him of the manner of presenting himself before so great a dignitary.

Luther enters, prostrates himself before the cardinal after the manner prescribed. At the first order to rise, he raises his body only, remaining on his knees; at a second order he rises to his feet. Now, standing erect, he awaits what his eminence has to say to him. (Sensation!) His eminence and his clerical satellites are confounded! Surely the monk has not quite comprehended the meaning of the ceremony! As a penitent he should have remained in that abject posture and humbly whined *peccavi*, or chanted the *palinode*.

As the legate does not address him, Luther respectfully inquires of what he is accused. His amazing audacity astonishes the assembled ecclesiastics. But Da Vio is inclined to be lenient. He is fond, too, of disputation, and is considered by himself and his order the most learned of the Dominicans. He, however, deigns to inform his "dear son" that he is accused of exciting the whole of Germany by the errors he had uttered with regard to Indulgences and the nature of faith. But being informed that he is one of the learned doctors of his university, well acquainted with the Scriptures, and that he has a large number of pupils, he benignantly desires that he will attentively listen to him.

"If he would remain a member of the Church and find in the Holy Father a gracious master, ready to pardon the penitent sinner and to welcome him back into the fold of the faithful, he must retract. He must promise to be more guarded for the future—abstaining wholly from heretical teaching, and the publication of new and erroneous doctrines." But Luther firmly replies that he cannot retract until it is proved to him that he is in error. This irritates the cardinal legate, who, in a high tone of authority, explains that he came not there to argue, but to receive his retractation. However, he did condescend to argue; confident in his ability to confute his humble opponent. But papal decrees and scholastic opinions were proofs rejected by Luther, who, in support of his own views, referred to Scripture.

"The Pope has authority and power over all things," said the cardinal.

"Save Scripture," replied Luther.

"Save Scripture!" repeated his adversary in a mocking tone, shrugging his shoulders, and pouring forth a torrent of words, contemptuous, menacing, and ironical.

So ended their first interview. A second and a third followed, with no better result. The volubility of the cardinal stopped Luther's every attempt to reply. At his written declarations my lord cardinal affected to laugh. "Retract, my friend, retract," he said; "such is the Holy Father's will. But whether you choose to obey or not — no matter. My friend," he said, jeeringly, "you will find it difficult to kick against the pricks."

Some days having elapsed without any fresh summons from his eminence, Luther's friends urged him to leave Augsburg, suspecting that the legate's silence boded evil, and that an order to seize him and send him to Rome might at any hour arrive. A safe conduct was procured from the emperor at a happy moment, when, eager to set out for his favourite pursuit — hunting the chamois — he gave little heed for whom it was granted. A guide was provided, and a pony, without either saddle or bridle, was lent by Luther's friend Staupitz. A letter was left for Da Vio, and at midnight he and his guide passed unmolested through the dark and silent streets of Augsburg. A door in the city wall was opened to him by order of his friend Langemantel, one of the councillors of Augsburg, and Luther was soon beyond the power of the cardinal legate.

At all the towns through which he passed on his journey, he was the object of great and general interest, and everywhere offers of hospitality awaited him. But Luther was anxious to reach Wittemberg. The tenour of the Pope's letter to his legate at Augsburg concerning him had been made known to Luther for the first time at Nuremberg by the prior of his convent. Only then did he become aware of the perilous position in which he was placed, and the probability of his losing the protection of the elector, from the necessity he would be under of leaving Wittemberg.

He arrived on the eve of the feast of All Saints. The elector was absent. On his return, letters breathing vengeance on the heretic monk who had fled from Augsburg desired the elector to send him to Rome, or to banish him from his dominions. At first he hesitated, then refused to do either. Soon after, in a letter to Luther, he expressed a wish that he would leave Wittemberg, and in a second letter urged him to do so without delay.

He was on the point of obeying, and had determined to seek refuge in France, where he believed he would be able to make known his views and preach the truth without hindrance. The doctors of the University of Paris appeared to him to enjoy much enviable liberty in the expression of their opinions; besides, he then agreed with them in many points of doctrine. Another letter from the elector bids him remain. A communication from the Pope had given another turn to the matter. There was a change of tactics on the Holy Father's part. Luther was saved for the present.

Another event — the death of the Emperor Maximilian (January the 12th, 1519) — still further favoured the reformer and conduced to the progress of the Reformation. The attention both of the Pontiff and the dignitaries of the Church of Rome, as also that of the sovereigns of Europe, was diverted by it from religious strife and theological disputation to the political struggle about to ensue for the sceptre of the Holy Roman Empire. During the interregnum the Elector Frederick of Saxony, the most powerful of the seven electoral princes, became administrator of the empire.

Leo was very anxious to prevent the election of Charles of Austria, already King of Naples and of Spain, to the imperial throne, and for that object desirous of conciliating the Elector of Saxony; hoping to bring him over to his views and to induce him to oppose Charles's election on the ground also of his youth incapacitating him for so important and responsible a dignity. Therefore, the elector's *protégé*, the "monk of Wittemberg," was for a time to be left in peace. Thus, under the shadow of the elector's vicariate, the Reformation for the next eighteen months spread and prospered.

CHAPTER X.

The Emperor Maximilian. — Maximilian's Poverty. — Rival Claims for Empire. — The Infidel Turk. — The Bankers Fugger. — Too Late in the Field. — Frederick of Saxony. — A Stripling of Limited Capacity. — Emerging from Obscurity. — The Spaniards Dissatisfied. — The Title of Majesty.

THE Emperor Maximilian, though endowed with none of the qualities of a great prince, was yet much regretted by his subjects. He was of an easy temper, good-natured, pleasant-mannered, and in his younger days very handsome. He was possessed of a sort of ready wit, and many *bons mots*, generally amusing and often piquant, are attributed to him. Hunting the chamois was his favourite diversion. But he was always full of great projects, which usually came to nothing, because always asking money of others in order to carry them out.

He had been needy from his youth. His father, Frederick III., who wore the imperial crown for fifty-four years, had the reputation of being the most niggardly of men (*"Le plus chiche homme du monde"*). When his son Maximilian was betrothed and married by proxy to Mary of Burgundy, daughter of Charles the Bold, he was unable for months to make the journey to

Flanders to join his bride in her own dominions; and only then when she furnished him with the means of making his appearance there in a manner befitting his rank.

Again, when left a young widower (Mary having died in her twenty-fifth year, of injuries sustained by a fall from her horse), he was once more betrothed to a great princess — on this occasion Anne of Brittany — want of means prevented him from going in person to marry his *fiancée*. Charles VIII., taking advantage of this, and political matters favouring his suit, Madame Anne, rather against her will, became the bride of the King of France instead of the Emperor-elect of Germany. He seems to have been equally needy even after his father's death, and to have been always ready to sell himself to the highest bidder, when required to take part in wars or to enter into treaties of peace and amity — "thus reaping advantages from every war and every negotiation in Italy during his reign."

His efforts to obtain the election of his grandson as King of the Romans by bribes and promises, though unsuccessful, yet in some measure prepared the way for his election to the empire. *

No sooner was Maximilian's death announced,

---

* Maximilian was elected emperor in the lifetime of his father; but, as the ceremony of receiving the crown from the Pope had never taken place, he was, in fact, only King of the Romans himself; therefore no other king could be elected while he lived.

Charles VIII.
Steel engraving by W. Wellstood.

than Charles and Francis hastened to put forward their several claims to the succession, — the electors being assembled at Frankfort to consider and decide on them. Both candidates had declared their determination to leave no means untried to secure the realisation of their respective hopes; the "chevalier king" courteously announcing that he should seek the great prize they contended for as he would woo the favours of a mistress, with generous and chivalrous feelings towards his rival.

The sceptre of the Holy Roman Empire had so long been swayed by princes of the House of Austria, that Charles considered that it descended to him by right. Francis, on the other hand, urged, or his emissaries did so for him, that the time had arrived to convince the House of Austria that the imperial crown was not hereditary but elective. Very eloquently the ambassadors,—of whom Admiral Bonnivet was the most fluent,—and other agents sent by Francis to Frankfort and other parts of the empire, supported his cause; enforcing their arguments by the lavish distribution of 400,000 gold crowns, either in presents for purchasing votes, or in banquets and *fêtes* to persons of distinction, whose approval of the French candidature might be likely to influence the votes of the electors.

Large sums were also remitted from Spain for the same purpose, and every possible stratagem employed by Charles's agents to remove the objections of those who were too conscientious to be won by bribes to give their support to either candidate. Francis had said "he would spend three millions to obtain the imperial crown," and further "had sworn"—probably to excuse and in some degree to sanctify all this intriguing, bribing, and bargaining—"that three years after his election he would be in possession of Constantinople, or would have ceased to live."

To conquer the infidel Turk was then regarded as a noble, a holy ambition. It must have been pleasant also for his agents to allude to it, in mitigation of the discredit attaching to their mission, as they travelled with the train of horses laden with treasure, and an armed escort to protect it. Their pockets were also filled with the king's signatures in blank; the reason being that the great house of Fugger and other bankers were prohibited by the Free Cities of the League of Suabia from issuing bills of exchange for the King of France.*

Henry VIII. of England was also disposed to put in a claim to the imperial crown. It was mortifying to his vanity that either of the young

---

*"To the bankers Fugger," says Michelet, "were due the two great events that changed the face of the world—the election of Charles V. and the Reformation; the former by closing the bank to Francis I., and supplying Charles with the funds he needed; the latter by becoming the bankers or receivers of the product of the sale of the Indulgences farmed by Albert of Brandenburg, Archbishop of Mayence.

sovereigns should be elevated to a dignity placing them, as it was then considered, so far above other monarchs, and consequently above himself. It was late in the day to enter the lists. Nevertheless, he sent off his ambassador to Germany. Though no decision had yet been come to, the election was an affair so complicated, and the electors already so besieged by artful and cunning devices to wrest from them their votes for this or that candidate, that a new claim preferred at the eleventh hour had no chance of success.

So Henry was told; and of course with many expressions of sincere regret, both from German princes and the Pope's representatives, that he should so long have held aloof from the contest. But he was thus enabled to withdraw his claim with dignity, and with the full conviction that, had he sooner preferred it, he would have had every chance of thwarting both his rivals.

Four of the electors had, on very high terms during the preceding year, secretly sold themselves to Francis, and as secretly disposed of their votes to Charles. But the death of Maximilian, they contended, absolved them from their promises. They were, however, willing to renew the bargain at a higher figure, and Francis recklessly wrote to his ambassador, Bonnivet, to "stuff those gluttons to their hearts' content."* Considering the object

* See Fleuranges, "*Mémoires;*" Fiddes, "Life of Charles V.;" Robertson; H. Martin.

in view, as well as the pleasure of overcoming his rival, the more prudent Charles, having also the Fuggers to support him, may for once have been as prodigal as the "chevalier king."

Leo X. was very desirous of excluding both Charles and Francis from the dignity they so ardently sought. The imperial and papal authority often came into collision. It suited, therefore, the views of the papacy that the sceptre of the Holy Roman Empire should be in the hands of a less powerful sovereign than either the king of France or of Spain. "Choose neither a Frenchman nor a Spaniard, but a German — one of yourselves," he said to the electors. "More than one among you has sufficient power and capacity to be invested with the imperial dignity." The electors were of the same opinion, and believing none more worthy of it than the Elector Frederick of Saxony, to him the sceptre of the empire was unanimously offered.

But Frederick declined to accept it. "The interests of the German states," he said, "required that it should be placed in the hands of a sovereign whose dominions, revenues, and authority far exceeded his, or those of any prince of the empire, one who, for their defence, could bring into the field a sufficient force to meet an enemy" (alluding to the Turks) "whom he would be powerless to encounter."

Of the two candidates he thought the King of

Spain should be preferred. He was of German extraction, a prince of the empire, and his hereditary dominions lay on the frontier most open to attack. The King of France was of alien race, a stranger to their language, manners, and customs. He therefore gave his voice for the King of Spain.

This was decisive, the other electors voting also for Charles V. The Pope withdrew his protest, and as no king of Naples could, by the laws of the Germanic Constitution, succeed to the empire, Leo, finding opposition useless, absolved him from that legal impediment.

As a precaution, however, against the possible violation by so powerful a prince, of the rights, privileges, and customs, of the German states, the Diet drew up a formal statement of them, called "The Capitulation," and by it the Emperor Charles V., and his successors, were required to promise, solemnly on oath, faithfully to observe all the stipulations contained therein. The ambassador signed this document on behalf of his absent master, and Charles afterwards confirmed it by his own signature.

Great indeed was the French king's disappointment — extreme his sense of humiliation at the triumph of a rival whom hitherto he had almost contemned; looking on him as a stripling of limited capacity, under the sway of his governor, Chièvres, for Charles had shown himself humbly submissive to the wishes of his "good father," the brilliant young monarch of France, the ruler of a nation foremost among the enemies of his house. Until now hidden, as it were, in the marshes of Flanders, Charles is scarcely known in Italy, and is but ill at ease in Spain, where the title of king is accorded him only under protest.

But with imposing effect the youthful monarch emerges from this obscurity by the distinguished success of his first effort to cast off the trammels that interfere with his freedom of action, and the realisation of that ambitious dream — universal dominion — which he has cherished from boyhood. All the schemes of his rival are at once disconcerted, while, at the same time, a blow is given to that high consideration, which, though ill-deserved, Francis I. has enjoyed throughout Europe since the murderous conflict with the Swiss, and triumph over them at Marignan.

Very keenly did Francis feel the ignominious defeat he considered he had met with. For a time it even preyed so much on his mind that all the blandishments of the fair ladies of his court, anxious to console him, could not put to flight his gloomy thoughts. He sometimes affected to consider himself much indebted to the electors for relieving him from so heavy a burden and its attendant anxieties, yet cherished no less a deep resentment towards the young Emperor Charles V., preferred before him in the sight of Europe; thus sorely wounding his *amour propre*. From this sprang that personal jealousy and rivalry in which some historians see the true principle of those almost ceaseless wars by which, during the reign of those two monarchs, France and Italy were ravaged.

Charles was elected emperor on the 18th of June, 1519. He was at Barcelona when, nine days after, he was informed of it. The Spaniards were as much dissatisfied with this elevation of their king to the imperial dignity as he himself was gratified by it. They urged him to decline the proffered honour, as they desired their sovereign to reside among them, and objected to the government of a viceroy. Charles, however, heeded not their remonstrances; but gave a very gracious reception to the German embassy, headed by the Count Palatine, and accepted the dignity conferred on him by the electors, promising to speedily set out for Germany for his public coronation.

Murmurs grew louder, the Spaniards exhibiting a most refractory spirit. Serious commotions occurred in Valencia, and a mutinous disposition showed itself with no less violence in Castile. Charles's Flemish ministers were in the highest disfavour, but were as anxious to leave Spain as their master, who, after near a twelvemonth's delay, disregarding a threatened insurrection in Toledo, embarked at Corunna on the 22d of May, 1520, having arranged to meet Henry VIII. at Sandwich.

It is remarked by Robertson * that the effect on Charles's mind of this great elevation was noticeable by his assumption from that time of the title of majesty in all public writs which he issued as King of Spain, and his requirement of it from his subjects as a mark of their respect. Until then, he continues, all the monarchs of Europe were satisfied with the appellation of "Highness," or "Grace;" but the vanity of other sovereigns soon led them to follow the example of the Spanish king.

According, however, to French historians, it was not the Emperor Charles V. who was the first monarch that bestowed on himself the title of majesty, but that most ignoble of the kings of France, Louis XI.

* "Reign of Charles V."

CHAPTER XI.

A Dream of Glory and Grandeur. — Constantinople, or Death! — Sickness and Famine. — Free Gifts to the King. — The Most Learned Prince. — A Good Calf to His Leg. — England's True King. — Young, Gay, and Gallant. — The Rival Monarchs. — Mutual Courtesies. — Journeying Toward the Sea. — A Halt in the Preparations. — Europe Astounded. — The Feast of Pentecost. — Europe's Mightiest Prince. —The Old Spanish Doubloons. — Espials and Counter-espials. — The Cardinal Visits the King. — The Signal to Advance. — The Royal Retinue. — The Chevalier King Approaches. — — An Embrace on Horseback. — Dwelling in Tents. — Henry's Visit to Queen Claude.—Incurring a Risk. — The Royal Wrestlers.— French and English Fashions. — A More Business-like Meeting.

THE king's signal defeat at Frankfort was a no less mortifying blow to the paladins and fair damsels of the corrupt Court of France — where, under the protection of Madame Louise, vice still grew and flourished, masked by the varnish of external elegance, great politeness and distinguished manners — than to the king himself. If Charles V., dominated by the one passion of ambition, as described by some historians, looked forward to girding himself with the powerful sword, as well as wearing the crown, of the great Charlemagne, and with it reviving the Empire of the West, Francis I. had also his dream of glory and grandeur.

He beheld, in mental vision, the scenes described in romances of chivalry, which, as a youth, had formed his chief study, often guided his conduct, and partly formed his character. He saw the hosts of the faithful once more assembled, and, led by invincible steel-clad warriors—*preux chevaliers* all of them — ready to go forth to fight the Crescent under the sacred banner of the Cross; to put down the power of the infidel, and recover the Holy Sepulchre. He, too, would be the foremost of a band of Christian knights, for had he not promised the electors to conquer the Turks within three years or die?

Papal opposition to the teaching of Luther had agitated men's minds, and filled Christendom with religious strife. Anxiety was further increased by the Pope's penitential processions, and the proposal of a new crusade against the invading Turks. The religious spirit of the times, therefore, seemed at that particular moment not altogether out of harmony with the idea of a ninth holy war, whether conducted according to the chivalric views of Saint Francis, or the more matter-of-fact views of Saint Charles.

Francis had never been very popular, except with the young nobility who had grown up with him. Amongst the people he enjoyed a sort of *prestige*, on coming to the throne, as the husband of the "saintly Madame Claude," the daughter of their father, the "good King Louis XII." But when they came to know him better, his popularity vanished. At the period now in question, murmuring, discontent, and great distress were general, and in some parts of the kingdom sickness and famine, that frequent scourge of the land, prevailed.

To obtain the enormous sums he had squandered with the vain hope that the German states would elect him as their head, Francis and his chancellor, Duprat, had had recourse to the most oppressive measures, the most unjust exactions, always enforcing them with the utmost rigour. The vast amount thus iniquitously raised was now expended. Further supplies were needed, and Francis, who had returned to his usual course of libertine pleasures, with his accustomed reckless indifference to the affairs of his kingdom, trusted to the inventive brain of his chancellor to procure them.

The already heavy *taille*, or tax on the commonalty, was much increased. The people were enraged at this, and complained that the burden imposed on them was heavier than they could bear. Vain were their remonstrances. Driven to despair, they cried aloud for vengeance, and were punished for their presumption by whipping, imprisonment, and hanging. Francis and his infamous mother — he squandering, she (continuing her depredations on the public treasury) hoarding — had no sympathy whatever with the people.

The Venetian, Giustiniani, writes that "words were powerless to express the hatred and indignation of the feelings of the people towards them. The king," he continues, "has taken the gold and silver plate of the princes and prelates; has exacted fines for the customs and usages enjoyed by the gentry on their own domains, and attempted to levy a fifth penny on all their receipts for thirty years back. He has taken loans from his officers; accepted 'benevolences' (free gifts of money) from them, and is about to sell his own private domain, already mortgaged to the amount of 300,000 or 400,000 *livres*."* In short, this Christian King of France had begged, borrowed, and plundered in all directions.

Notwithstanding the necessitous position of both king and people, preparations were about to be made, on a scale of splendour that were to throw all former festivities into the shade, for the long deferred interview shortly to take place between Henry VIII. and Francis I., at a spot between Ardres and Guines. Henry had been very jealous of the military renown acquired by Francis at Marignan, and was most desirous of seeing him. He made frequent inquiries of those who had had any intercourse with him respecting his personal

---

* See "State Papers," reports of Venetian ambassadors; also "*Mémoires du Seigneur de Tavannes.*"

appearance, his manner of bearing himself, his tastes and acquirements. For Henry himself was perhaps the most learned prince of that age, though he was not unmindful of his personal advantages.

If they were rather of the burly kind, it is yet probable that Henry was a man of finer physique than Francis. For although his courtiers attributed to the French king the form and stature of a demigod — which may have led to his being regarded with an unusually critical eye by foreign ambassadors and others, when for the first time they found themselves in his godship's presence — yet it is certain that all were struck by the length and slenderness of his legs, compared with the shortness of his body, which was also inclined to corpulence. The exaggerated size of the puffed-out, padded trunk-hose, introduced by him at the beginning of his reign, may have partially concealed this defect, aided by the mantle.

When the Venetian ambassador, Pasqualigo, arrived in England — having been received by Francis on passing through Paris — Henry inquired of him, at his first interview, whether the King of France was really as tall as he was. The Venetian replied, "He thought there was but little difference."

"Is he as stout?" asked Henry.

"Not quite, I think," was the rejoinder.

"What sort of legs has he?"

"Very spare ones.'

"Whereupon," says the ambassador, "the king opened the front of his doublet, and, placing his hand on his thigh, said, 'Look here; you see there's a good calf to my leg.'"

Soon, however, he would be able to judge for himself as to their respective claims to be the Adonis of that age among princes.

Various circumstances had concurred to defer from time to time the desired interview between the sovereigns of France and England, first projected in 1518, when Tournay was restored to France, and the betrothal of the infant dauphin and princess took place.

But Francis, in his turn, was now urgent that the meeting should not be longer delayed, and Wolsey, whom he treated with the greatest deference while adequately bribing him — at least, so far as it was in his power to administer to that magnificent and haughty prelate's insatiable love of wealth — was humbly entreated to press his master definitively to fix a date for it, and to suggest an early one. He was very anxious to secure Henry's friendship, but more especially sought it through that of England's true king — Wolsey. He believed that his own fascinations and the support of the all-powerful minister would prevail on the English monarch to enter into such an alliance with him as would, in some measure, serve to check any attempt of the young emperor to acquire a preponderance of power fatal or formidable to the rest of Europe.

Wolsey's interest in the French alliance, towards which he had hitherto shown so much favour, had considerably cooled since the French king's influence in the College of Cardinals (promised to him in furtherance of his pretensions to the papacy) had fallen so low, while that of Charles had risen so greatly. Veer round and abruptly oppose what, until now, he had sought to promote, he could not; but he could interpose delay, and further delay, until circumstances arose (the war looming in the distance) affording a pretext for evading the interview altogether.

England held a distinguished position at that time among the states of Europe. "All sought the monarch's friendship, and obsequiously courted the favour of his minister, striving by presents, promises, or flattery, to work on his avarice, his ambition, or his pride. Nor was Henry insensible to the singular advantage he derived from the deference paid to him as the natural guardian of the liberties of Europe." * But he was also young, gay, and gallant, fond of amusement, pomp, and show, and by no means disposed on this occasion to yield to any suggestion to forego the gratification of his long-cherished wish to meet his chivalric brother of France.

* See Robertson, also Fiddes's "Life of Wolsey," and "Foreign State Papers."

After some correspondence respecting the general arrangements, the etiquette to be observed, the order of precedence, and other important preliminaries, Wolsey proposed the month of July for the interview. Francis was annoyed at this unreasonable delay. It was early in the spring; and in reply he suggested that April, or May at latest, was a more suitable time of the year. Further, it was stated that the queen's accouchement was expected in July, and that if the interview were deferred till that month she would be unable to be present.

This was sufficient for the then gallant Henry, who immediately charged his ambassador, Sir Richard Wingfield, to declare "that he would not for anything that the queen should be absent. Wanting her presence, he should then be lack of one great part of the perfection of the feast." The 31st of May was then appointed for the meeting of the young monarchs of France and England.

Charles being informed of this, hastened his departure from Spain. For while he, too, was anxious for a friendly alliance with Henry, he desired no less to defeat his rival's views of drawing England nearer to France by closer bonds of amity. As some French historians assert, and events seem to confirm it, Charles had outbid Francis for the services of Wolsey by larger pensions, presents, and, above all, the promise of his influence at Rome when the chair of Saint Peter became vacant.* Francis was aware that a meeting was arranged between Henry and Charles. His secret agents watched and reported all the young emperor's movements, while the latter, of course, was kept equally well informed of all that was passing between Henry and Francis. To give the emperor more time for his voyage, Francis was again requested to name a later date for the interview, Henry informing Queen Katharine — who would have been glad that the visit to France, which she did all in her power to obstruct, should have been put off altogether — that he was in hopes of a favourable answer.

"The French king," he said, "cannot yet know, Madam, how matters stand between me and my brother the emperor, your nephew. If he did, he would never grant the request; so the thing must be kept as secret as possible. On this the queen, clasping her hands and raising her eyes to heaven, gave laud unto God for the grace she hoped He would do her, that she might behold her nephew, which was her greatest desire in the world. So saying, she thanked the king and made him a very low curtsey. The king, removing his bon-

---

*Leo X. was still in the prime of life; but his extremely licentious habits did not seem to promise length of years. He believed that he was destined to an early death, and had determined that while he lived he would have a double portion of what he considered life's pleasures.

net, assured her he would do all that on his part was possible." *

It was hoped that Charles would land at Sandwich about the middle of May, when he and the king would proceed to Canterbury, where the queen was to receive her nephew. In honour of the event, Wolsey had obtained from the Pope a plenary indulgence and jubilee, which probably absolved the whole party from any blame that might otherwise attach to them for the chicanery, falsehood, and deceit employed to make it appear that the emperor's visit was an unexpected one.

The request for further delay was refused. Francis desired that his interview with Henry should precede, not follow, his rival's visit to England, and complained to Wolsey of the arrangement between Henry VIII. and "the King of Castile" as a sort of discourtesy. Wolsey replied that, "if the King of Castile should offer to land at Sandwich, or about those parts, to visit his uncle and aunt, they being in journeying toward the sea and next thereunto, it were too marvellous ingratitude to refuse the same."

The preparations meanwhile were being pushed forward with great diligence, and wondrous edifices were rising, as if by magic, on either side of the sandy borderland of the French and English possessions. Yet more than once it had

* See "Calendar of Foreign State Papers, Letters," etc.; and Brewer's Introduction.

seemed that the great event, after all the anxiety and trouble it had occasioned, was destined never to take place.

The enemies of the French king had whispered in Wolsey's ear — or he may have feigned it, in order to please his royal mistress and alarm his royal master — that Francis entertained sinister intentions towards the English monarch. That under cover of sending escorts to Ardres to accompany the pictures, statues, jewels, tapestry hangings, velvets, cloth of gold, and other finery transported thither for the concealment of the lath, plaster, and boards of those truly imposing erections that Europe was to be called upon "to come, to see, and admire," he was really assembling a large body of troops and bringing up supplies of ammunition. Several large vessels were also said to be fitting out on the coasts of Normandy and Brittany.

Until this serious matter was satisfactorily arranged — by an assurance given under the king's sign-manual that no vessel should leave any port of Normandy or Brittany before the meeting of Francis and Henry had taken place, and its attendant festivities were ended — no further progress was made towards completing the preparations.

What hopes and fears, too, during that interval had agitated the breasts of those fair ladies who were appointed to accompany Queen Claude, Madame Louise, and the Duchesse d'Alençon to

Guines! Their number, of course, was limited, if only because of the difficulty of providing a shelter for them, even from the weather. Those alone who were considered the most beautiful of the throng of sirens composing the gay court of Francis I. were selected for the special honour of fascinating the English king; and many must have been the heartburnings occasioned by so invidious a distinction.

All was suspense and anxiety as to the result of Wolsey's newly raised obstacles, suggested, probably, to afford Charles — detained in Spain by the rebellious attitude of the people — the opportunity, by a short delay, of still arriving at Sandwich before the 31st, when Henry was to enter Guines. If so, the ruse succeeded. Europe, it appears, was astounded at the condescension of "the greatest monarch of the earth visiting a king of England," or, as it was termed, "vailing his bonnet to him." The Pope could scarce conceal his surprise and indignation. The English people, however, were quite elated that the sovereign who held in his grasp so many sceptres had "degraded himself" to go out of his way to do so much honour to England and its monarch. They were greatly pleased, too, with the "benignity of his manner, and the meekness of so high a prince in dispensing with all pomp and state."

Henry VIII. and Queen Katharine "left Greenwich for the seaside on the 21st of May, and arrived at Canterbury on the 25th." On the same day the emperor's fleet was reported in sight. Wolsey being at Dover to receive him, Charles landed there next morning,* and the king rode over to greet him early. It was the feast of Pentecost, and in order more worthily to solemnise it and to sanctify the family meeting, the pious uncle and nephew took horse for Canterbury, there to join Queen Katharine, and together to celebrate the feast.

Charles spent four days with his kinsfolk. What topics they discussed, what advice Wolsey gave them, or what resolutions they came to, remained a close secret. It got whispered about, however, that the queen's ardent desire that the hand of her daughter, the Lady Mary, should be transferred from the dauphin to her nephew was one subject of their conference. But Charles, it was also reported, seemed inclined to a renewal of his betrothal to Madame Renée of France.

If so, nothing final resulted from it; but as he always took time to make up his mind, he may have thought that, as the young ladies were respectively but four and nine years of age, there was no need for a hasty decision. On the 31st, Charles re-embarked and sailed for Flanders,

* He seems to have had a remarkably quick passage, if the date of his departure from Corunna (22d of May) is given correctly — wind in the poop surely all the way — the vessels of those days being very slow sailers.

where he remained during Henry's festive visit to France.

The impression he made on the gentlemen of the English king's suite was naturally not so favourable as the opinion of the people. "There was something sad," writes a contemporary, "in the expression of his long, thin sallow face, his pale blue eyes, his projecting under jaw, and discoloured, defective teeth." There was in his manner, too, in those early days, a want of self-possession, an embarrassment, which scarcely seemed to announce a mind full of mighty projects. He had also a slight impediment in his utterance, afterwards almost entirely overcome, and was naturally reserved.

He had studied several of the modern languages — English, French, Italian, German, Spanish. His French was that imperfect idiom spoken in the Netherlands, then called Walloon French. His proficiency in the other languages by no means justified the application to himself of the well-known *mot*, attributed to him by his panegyrist, M. A. Pichot, that "*On est autant de fois homme qu'on sait de langues differentes.*" M. Michelet says Henry was pleased that Charles was of inferior stature and mean appearance; that he was simply dressed in black, leaving every advantage to him; declaring that he would have no judge but him in his disputes with Francis, and would sign whatever he approved.

In personal appearance Charles V. doubtless showed to great disadvantage in the presence of Henry VIII. But the want of his stalwart graces might have been condoned by the English courtiers had Charles's dress and equipage, plain and unpretending, corresponded better with his rank of "Europe's mightiest prince." In his retinue were several of his favourite Flemish courtiers and ministers, driven out of Spain for their rapacity by the indignant Spaniards.

They are said to have carried out of the country nearly all the fine old gold doubloons of the Ferdinand and Isabella reign. "So rare had they become," says Michelet, "that when a Spaniard by chance met with one, he was accustomed to take off his hat to it, saying devoutly, 'God preserve thee, doubloon with the double head, since M. de Chièvres has failed to find and grasp thee.'"

His brother Ferdinand, two years his junior, also accompanied him. Charles was unwilling to leave this disinherited youth in Spain, lest the crowns of perhaps both Aragon and Castile should have been placed on his head in his absence. The Spaniards looked on Charles as a foreigner; while Joanna's younger son, born and brought up amongst them, and expecting to be Ferdinand's heir, they regarded as one of themselves.

Henry VIII. and his queen, with their retinue, also left Dover on the 31st, and Guines was entered only on the 4th of June. As their retinue is said to have consisted of 5,172 persons and 3,465 horses, one may suppose that the greater part had been despatched some time before the departure of the royal visitors. No doubt, in all the accounts of this famous event there is much exaggeration; so that this very numerous retinue may have included "the body of gentlemen appointed to attend on the king in case of surprises," as well as those employed in the arrangements for "espials," for great distrust existed on both sides, as the "counter-espials" of the French king testified. Then there was a large number, also, of workmen — a part of whom may have come from Calais — who put the wooden palaces, chapels, and other constructions together, and made them "so brave" with cloth of gold brocade.

All the grand altar-cloths, sumptuous vestments and ecclesiastical decorations that Henry VII. had given to the Abbey of Westminster, were brought over for the adornment of the king's temporary chapel and the queen's oratory; while Francis, on his part, ransacked churches and palaces, and put into requisition all that could be obtained from the private hôtels of the nobility, of Turkey work, silk and satin hangings, or rich embroidery. Anything, in fact, that was sumptuous or costly, for the indispensable chapel (piety and revelry walking hand in hand), as well as for the state apartments of his royal pavilion, which was to rival in splendour Henry's wonderful summer palace.

Wolsey, haughty and arrogant, strove to outvie both sovereigns in the pomp and magnificence he displayed. The proceedings began with the cardinal's visit to the French king. He rode a splendidly barded mule, and wore the richest ecclesiastical vestments. His arrival was announced by a salvo of artillery and a deafening noise of trumpets, drums and fifes. The king, bonnet in hand, received him with profound respect and many demonstrations of affection.

On the following day he returned my lord cardinal's visit, and, after what seems a strangely unnecessary delay of three days — as though the monarchs of England and France, on the point of meeting, were really afraid to face each other — the long-projected interview took place. Such was the extreme punctiliousness observed on both sides, that not until the signal was given to fire simultaneously from the castles of Guines and Ardres, might either sovereign advance a step to meet the other.

Henry slowly rode towards the valley of Ardres, preceded by the Marquis of Dorset, bearing the sword of state. Immediately behind him rode my lord cardinal, several noblemen following, amongst whom was Brandon; but it does not appear that Mary, the duchess, Dowager-Queen of France, accompanied Queen Katharine to Guines. Nine henchmen, in silver tissue, formed the escort of this grand cavalcade, so resplendently arrayed in damasks and cloths of gold, velvets, satins, feathers and jewels, as the costume of the time required for cavaliers of such high distinction. A little in the rear marched a rather numerous guard of honour.

"It is worthy of remark," says a French writer (Servan), "that good taste was more conspicuous in the English arrangements than in the French, to which was decreed the palm of greater magnificence."

Doubtless both the young sovereigns looked well. Henry, tall and muscular, ruddy complexioned, and with an ample red beard, was "the most goodliest prince," says Hall, "that ever reigned over the realm of England." The French accounts are scarcely less complimentary.

Henry and Francis were alike excellent horsemen; though on this occasion little could be seen of their horses. So brilliant a part did the poor animals play in this grand pageant, with their housings of cloth of gold and jewelled trappings, that only their eyes and a part of their elaborately decorated tails were visible.

The description given of the costume of the King of France would lead one to think that he had really designed to outshine his brother of England, at least in the sumptuousness of his dress. The manner, too, in which his retinue advanced was evidently intended to prepare for the appearance of the king with greater *éclat*. The provost-marshal and his archers rode forward some distance before him to clear the way. At short intervals appeared the marshals of France, each with several attendants, all wearing cloth of gold, plumed hats, and many jewels, and riding richly caparisoned horses. Following them, and even more dazzlingly arrayed, were the princes of the blood with the King of Navarre, escorted by the Swiss guard in "new liveries," and accompanied by their drums, flutes, hautbois, and clarions.

But surely majesty itself approaches! Not yet. It is but a cavalier of majestic bearing, the grand constable of France, Charles de Bourbon, carrying his sword of office. With him rides the *grand écuyer*, with the sword of state, decorated with *fleur-de-lys* in gold. There now looms in sight a glittering object, almost literally a mass of jewels. He wears a full-skirted doublet and short casaque of violet velvet interwoven with gold. His mantle of cloth of gold is thickly incrusted or inlaid, as it seems, with rubies and emeralds, pearls, and diamonds, and his velvet hat is studded over with the same precious gems, and ornamented with a magnificent white plume. Golden spurs, gold-fringed gloves, and square-toed shoes are all glittering with jewels, which flash and sparkle also, in the sunlight of a summer's morn, on the elaborately embroidered and gold-fringed housings of his curveting charger.

This brilliant personage is Francis I., the

"chevalier king," the great patron of art, and "father of letters." Like many of the nobility whose ambition it was to appear at this meeting of the kings with great pomp and magnificence, and whom Martin du Bellay describes as "carrying thither their mills, their forests, their lands on their shoulders," so Francis, in order to surpass the English king in the splendour of his appearance, and to give a general impression of his wealth and grandeur, had sold his private domain, raised loans at ruinous rates, and grievously oppressed his suffering people.

A body of troops followed the king. Their number appearing greatly to exceed the small detachment attendant on Henry, a moment of distrust caused the English party to come to a sudden halt. However, the two kings set the example of casting aside all suspicion by separating themselves from their retinues, putting spurs to their horses, and approaching each other at a gallop, uncovering as they drew near, and embracing each other on horseback. This feat performed, they dismounted, again embraced, and, attended only by Wolsey and the chief favourite, Bonnivet, walked arm in arm for private discourse to a pavilion. The English and French troops meanwhile fraternised, and "drank to each other with good courage."

The fanciful usages of the courts of Love and Beauty were revived; the jousts and tournaments to begin on the morrow were arranged, and a glazed pavilion set apart for the two queens conveniently to view the sport, galleries being arranged for the numerous fair dames of their respective retinues. Strictly for the royal personages everything was, no doubt, made as comfortable as the many difficulties of the situation permitted. But for the dwellers in those two or three thousand picturesque-looking white tents, with a bundle of straw or grass for carpet and couch, and often only the sky for a covering — the winds making high festival also during this grand gathering, and causing sad havoc amongst those frail tenements — there was nothing but disappointment, regrets, and vexation of spirit. The ladies attending the tournaments displayed as best they could, but by no means satisfactorily, the rich and costly *toilettes* prepared with so much toil and expense, and transported with so much difficulty to the scene of the revels.

"When the two kings," says Michelet, "opened the tournament, Francis gave Henry so vigourous a blow that he was unhorsed, and could not rise. He was taken up by his attendants and carried to his tent. The horse was found to be in as bad a plight as his master;" one may even say worse, for, according to the same authority, "he died from the blow he had received the same night." This unfortunate commencement of the festivities is not mentioned by other writers.

On Sunday, June the 10th, Henry dined at Ardres, with Queen Claude and Madame d' Alençon. Madame Louise of Savoy, attended by a bevy of young ladies, the beauties of the court, splendidly arrayed, received the royal guest. He is said to have been so struck by the loveliness of this youthful group of fair damsels, as to have lingered long to gaze on them with admiration.

At last he awakes to a consciousness of the presence of the gentlemen-in-waiting, who are to conduct him to the queen's apartment. Claude rises from her chair of state to meet him. Henry falls on one knee, and, bonnet in hand, kisses the queen; then he salutes Madame Louise and the Duchesse d' Alençon; and, finally, all the ladies of the company are thus honoured. A flourish of trumpets soon after announced that the banquet was served. This grand state dinner was ended by five o'clock, when Henry, with many compliments to the ladies generally, and gracious speeches to the queen in particular, took his leave, mounting his high-mettled charger with much graceful agility, prancing and curveting as he rode off, to the great admiration of the ladies.

While this pretty scene was enacting at Ardres, a similar one was taking place at Guines, where Francis dined with Queen Katharine and her ladies; leaving, after the banquet, at the same hour as Henry left Ardres. Each monarch thus, for three successive Sundays, played the part of hostage for the other's safety while dining with his wife; distrust preventing them from entertaining each other, in person, on territory not strictly neutral.

Francis broke through these restraints by one morning paying Henry an unexpected visit before he was up, to the surprise and alarm of attendants French and English. But Henry expressed himself delighted. The monarchs cordially embraced and exchanged presents; but the French king's compliment was not returned by the English one. Fleuranges thought it an act of madness on the part of Francis to have incurred such a risk.

But these monotonous festivities, these daily jousts and tournaments, wrestlings, and tiltings, varied by much feasting, high mass, and Latin sermons, were drawing to a close. Unfortunately the last day's sport was a wrestling match, at which the two kings and their queens, with the princesses and the ladies of their respective suites, were present, the ladies "benignly" awarding the prizes to the victors.

Many stout wrestlers were there, and the pastime excellent; but as the King of France had neglected to send for any of the famous wrestlers of Brittany, the English gained the prizes. The Kings of England and France then retired to a pavilion, where they drank together; and the King of England, seizing the King of France by the collar, said, "My brother, I must wrestle with you," and once or twice strove to trip up his heels. But the King of France, who is a dexterous wrestler, twisted him round and threw him on the earth with prodigious violence. The King of England, rising, desired to renew the contest, but, according to Fleuranges, "was prevented by his lords."

Thus Francis, by a rather impolitic act, avenged the defeat of the French wrestlers. But Henry, who was exceedingly vain of his own dexterity in that sport, was deeply humiliated, and the resentment he felt is supposed to have aided Wolsey in preventing Henry from entering into any engagement with Francis prejudicial to the views of Charles V.*

They, however, separated on the 24th of June with a show of great cordiality, exchanging costly presents, and "embracing each other most lovingly."

The treaties concerning the restitution of Tournay and the betrothal of Mary and the dauphin were confirmed; this being all that was achieved for France by the king's prodigal expenditure of the resources of the state on that pompous royal meeting — the Field of the Cloth of Gold; † "that final expression of the Middle Ages; the last

---

* Henri Martin.

† For further details see "*Mémoires de Fleuranges;*" also "Calendar of State Papers," Foreign Series, and Mr. Brewer's Introduction to same.

public display of habits acquired during five centuries; the efflorescence of a completely bygone age, which seemed not to belong to the sixteenth century" (Paul Lacroix).

There was, however, one other result which, perhaps, should not be overlooked — the demand which from that time arose in England for French fashions. The *belles* of the French court who attended the festivities at Guines were not only dressed superbly but with exceeding elegance and such perfect taste that they greatly excited the admiration, and, perhaps, a little of the envy, of the English ladies of the suite of Queen Katharine. Henceforth the *toilettes* of the French court became the models for that of England.

The influence of Queen Claude was small, yet she had endeavoured to sustain the vogue of the graceful fashions introduced by her mother, Anne of Brittany, — the long training robes, open in front, displaying a rich brocade or embroidered skirt; the hat or cap similar to the Mary Stuart; the flowing veil of Italian tissue, with some slight modifications, still retained their favour; probably because of their gracefulness, and that they were generally becoming.

The gallant knights and their ladies fair had all forsaken Ardres and Guines by the evening of the 24th; Francis I. and his court for Abbeville; that of Henry VIII. and Queen Katharine for Calais. From Calais the English king, accompanied by my lord cardinal, repaired to Gravelines to return the emperor's visit to Dover. There Charles and his brother Ferdinand, with his minister Chièvres and the Archbishop of Cologne, awaited Henry's arrival. No splendour dignified this meeting — the cloth of estate with the black eagle splayed in gold being the only conspicuous mark of dignity — but there is said to have been much cordiality. At all events, there was more attention to business — for a new convention between Henry VIII. and the Emperor Charles V. was signed there, of which the terms were far from favourable to the King of France.

Henry VIII.
Steel engraving by Bosselman.

CHAPTER XII.

A Round of Flying Visits. — Check to the King of France. — The Crown of Charlemagne. — Compensating Ferdinand. — Ignacio da Loyola. — Dona Maria Pacheco. — The Romance of War. — The Monk of Wittemberg. — Burning the Papal Bull. — A Revolution. — Just and Generous. — Cropped Hair and Flowing Beard. — A Mark of Noble Birth. — More Red Hats than Helmets. — "The Hundred and One Grievances." — The Promise Given Must Be Kept. — "The Lord Is My Defence." — "If I Am Wrong, Prove It to Me." — A Fearless Spirit. — Captured by Armed Horsemen. — A Transformation. — Mind and Body Benefited. — The Defence of the Faith.

AFTER those three weeks of formal, fatiguing festivities of the Field of the Cloth of Gold, Francis and his court left Abbeville with "bag and baggage" for the customary summer series of flying visits from château to château, forest to forest — a *pèlerinage pantagruelesque*, as termed by Michelet — a moving romance of gaiety and pleasure, from which all that was serious, whether of affairs of state or the concerns of every-day life, was rigourously banished.

These roving habits of Francis and his court often occasioned considerable expense and much vexation to foreign envoys and ambassadors, and were the frequent subject of complaint in their reports to their respective governments. New arrivals never knew where to find the king — or "that other king," his mother; and business was wholly at a standstill when she, with her ladies, accompanied her son. On reaching the place where last they were heard of, it was too often only to find that the king and his court had just struck their tents and were on their way to some new encampment; to feast and make mirth on some fresh grassy slope, to hunt in the forests, or to disport themselves 'neath the greenwood tree.

Notwithstanding this rambling life, so fitted to dispel anxiety and care, Francis could not quite forget his recent second defeat. Again the emperor, King of Castile, had checkmated the King of France, and no advantage that he had promised himself from the interview with Henry VIII. had been secured. In the midst of his pleasures his thoughts turned towards Leo X., whose aims and interests he believed would be served by an alliance with France against the emperor; and an ambassador was forthwith despatched to Rome.

That wary young gentleman, who carried such a very old head on his youthful shoulders, had not been too obedient to the urgent call of the electoral princes to come and be crowned. He, indeed, began his reign surrounded by difficulties and dangers, all claiming immediate attention. Rebellion was rife in Spain, and jealousy of Spain prevailed in Flanders — his ministers, Flemish and Spanish, being at daggers drawn. There was a fitting provision to be made for his victimised brother, and a new heresy was represented to him as spreading so rapidly in the German states as to call for measures prompt and peremptory to suppress it. Like Francis, Charles coveted the alliance of the Pope. He was able to serve the papacy by "stopping," as he thought, the spread of the "new opinions;" the Pope, in return, being willing to unite his forces with his against France. An imperial envoy was, therefore, soon on his way to Rome.

The plague was then raging in parts of Germany, and many persons had fallen victims to it in Aix-la-Chapelle, where the coronation, according to the Golden Bull, was to take place. Nevertheless, the electors being impatient of further delay, Charles bade adieu to his native Netherlands, and was crowned with the crown of Charlemagne on the 23d of October, 1520, with exceeding pomp and splendour — no previous imperial coronation having occurred since 1439.

Besides the electors the rest of the German princes and the Roman officials, visitors of rank from Italy, Spain, and Germany, filled the town to overflowing. But no sooner was the ceremony ended than all this grand company, as though seized by panic, fled from the plague-stricken spot and reassembled at Cologne. Cologne, now, then, and from all time, notorious for the variety of its *mauvaises odeurs*, each street having one peculiar to itself, differing from all the rest, had yet wholly escaped the plague! While Charles was receiving the homage of the princes of the empire, and very wisely ceding to his brother, in lieu of Aragon, a large part of the Austrian dominions left by Maximilian, — as well as securing the consent of the Electoral Diet to the regency of the empire, when compelled to absent himself from Germany, being confided to Ferdinand, assisted by a council chosen by the Diet, — Francis, taking advantage of the rebellion in Spain, was sending troops to Navarre.

This step, though it added fuel to the flames of sedition then raging in Castile, was not a formal infraction of peace. The French troops, under the command of Lesparre, the youngest of the three brothers De Foix, invaded Navarre in the name of Henri d' Albret, whom Francis was bound by the treaty of Noyon — whose stipulations Charles had wholly neglected to carry out — to assist in recovering his hereditary dominions, of which Ferdinand V. had deprived him, and which Charles had promised to restore.

Lesparre, though brave, had neither experience nor the qualities that form a great general. He is said to have owed his command to the all powerful influence of his sister, the Comtesse de Châteaubriand. Nevertheless, in the course of a few days the whole of Navarre was conquered in a sort of triumphal march, the people hailing with enthusiasm the expulsion of the Spaniards and the return of their dispossessed but legitimate sovereign.

The somewhat dilapidated citadel of Pampeluna was held by a small garrison, under a young Biscayan officer, Ignacio da Loyola, and here some resistance was encountered. After a few hours of alternate attack and repulse, the citadel surrendered, the commandant being dangerously wounded. To the shot that disabled him, and to the dreams of spiritual influence suggested by the study of the lives of saints, during a long convalescence, were due, after some wild and perilous adventures, the organisation of the powerful Society of Jesus. In the strict discipline Loyola introduced into this monastic order, and the title of general assumed by him as its head, he revived the regulations and subordination to authority to which, as a soldier, he had been subjected during his short military career. As a priest, he adopted them as necessary to ensure the united action of those under his control, and the attainment of that wide-spread power and influence to which he aspired, both for himself and the new fraternity.

Lesparre, elated by his great success, was not content with having so rapidly and thoroughly accomplished the mission confided to him, but must carry his invincible arms into Spain. He had the imprudence to enter Castile, where he took the small town of Lagroño, incited, it is said, by the heroic Doña Maria Pacheco, who, after the execution of her husband, Don Juan de Padilla, who headed the insurgent Castilians, took up arms herself to avenge his death, and held the citadel of the Alcazar of Toledo four months after the town had submitted to the imperial troops.

Incited by the courage of the heroine who sought his aid, Lesparre, young and brave, instead of waiting for a reinforcement from Henri d'Albret, offered battle to the imperialists with a force far inferior in numbers. He was overwhelmed, taken prisoner, and personally attacked with so much fury, that, powerless to defend himself, he fell dead in the midst of his foes, his armour battered and broken, his body a mass of wounds. Pursuing their victory, the imperialists entered Navarre, and Henri d'Albret's dominions were lost to him as speedily as they had been regained, nothing remaining to him but the small town of St. Jean-Pied-de-Port.*

This unhappy yet romantic incident of the changes and chances of war was followed by much indirect skirmishing in the Netherlands and elsewhere, and menaces of invasion — yet without formal declaration of hostilities — on the part of both Francis and the emperor; preludes of that great war between France and the House of

* Servan, "*Guerres des Français;*" H. Martin, "*Histoire de France.*"

Austria, soon to burst forth and deluge Europe with blood. The unfortunate Lesparre's disaster was some months later avenged, and the cantons of Lower Navarre, with the province of Fontarabia, reconquered by a *corps d'armée* under the Comte de Guise and Bonnivet, the Albret family retaining henceforth that portion of their dominions.

Meanwhile, Charles's first act of administration was to convoke a Diet of the empire. Conformably to the Papal Bull, it should have been held at Nuremberg; but, as the plague was raging in that city, the emperor named Worms, and appointed the 6th of January, 1521, for the first solemn assembly over which he was to preside. Many matters of great public interest were alluded to as demanding the attention of the Diet. But the one subject in every one's thoughts was "the heresy of the monk of Wittemberg," "the progress of whose new and dangerous opinions, threatening to disturb the peace of Germany and overturn the religion of their ancestors, the emperor called on the assembled princes to concert with him the proper measures for effectually checking."

The "heresy" had, however, progressed far beyond his power to check. Luther's writings had been burnt in some towns by the agents of the papacy, though it was he rather than his books whom they wished to burn. The Pope had issued a Bull of excommunication against him, to which Luther replied, on the 10th of December, by leading a procession of the professors and students of his university to the market-place of Wittemberg, where a large pile of fagots had been heaped together. To this, the oldest of the professors applied a burning brand. When the flames began to rise, Luther advanced and threw into them the books of the Canon Law, the Decretals,* the Clementines,† and the "Extravagantes." ‡

When these were consumed, Luther took the Pope's Bull of excommunication, and, holding it up, said, "As thou hast vexed the spirit of the Lord, may eternal fire vex and consume thee!" at the same time casting it into the flames. All the spectators applauded, and, the last vestige of the Bull having disappeared, they accompanied Luther back to his university.

That he dared take such a step, showed that the time for checking him and his doctrine had long since passed. His object in taking it, as he explained, was by a solemn act to declare that he separated himself from the Pope and the Church; that he accepted the excommunication pronounced by Rome, and to make known to the Christian

---

*The Pope's decrees.
† Ordinances of Clement V.
‡ A collection of fundamental rules or principles of certain popes added to the body of the common law. (Merle d'Aubigné.)

world that henceforth there was war to the death between him and the papacy.

While these stirring scenes were enacting in Germany, the fermentation they excited spreading even to Switzerland — where Ulric Zwingle was already preaching doctrines similar to Luther's — others, of a very different kind, occupied the court of France.

On the 6th of January, the same day that Charles V. had appointed for an assembly of the princes of the empire, an accident occurred to Francis I. that for a while threatened to change the aspect of affairs in Europe. It, however, only occasioned a revolution in the fashion of wearing the hair and beard.

Francis and the court had repaired to the château of Madame Louise at Romorantin, in Berry, to amuse themselves with the revelry of the carnival. On the feast of the Epiphany, or *Fête des Rois*, a "King of the bean," or Twelfth-night king, having been made by one of the party assembled in the rooms of M. de Saint Pol (brother of the Duc de Vendôme), Francis sent one of his courtiers to challenge this king in his name. He then proceeded, accompanied by several of his favourite companions, to besiege his majesty of the bean in his castle, whence the besiegers were repulsed with snowballs from a balcony. This seasonable ammunition coming to an end, there was a demand for surrender, when some one of the besieged party ("*quelque mal avisé,*" Fleuranges says) seized a brand from the hearth and threw it amongst their assailants. It fell on the king's head. Francis was severely hurt (*grièvement blessé*); and for some days the surgeons were doubtful of his recovery. A report rapidly spread, both in France and abroad, first that the king was dead, next that blindness had resulted from the blow. Yet he seems really to have suffered but little, and speedily silenced those rumours by receiving the ambassadors who accompanied the court.

He would not allow, says Fleuranges, any inquiry to be made by whom the brand was thrown. "He had begun the foolery," he said, "and must take his share of its consequences." This was only just; but, considering what were the ideas and customs of the period, a generous view of the occurrence also. The thoughtless act was attributed, not at the time but many years after, to Montgomery of Lorges, the father of the Montgomery who caused the death of Henry II. in an encounter at a tournament. It may have been so; yet it was merely conjecture, simply a suggestion, which, after the second event, was assumed as a fact and an extraordinary coincidence.

But for the above misadventure, Francis had intended to take the queen and his sister and mother, with the ladies of the court, in great state to Milan ("Bourgeois de Paris").

A closely shaven beard and long flowing locks had been the fashion in France for several generations. But for more effectually dressing the king's wounds, it became necessary to cut off his hair. On his recovery he continued to wear it cropped, but allowed his beard to grow, as was the custom of the Italians. His courtiers followed his example, and gradually short hair and long beards became general in France — one class of the community, the magistracy, excepted.

They objected to the innovation as contrary to the dignity of the profession; and for a long time the Parliament prohibited its members from conforming to this infringement of ancient usages (*nouvelleté*), as in legal language they termed this change of fashion. By and by, however, as younger men supplanted the elder gentlemen of the long robe, the long beards also got into Parliament, and were soon in a majority, before which the remaining dissentients at last gave way. Beards continued in favour until the seventeenth century, when the magistracy, again opposing the change of fashion as *infra dig.*, declined as long and as resolutely to part with their beards as their predecessors had declined to adopt them.

Servan,* referring to the warrior Pope, Julian II., remarks that "he was the first Pope who wore a beard; thinking by that singularity to inspire the people with greater respect for him. The Italian

* "*Guerres en Italie.*"

nobility imitated the Pope; and from that time," says Servan, "beards became generally worn at the European courts." Boys continued to wear their hair long, except over the forehead, where it was cut short and straight, as is seen in old pictures, and worn by some children of the present day. But in the sixteenth century it was the distinguishing mark of children of noble birth, and permitted to no other.

To return to the important events which then agitated Europe. The Diet convoked by Charles V. for the 6th of January did not assemble at Worms till the 28th. Great preparations were needed, both public and private, to accommodate within its walls the large number of princes of the empire who had announced an intention of being present. They knew so little of their young emperor that all were anxious to see and hear him. What would he do with respect to Luther, placed as he was between Luther's protector, Frederick of Saxony, to whom he owed the coveted imperial crown, and the Pope's nuncio, who called on him to issue a decree that a second Bull of excommunication, of which he was the bearer, be rigourously carried out?

This was the burning question; and friends and foes alike among the princes were drawn by it to Worms. All, too, proposed to attend in state, and even to make some sacrifices, like the French nobility at the Field of the Cloth of Gold, for the sake of appearing at the Diet with *éclat*. It is stated, in order to give an idea of the concourse of visitors at Worms, that the young landgrave, Philip of Hesse, was attended by a retinue of six hundred cavaliers in splendid uniforms; other princes also, the sovereign rulers of small states, either to gratify their vanity or in compliment to the emperor, appearing with a more or less numerous train of officers and servitors.

The emperor was less pretending. Nevertheless, on this occasion he deemed it necessary to enter Worms with his brother, the Archduke Ferdinand, more brilliantly attended than usual — "the red hats of cardinals" (as Ulrich von Hutten wrote to Charles) "being more conspicuous in his retinue than, for a mighty prince, the more appropriate plumes and helmets of valiant warriors."

The Diet was opened by the emperor with a haughty speech, in which he expressed his desire "to revive the fallen glory of the Holy Roman Empire, and his hope to succeed in doing so by means of the numerous kingdoms over which he bore sway, and the aid of his powerful alliances" (H. Martin). The edict for executing the Papal Bull being laid before the Diet, was responded to by the vehement complaints of the electors against the Pope and clergy; and a document was subsequently prepared and laid before the emperor enumerating these complaints, and called "The Hundred and One Grievances."

Luther's presence being desired, he was ordered by Charles to appear at Worms and answer for himself, "whether or not he adhered to the opinions which had drawn on him the censures of the Church." A safe-conduct from the emperor and princes was sent to him by an imperial herald, who returned with Luther to Worms. His friends were alarmed. Remembering the fate of Huss, they would have dissuaded him from recklessly rushing, as they thought, into danger. "I should go," he replied, "though as many devils as there are tiles on the houses of Worms had combined together to oppose me." Luther was then in feeble health, and so ill when he set out that he was scarce able at times to continue his journey.

He arrived on the 16th of April. A rumour having spread that the famous "monk of Wittemberg" was on his way to Worms, people from far and near flocked to see him. His journey had been a sort of triumphal progress, and above two thousand persons waited at the gates of Worms to receive him, amongst them princes and nobles, many priests who shared his opinions, and men of eminent learning. Some, of course, were influenced by mere curiosity. Others, and the far greater part, were lead thither by sympathy, and by admiration of the unflinching courage of the humble monk who so boldly defied the papacy, and fearlessly appeared in the presence of the powerful monarch whom papal agents were urging to disregard his safe-conduct, and at once deliver the obstinate heretic into their hands. To this Charles is said to have simply replied, "The promise given must be kept."

On the 18th—a day's delay having been granted at Luther's request—the emperor, the electors and princes of Germany, the Archduke Ferdinand, Charles's Flemish and Spanish ministers, the ambassadors—amongst whom were those of France and England—the Pope's nuncios, cardinals, archbishops, bishops, abbots, priors, and other priests, were assembled in the town hall of Worms, where Luther was cited to appear to reply to two questions: "Was he the author of certain heretical books? and was he prepared to retract the opinions set forth in them?"

From the hôtel of the Knights of Rhodes—where Luther was lodged by the Elector Frederick of Saxony—to the town-hall, so dense was the crowd that the imperial guards, with their halberds, with difficulty opened a passage for him. Not only the streets were crowded, but the roofs of the houses were covered with spectators. The entry of Charles V. excited far less interest than that of the poor, weary-looking monk on his way to his condemnation; for all believed that not his books alone would be committed to the flames, but that the stake was his own doom.

Jeers and gibes, mingled with words of consolation, meet his ear; but he, unmoved, utters only, "The Lord is my defence." * At last he is in the presence of the young monarch who is to decide his fate, who has already declared that "he will support the old faith." But Charles's zeal is not so ardent as Rome had hoped to find it. His political views clashed with his piety, and his ministers had made known to the nuncio that "the emperor would act towards the Pope as the Pope was inclined to act towards him; but that he in no case proposed to assist an ally of the King of France." †

Luther, repressing his natural impetuosity, had acknowledged in mild, respectful terms, on the previous day, that the books of which the titles were read to him were his writing. Charles had then contemptuously remarked, "that certainly such a man as that would never make a heretic of him." The question of a retractation of the doctrines contained in those books was now to be answered.

Forcibly and eloquently Luther defended those doctrines; his enthusiasm, as he proceeded, overcoming the bodily weakness from which he was then suffering. "If I am wrong," he said—"and, as I am but a man, of course I may be—prove it to me by the writings of the prophets and the apostles; and when convinced I will immediately

---

* Merle d'Aubigné, " Réformation."
† Pallavicini, quoted by Henri Martin.

retract all my errors, and be the first to cast my writings into the flames."

Luther had spoken in German. When he concluded he appeared to be nearly prostrated by fatigue, emotion, and heat (every available inch of standing-room having been taken possession of, in spite of all efforts to exclude the people). His discourse had made a deep impression; but the emperor, it was said, disliked the German language, and Luther was ordered to repeat his discourse in Latin. Several of the German princes objected, and sent him word that, if too much exhausted, what he had said sufficed.

After a few minutes, the agitation of the assembly beginning to subside, Luther resumed his defence in Latin, and with the same clearness and force of expression, the same warmth and fluency as had characterised his discourse in his native tongue. A feeling of admiration pervaded the assembly. The Chancellor of Trèves, who spoke for the Diet, perceiving this, said, "The question put to you is, 'Will you or not retract?' You have not replied to it." But Luther declared that he neither could nor would retract, unless convinced of error by the witness of Scripture. As that was refused, he had no other answer. "I am in your hands; God assist me!" he said, "for I can retract nothing."

"The monk speaks with a fearless spirit, and unshaken courage!" exclaimed the emperor. Admiration had overcome anger, and he might with truth, perhaps, have added, in words similar to those of King Agrippa to Paul — "Almost thou persuadest me to be a heretic."

Luther was then ordered to retire, the assembly remaining to deliberate on the steps to be taken for punishing this pestilent heretic. A servant of the old Duke Erick of Brunswick followed Luther from the hall with a large goblet of Eimbeck beer, and a message from his master desiring the monk to drink and refresh himself, assuring him, also, that he had tasted the beer before sending it.

The German princes, friends and foes, would not allow the violation, as proposed by the nuncio Aleandro, of Luther's safe conduct. A repetition of the fate of John Huss, in the person of Luther, "should not again bring disgrace and misfortune on Germany." So "the monk of Wittemberg" was allowed to depart; but three days after, a very severe decree against him was obtained from the emperor. This was of more force than a papal Bull, which, being published in Italy, could not be executed in Germany. He, meanwhile, was journeying homeward in the company of friends; but, when arrived on the borders of the forest of Thuringia, there occurred that well-known romantic incident in his career — his capture.

Five horsemen, armed, and wearing masks, suddenly issued from the woods. Seizing Luther, they placed him on a horse, and galloped off with him into the forest, making many turnings and windings and changes of route to lead possible pursuers astray as to their destination. But Luther's companions were too much alarmed to pursue. They saw in the occurrence the hand of the papacy, and, making the best of their way to Wittemberg, spread the report in every village and town on their route of his having fallen into the hands of his enemies. A cry of astonishment and indignation rose throughout Germany on the part of his friends, of fiendish delight on that of his foes.

Not until night was closing in did Luther's captors venture to approach the isolated, frowning old fortress of Wartbourg, to which they were bearing their prisoner. The drawbridge being passed, was immediately drawn up; the bolts and bars of the ponderous doors removed, were replaced as soon as he had crossed the threshold. An apartment had been prepared for him, also a change of costume, with a feathered hat, spurs, and sword. The friar's frock and hood were cast aside, and "the monk of Wittemberg" was transformed almost — as he said, beyond his own recognition — into a cavalier; while, as a further disguise, that none of the inmates of the fortress might recognise him, his hair and beard were to be allowed to grow.

He now knew that the masked cavaliers were

his friends, and that the scheme to save him from the fate to which he had been doomed by emperor and Pope was devised by the Elector Frederick of Saxony, who supplied him with all that he required, or that was agreeable to him, while in his solitary retreat. He remained at Wartbourg nearly a year, rest and quietude benefiting both mind and body. The secret of his retreat was known to only his most trusted friends; for others he had disappeared from the scene of the world. Rome apparently had triumphed, and the cause of reform, as some feared, was lost. But his opinions continued to gain ground, and the light of truth became more widely diffused. The decree against him became by and by a dead letter; meanwhile, the courageous reformer revived the spirits of his disheartened followers by publishing several treatises in confutation of his adversaries. (See Merle d'Aubigné, "Réformation.")

He seems to have been disappointed and a little grieved, during his sojourn in what is called his Patmos, at the issuing of an edict by the University of Paris, condemning his doctrines. He had once thought to be able to preach them there with freedom; but Francis, no less intolerant of reform than his rival Charles, had prohibited the introduction of Luther's writings into France.

At about the same time, too, Henry VIII. wrote his reply to Luther's "Babylonish Captivity." The praises lavished on it by his favourites and courtiers flattered his vanity greatly. It was presented to the Pope in full consistory. Leo rewarded the royal author's pious zeal in defence of popery with the title of "Defender of the Faith" —an appellation so strangely retained by English sovereigns after the erring faith defended was abjured by both sovereign and people.

CHAPTER XIII.

Rigid Ideas of Morality.— As Insensible as Ever.— Bent on Wearing the Papal Crown.— War Begins in Earnest.— Humiliating the Constable.— A Victory Missed. — An Anxious Mother's Fears.— The Mother and the Mistress.— Tardy Repentance.— Promises and Assurances.— Despotic Measures.— Dying of Laughter.— A Sudden Holy Inspiration. — Driven Out of Lombardy. — The Proceeds of Her Savings. — Stormy Family Scenes. — Vengeance Accomplished.

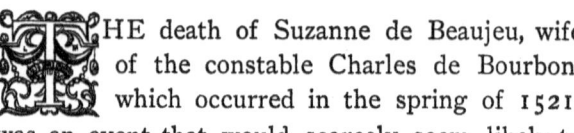HE death of Suzanne de Beaujeu, wife of the constable Charles de Bourbon, which occurred in the spring of 1521, was an event that would scarcely seem likely to influence the affairs of France, whether for good or evil.

It, however, revived in the depraved mind of Louise of Savoy the vain hope she yet cherished of subduing the cold disdain, and exciting a tender feeling in the breast of the man who had hitherto treated her advances with haughty indifference. A restraint was now removed, as she flattered herself, that, according to the constable's rigid ideas of morality — the source of so much amusement and banter to the less severe moralists of the court of France — might have prevented him from reciprocating her love.

Francis sympathised with that loving injured mother, even as she would have sympathised with him, had any lady turned a deaf ear to his pleadings and treated with supreme contempt his protestations of devoted love. He had long cherished an antipathy towards the grave constable, but was induced by his mother's infatuation to tolerate him.

The time of deep mourning may in strictness, perhaps, be said to have passed; for the constable had been some months a widower. It was not known that he had yet sought the love of any lady of the court; but whispers again reached the king's ear that the countess smiled more graciously on him than ever. Whether he responded to her smiles or not, it was certain that he was as insensible as ever to the gracious encouragements of Madame Louise. But, if she was powerless to inspire him with love for her, she could find the means of wounding his self-love and grievously vexing his haughty spirit.

A congress is being held at Calais, and Wolsey presides — the mediation of Henry VIII. having been sought to settle, if possible, the rival claims of Francis I. and the Emperor Charles V. Notwithstanding, both were preparing for war, so small was the expectation of an amicable arrangement being arrived at. Charles demanded his heritage of Burgundy and release from doing homage, as his ancestors had done, to the crown of France for his counties of Flanders and Artois. Francis required the cession of Naples, and the restitution of Navarre to Henri d' Albret. Both sovereigns had made a secret treaty with the Pope, — Charles to invade Milan and Genoa, and, aided by papal troops, to drive the French out of Italy; Francis similarly aided, to wrest the kingdom of Naples from Charles.

The propositions on both sides were, therefore, rejected. Wolsey, bent on wearing the papal crown, was incapable of judging between them impartially, or of recommending any solution of their difficulties not wholly in favour of Charles, to whom he looked to support his pretensions to sit in the chair of Saint Peter. Consequently, increased irritation on the part both of Charles and Francis was the only result of the congress.

As soon as his labours were ended, Wolsey set off for Bruges, where Charles was then staying. My lord cardinal was received with as great ceremony and state as though he had been Henry of England in person, and a treaty was concluded by which Henry undertook to invade France on the side of Picardy with an army, 40,000 strong, while Charles, with an equal number, was to enter France on the side of Spain. Of course, there was the usual marriage contract, which gave so much force to the treaties of that day.

The little Princess Mary, the heiress-presumptive of the throne — betrothed to the dauphin with such extraordinary splendour, festivity, and expense on both sides of the channel — was now transferred to the emperor, to the great satisfaction, at least, of Queen Katharine; while Henry then flattered himself that on him was to rest the glory of reannexing to the crown of England the ancient heritage of the English monarchs in France.

War now began in earnest; the struggle of arms side by side with the struggle of ideas, — the conflagration soon enveloping all Europe, — Solyman "the Magnificent" taking possession of Rhodes, — fighting in the north, the south, the east, the west going on at the same time and with the most savage ferocity. "One might believe at this crisis," writes M. Michelet, "that Europe was about to sink into profound barbarism. Yet, so far from it, the delicate blossom of the arts and civilisation grew and strengthened itself in the midst of these violent conflicts, which seemed ready to crush it."

Charles had blockaded Tournay and besieged Mezières. To oppose him, an army was advancing, which the King had left Chambord to head in person. To the constable — one of the ablest generals of that day — belonged, in virtue of his office, the command of the vanguard of a royal army.

To his surprise, he found that this honourable post had been given by the king to the Duc d'Alençon, whose command was that of the rear guard. The duke had not sought to supplant the constable. He possessed no military talent, and was not ambitious of military fame. But he was first prince of the blood, a degree nearer the throne than Charles de Bourbon, and ought to be a degree above him in command; so suggested Madame Louise to her son. It offered an opportunity of humiliating Bourbon, of affronting him in the presence of the whole army, by an apparent slight on his ability as a commander, of which he would probably complain, and thus open a way for further indignities and the widening of the breach between him and the king.

Francis, like an obedient son, adopted the views of his excellent mother, who had never thwarted him in any of the vices he was inclined to, and in whose hands he had become a mere automaton. The constable was well aware whence the affront came, and, dissembling his resentment, would not condescend to complain.

On the departure of the king, Louise resumed the government of the kingdom as regent. Though this title was assumed and laid aside during the absence or presence of the king, the power it gave her she at no time relinquished, and to the end of her life was, in fact, more the sovereign of the country than Francis himself, his ministers being for the most part, like her chancellor, Duprat, favourites of her own appointing.

The Chevalier Bayard had already compelled the imperialists to raise the seige of Mezières, and the royal army, it appears, might, on its arrival, have gained a decisive victory over Charles's troops, had a favourable opportunity that presented itself of charging and routing them been taken immediate advantage of. It was strongly urged by the constable, which sufficed to induce Francis to adopt other counsels, though Bourbon's advice was supported by that of such experienced generals as La Palice and La Trémouille.

Francis had preferred to listen to Général de Châtillon, a courtier rather than a soldier, and high in the favour of Madame Louise. He was one of the staff officers attending the king, and the mission confided to him by the anxious mother was to prevent the king, as far as he was able, from recklessly exposing himself to danger. He therefore advised Francis, at least, to delay the attack. "The atmosphere was cloudy, and the enemy's full force might not be wholly revealed." The result was, that, from want of promptitude, the advantageous moment for attack was lost, and did not recur. Tournay fell into the hands of the enemy, who committed many atrocities.

The ambitious Louise, unscrupulous as she was, could hardly have desired that a battle should be declined and territory lost merely to offer another affront to the constable. Châtillon was, perhaps, over-zealous in his desire to carry out her wishes. The king had but recently recovered from the serious wounds in his head, which may have been a motive for fears for his safety. It would be a satisfaction to be able to attribute some of his actions to injury to the brain.

The accident at Romorantin was not the first of the kind he had met with. Some few years before, in a violent encounter in an assault-of-arms, a lance is said to have deeply pierced his head and broke in it. The surgeon in attendance drew it out, Francis not uttering a groan (Michelet). That he should have survived such an injury seems extraordinary. The story is one of many of a similar nature, told by panegyrists with the view of giving an exaggerated idea of his great courage and strength, and having probably some slight foundation in truth.

The French arms were not successful in Italy; and again it was the intriguing Madame Louise — the evil genius of Francis and his kingdom — to whom disaster, defeat, and expulsion were in a great measure due. There was always some rival of hers to displace, some favourite to elevate, no matter by what means, if her object could be attained. Her insinuations had induced the king, after the battle of Marignan, as already mentioned, to recall Bourbon from Milan; but it had sorely vexed her when Marshal Lautrec, at the instance of the king's mistress, was appointed to replace him. The king, no less unjust than his mother, had gratified both her and his wily mistress, to the prejudice, not only of Bourbon, but of the claim to the post of a man much beloved by the people — the brave Milanese veteran, Marshal Trivulzio.

Lautrec, by his tyranny, had rendered the French rule hateful to the Milanese. The smallest offences were punished as heavy crimes. Imprisonment, chains, confiscation, and banishment led to numbers of the inhabitants seeking a refuge from the ferocity of the Milanese governor in other Italian states. Plots were formed to displace Lautrec, or to turn the French out of Milan, and Leo X. was known to have encouraged them. Lautrec, however, chose to accuse Trivulzio of fomenting these troubles.

The old marshal had been a faithful ally of the French, during the reigns of Francis and his two predecessors. He was now eighty years of age; yet to justify himself from such accusations he crossed the Alps in mid-winter. But Francis refused to see him — influenced by the countess, in her brother's interest. To compel the king to hear him, he placed himself in his way as he was riding out to Montlhéry. But the ungrateful prince, on perceiving him, disdainfully averted his eyes and rode on.

This unworthy treatment so deeply grieved

Trivulzio that he took to his bed, and, being too ill to return to Milan, soon after died at Châtre. The king afterwards expressed some regret for the pain he had caused this old and faithful ally; but his tardy repentance could not remove the sting of the great indignity he had inflicted on a brave commander, who had so long fought the battles of France. When the insult offered by the king to a man so much beloved by his countrymen became known in Milan, both grief and indignation were general, and contributed greatly to the success of the intrigues of the Pope and emperor.

Lautrec's turn was soon to follow. One of the difficulties of his government was the want of money to carry it on efficiently. Milan, he constantly declared, could not be retained without a free expenditure of money to keep on foot a large, punctually paid, and well-provisioned body of troops — the Swiss being so prone to rebel and desert when their pay fell into arrears. To get money from either Francis or his mother was exceedingly difficult; she unwillingly allowing it to pass out of her hands, he eagerly scattering it as soon as it came into his. Lautrec was well aware that Madame Louise was his enemy. But, unable to pay his turbulent Swiss troops, he returned to France to make known his imperative need of funds, — his brother Lescun (Maréchal de Foix) acting as governor in his absence.

Promises and assurances were always forthcoming; but, knowing how little they were to be relied on, Lautrec was loth to depart without the money required for paying the Swiss. The formal guarantee, the solemn promise of the king and his mother, and of Semblançay, the superintendent of the finances, that on his return to Milan 400,000 crowns should be ready for him at the bankers of Florence or of Languedoc, induced him at last to leave.

The promised remittance, however, did not arrive. The Florentine bankers, under pressure from the Pope, would not advance the sum, but lent to the emperor the money reserved for the king. Nor were the funds forthcoming from Languedoc. To levy taxes, exact contributions, and order the confiscation of the property (and in some instances the execution) of those who rebelled against measures so despotic, were the only means Lautrec could devise to quell the clamour of the troops for their pay.

Many of the victims of his oppression fled to Reggio in the papal states, and were pursued thither by Maréchal de Foix. This infraction of the territory of the Church led to immediate hostilities. The papal and imperial troops invaded Lombardy; Parma and Placentia and other towns were taken — the Milanese turning against their despotic French governor, and receiving the Italian visitors with delight.

The news from the papal general, Prospero Colonna, of the realisation of Leo X.'s long deeply cherished wish for the recovery of Parma and Placentia—the conquest of Julian II., afterwards taken by the French—had an extraordinary effect on his holiness. "He died of laughter," writes one historian; and, although that is not strictly true, yet his exultation on learning that the French were driven out of Milan was so excessive, that his enfeebled, worn-out frame was unable to bear the sudden shock of the rapturous rejoicing to which he gave way. The reaction brought on low fever, of which he died a few days after (December 1st, 1521).

The Pope's death caused a suspension of the war. A new pontiff was to be elected; and Wolsey's hopes ran high of succeeding the magnificent Leo, and of rivalling him in papal splendour. Charles V. recommended him (not very warmly, it is said) to the conclave; but Wolsey seems not to have received the suffrages of any one of the cardinals. They were divided in their choice between the cardinals Giulio de' Medici, Leo's nephew, and Soderini, supported by France, neither attaining the majority of voices that ensured election. Cardinal Giulio therefore determined, in order merely to gain time, to transfer his votes to the former preceptor of Charles V., Cardinal Adrian d' Utrecht, then Regent of Castile. The rest of the members of the Sacred

College followed the impulse of Cardinal de' Medici, doubtless with the idea at the moment of gratifying the emperor. But as soon as the deed was done they began to reflect on its strangeness. They had chosen for Pope a man whom none of them knew; who had never been in Rome; and, worse than all, was a "barbarian"—a Fleming. As the cardinals afterwards walked in procession from the conclave, the Roman people, being informed of their choice of a Pope, loaded them with insult. They, however, could only attribute the course they had taken to a sudden inspiration of the Holy Ghost.

Spain was much pleased to get rid of Adrian. It was deemed by the Spaniards as great an offence to the nation that a foreigner and a Fleming should be regent of Castile as that the rapacious Guillaume de Chièvres should be nominated to so important a see as that of the archbishopric of Toledo. The death of Chièvres at Worms, while the emperor was holding the Diet, and the nomination of a Castilian to succeed him, went far towards quelling the Castilian insurrection.

Adrian received the news of his elevation to the papacy with much surprise, and many misgivings of his fitness for so high an office; and some months elapsed before he left Spain to take possession of it. Meanwhile the war went on; until, after many defeats, partial successes, troubles with the soldiery, and errors in the conduct of the hostilities on the part of the brothers De Foix, the French were driven out of Lombardy. Genoa, too, became lost to France; and on the 30th of May, 1522, was given up to pillage and all the horrors of war.

Lautrec returned to France; but the king refused to see him, and was even unmoved by the entreaties of the countess. Yet, strangely enough, the constable prevailed on Francis to allow Lautrec to offer explanations of his conduct. Bourbon and Lautrec were supposed to be acting in concert to deprive Louise of her great influence over the king, by exposing her artifices and appropriation of the public moneys. The king received the marshal very frigidly; then, giving way to one of those violent ebullitions of anger he was subject to, accused him of losing his "heritage of Milan."

"It is your majesty who has lost it, not I," answered Lautrec, with difficulty restraining his anger — being as haughty and violent in temper as the king himself. "The troops had served eighteen months," he continued, " without receiving a fraction of their pay; and the Swiss, threatening desertion, compelled me to give battle at a disadvantage."

"What became, then, of the 400,000 crowns which, at your request, I sent you last year?"

"The letters announcing their despatch were received, but the money never arrived."

How was this to be explained? The superintendent of the finances was sent for. Perhaps there had been remissness on his part. But Semblançay, while acknowledging that the king had ordered the 400,000 crowns to be forwarded without delay, and that they had been forthwith prepared for despatch, informed his majesty that Madame d'Angoulême had taken the money, as he would immediately prove to him.

The king, enraged, rushed to his mother's apartment, and demanded an explanation of an act that had caused his losses in Italy. Madame Louise denied M. Semblançay's statement. "The money for which he had produced her receipt was," she said, "the proceeds of her savings, which for some time had been in his keeping; but the king's money she had never touched." Francis did not place much faith in this attempted refutation of his minister's account of the matter, and would not dismiss him. For a while some estrangement occurred between mother and son. Stormy family scenes took place, partly fomented by his mistress to exculpate her brother, the office of peacemaker devolving on Marguerite, the queen's sister. But Madame Louise soon regained her sway.

It seems extraordinary that Semblançay should not have mentioned the circumstance to the king at the time it occurred, as his word was also pledged to Lautrec for the due despatch of the money, and was probably more relied on than either the king's or his mother's. Some unexplained mystery enveloped this affair, and Madame Louise was all-powerful; but whether her implication in it was due to avarice or perfidy, Semblançay, "for speaking the truth," became a victim to her vengeance — slowly but effectually accomplished.

His voluntary retirement, in favour of his son, from the office he had held ever since the accession of the economical and methodical Louis XII., did not satisfy that most corrupt of women, the mother of Francis I. Accusations from time to time were brought against him, either by her or at her instigation; sometimes eagerly pursued, then dropped for awhile, and again resumed, as political affairs, her persecution of Bourbon, and the training of rivals to supplant the countess, occupied more or less of her attention.

Five years after her appropriation of the 400,000 crowns destined for the army of Italy, she and her worthy chancellor, Duprat, succeeded in obtaining the condemnation of the aged minister. He died on the public scaffold (1527) as related in that strange record of the occurrences in Paris during the reign of the libertine "chevalier king" and his worthless mother — the "*Journal d'un Bourgeois de Paris.*"

CHAPTER XIV.

A New Complication. — A Shock for the Cardinals. — Full of Good Intentions. — The Inquisition. — The Imperial Guest. — The Italian Emigrants. — The Rebuilding of Chambord. — The Ambassador's Report. — Duprat at His Wits' End. — Colonel of the Scotch Guards. — The Insignia of Royal Justice. — Such Was His Good Pleasure. — Louise and Her Chancellor. — A Contribution to the Treasury. — Avenging a Private Pique. — A Strange Infatuation. — Madame Renée's Reply. — Advice of Anne de Beaujeu. — Was He Legitimate? — Mother and Son. — Charles and Suzanne de Bourbon. — Too Absurd to Believe.

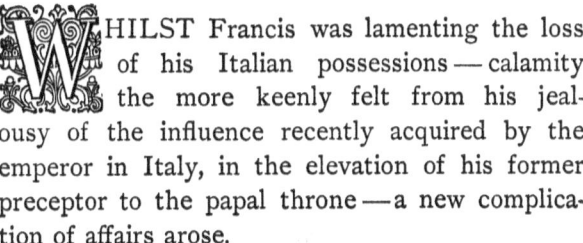WHILST Francis was lamenting the loss of his Italian possessions — calamity the more keenly felt from his jealousy of the influence recently acquired by the emperor in Italy, in the elevation of his former preceptor to the papal throne — a new complication of affairs arose.

On the 29th of May a herald arrived at the Court of France, the bearer of a formal declaration of war from Henry VIII. Charles V. was then at the English Court, visiting his relatives and bride-elect (then nearly six years old), on his way to Spain to relieve Pope Adrian of his duties as regent. The cardinals and the Roman people had become very anxious for the appearance of this pontiff elected under Divine inspiration.

As for the brilliant, the intellectual, the dissipated, and luxury-loving society of the Vatican, Adrian VI.* was a little, wizened, infirm, and humble-looking old man; rigidly pious, severely moral, an enemy to "pagan pomp and show;" knowing nothing of the arts of Italy, caring nothing for the society of painters, sculptors, poets, and learned philologists; keeping no sumptuous table; having in his pay no company of comedians, dancers, musicians, but wholly absorbed by the duties of his office—the most pressing of which he thought was to endeavour to reform both the Church and Court of Rome. An Herculean task indeed, which he had the will to accomplish, but, unhappily, had not the genius to discover the way.

But what a shock for the cardinals and others, ecclesiastics or laymen, who had formed part of the court of Adrian's three predecessors; who had witnessed the magnificence and licentious revelry of the infamous Alexander VI.; the pompous military surroundings of the martial Julian II.; the elegance, the luxury, the courtly refinement and courtesy, masking the libertinism of the munificent patron of art and learning—the profligate Leo X.

Yet Adrian was full of good intentions; desired to be impartial, and to promote peace in Europe. Though naturally devoted to the emperor, and in-

---

*Contrary to papal custom he retained his own name.

clining to his views, he on leaving Spain wrote to Francis, assuring him of his paternal sentiments. His first attempts at reforming the abuses of the Church were received in Italy with astonishment, and general murmurs of disapprobation. For he acknowledged and condemned what, it was contended, he ought to have concealed, the excesses of the Papal Court; admitted that the Roman pontiff was not infallible in matters of faith, and would have been willing to abolish the Indulgences, replacing them by the severe penances of the Primitive Church.

By these concessions made to Germany, he hoped to lure back the stray sheep from the false shepherds of heresy to the fold of the faithful. But, while in some sense a reformer, he was nevertheless a persecutor; being anxious that the decree against Luther—who had left Wartbourg and resumed his professorial chair in the University of Wittemberg—should be fully carried out. The Diet replied to the Pope's pastoral letter by a severe remonstrance, another "Hundred Grievances," and the adoption by the church at Wittemberg, and other now Protestant states, of a new form of religious service organised by Luther.

The first martyrs to Protestantism were burnt in the emperor's dominions during Adrian's short pontificate. They were three Augustine monks of Antwerp, who had adopted Luther's opinions. The Inquisition, further to frighten probable backsliders, ordered their convent to be burnt to the ground.

Adrian was not more fortunate in his efforts to persuade the sovereigns of Europe to desist from making war on their own account, and to unite their arms against the Turks, than in his efforts to reform the abuses of the Church of Rome. He proposed, in default of a treaty of peace, which he would have preferred, that the contending parties should consent to a three years' truce. Forgetting their private disputes, that they should make common cause to expel Solyman II. and his infidel hordes from Belgrade, which they had besieged and taken; also to compel the sultan to evacuate the Island of Rhodes, and reinstate the Knights of Saint John of Jerusalem.

This scheme did not at all meet the views of the parties addressed. Their common and chronic difficulty, want of money, would have made any feasible proposal for a truce welcome; but only in order to gain time to prepare more efficiently for breaking it. The ambassadors of the several powers, assembled to learn the pontiff's view of the matter, at once separated — knowing that the claims and counter-claims and demands for restitution that would be put forward on all sides rendered negotiation impossible.

Skirmishing had been resumed by the French, on the frontiers of Flanders, where the king's eagerness to play the part of commander-in-chief, when the tactics of his generals were on the point of securing some advantages, had again ended in frustrated plans and consequent defeat. Henry VIII., at the same time, was sending vessels to ravage the coasts of Brittany and Normandy. This was a compliment to his imperial guest, that he might witness, on his departure, the beginning of hostilities, the vessels afterwards joining the emperor's fleet, and convoying him into Spanish waters.

The plague, which, in the course of this year had raged in so many of the continental towns, at length appeared with extraordinary virulence in Paris — the chief plague-spot of Europe — the pestiferous open sewer surrounding the royal palace becoming every year more intolerable and more fatal to the inhabitants of the city. The court had fled to Blois; Francis had taken a fancy to the neighbouring Château de Chambord, which was about to undergo alteration and enlargement on a very extensive scale.

The misery following the unceasing wars of the French in Italy, the cruelty and oppression of the brothers De Foix in their government of Milan, and, recently, the death of Leo X., the great patron of art, had caused an influx of emigrants on this side of the Alps, the flower, often, of the Italian populations. Among them were many able artists, sculptors, and architects especially, who were induced to seek patronage and employment in the country of the devastators of their own fair land, if not exactly their conquerors (P. Lacroix). Francis is said to have had at least so much sense of the wrong he and his predecessors had done to Italy, as to seek to palliate it by favours to the Italians — only, however, those who were men of genius or learning — who sought refuge in France from the misfortune and ruin he had brought on their country.

It was then that the rage for building began. Many of the old feudal fortresses changed their military character, and, if not entirely rebuilt, were sufficiently transformed to receive and entertain within their walls, or in their newly laid-out grounds, large parties of pleasure. Constructed originally to keep enemies at bay and to stand a siege, they were now often the scene of royal revels and festivity.

The enlarging or rebuilding of the Château de Chambord had but recently been determined on, and for years after the work went on but slowly. Many interruptions occurred, either war, or want of money to pay the architects and sculptors. The men they employed were like the Swiss soldiers, often rebellious and inclined to desert, unless the arrears of their pay were forthcoming. Sometimes want of material brought the work to a standstill, funds being wanting to supply it, or to bring it from the quarries.

Such was the case at the time in question, when money was wanted, as well for war as building, Francis having determined on not losing "his heritage" without a struggle to recover it, or sparing blood or treasure to achieve its successful issue, though Europe was in arms against him. Even the Pope joined the coalition, persuaded that Francis alone had been the cause of the unfavourable result of his attempted mediation. Venice, the old and faithful and now only ally of France, yet hesitated to sign the pact for the defence of Italy against French invasion. The Senate waited for information from their ambassador respecting the extent of the preparations the king, menaced on all sides, was then making for war.

Shortly after, they were informed that the king was leading the life of a voluptuary, that he was wholly devoted to the pleasures of the chase and the society of courtesans, that the revenues of the state and the products of the heavy taxes levied on the people for the expenses of the war were wasted on his favourites, his mistresses, and in every kind of folly, and that, as to preparation for war, he was himself not occupied with it, and spoke of war only at table. Further, they were told that it was whispered about that a rich and powerful prince of the blood — Duc Charles de Bourbon — was suspected of being in secret correspondence with the emperor.

Venice hesitated no longer, but, on the 5th of

August, joined the league with the Pope, the emperor, the King of England, the Archduke Ferdinand of Austria, and the whole of the Italian states.* Francis had no friends now left but those doubtful ones, the Swiss, and, possibly, the Scotch, to whom he dispatched the Duke of Albany to invite them to invade England on the north, to divert Henry's attention from France. †

The king had at last torn himself from his libertine pleasures, and resolved on immediately assembling an army, of which he proposed to take the command in person, believing that Fortune would be more propitious to his arms than she had latterly been to those of his generals. Great efforts were making to raise funds. Duprat was at his wits' end for new devices. The clergy had been asked for the church-plate and the half of their revenues. They were to be rewarded by the nomination of twelve begging friars to preach in the provinces against the "erroneous doctrines of Luther." The massive silver railing surrounding the tomb of Saint Martin de Tours had already

* Adrian VI. died on the 14th of the following month, as weary of Rome and the cardinals as they were weary of him. The triple crown had oppressed him greatly. His poignant grief that he was unable to accomplish the good he desired, together with the feeling that he inspired only aversion, probably hastened his death. On the morning following it, the door of his physician's house was garlanded with flowers, with the inscription, "THE SENATE AND THE PEOPLE OF ROME TO THE LIBERATOR OF THE COUNTRY."

† Henri Martin, "*Histoire de France.*"

been appropriated. It was the offering of that pious king, Louis XI., as a bribe to the saint in order to secure his good offices for the success of some scheme whose happy issue he must have had greatly at heart, as he was not accustomed to be so liberal. Even for the holy virgin's aid he merely conferred on her the title of Comtesse de Boulogne and the honorary military rank of colonel of the Scotch guards, besides carrying in his hat a miniature statuette of her in lead.

The royal domains, by some new arrangement, were sold a second time, and numberless new offices created to be disposed of to the highest bidder. The magistracy was also increased in number, the provincial tribunals complaining in vain of the inconvenience and encumbrance of so many judges. All sorts of new taxes were invented, the old ones increased, and the national debt (*rentes perpetuelles*) was founded by Duprat; the only device of his that eventually was favourably received by the citizens of Paris (H. Martin).

The country appears to have been in a fearful state of turbulence and anarchy. The soldiery remaining unpaid, notwithstanding the vast sums raised, roamed about in bands, ravaging the country, pillaging the inhabitants, and levying contributions on the towns. The king and his mother, regarded as the cause of the alarm and distress that so generally prevailed, were in the highest degree unpopular. Expressions of hatred and contempt were on every lip. Tumultuous assemblages, violent brawls, and assassinations were of nightly occurrence in Paris.

The plague had abated, and the king was again at the Palais des Tournelles. The agitated state of the capital induced the bailiff or superintendent of the palace to take the precaution, on the king's arrival, of putting up scaffolds or gibbets at the entrances of the royal dwelling — a singular custom, intended, it appears, to intimidate refractory citizens. But the people responded to the menace by an act of bravado, and during the night these "sinister insignia of royal justice" were thrown down by a body of armed men.*

The police and the magistracy were not over-zealous in repressing this disorder in the capital. They, no less than the people, were dissatisfied with the rapacity of the king and his chancellor, who had recently instituted a second judicial chamber for Paris. Not that the requirements of justice called for such a measure. It was simply one of the devices to obtain money for the insatiable needs of the sovereign, the eighteen councillors and two presidents of whom the chamber was composed paying each for his office — which, to render it more attractive, was made hereditary — a sum of not less than 2,000 gold crowns.

Francis was desperately annoyed at the indocility of his subjects under his pillaging and exac-

* "*Journal d'un Bourgeois de Paris*, 1523."

tions. "Never was monarch so detested," wrote the English agent to Wolsey. Francis, however, was as much alarmed as irritated at the spirit of resistance he had provoked in Paris. Some of the most prominent offenders were imprisoned. On others, heavy fines were imposed (welcome additions to the king's treasury). A "bed of justice" was also held, when, after an angry reproof, Francis declared that he would not allow the anarchy of the Paris of Charles VI. and Charles VII. to be reintroduced into the capital during his reign. It must cease at once, or severe measures to compel it would be resorted to. Such was his good pleasure.

To put down the brigand bands who, under various appellations — "*Mille diables,*" "*Mauvais garçons,*" "*Adventuriers,*" etc. — were committing serious depredations in the provinces, an armed force was despatched, under the ferocious De Foix and other pitiless commanders, who soon captured most of the rioters, and slaughtered them, also, as they fell into their hands.

But other troubles were preparing for France. From the time when Marshal Lautrec and Charles de Bourbon had combined to expose the treachery and perfidy of Louise of Savoy, with the view of shaking her credit with the king, and thus diminishing her influence in affairs of state, that unprincipled woman had resolved on a great revenge. The minister Semblançay she slowly but surely pursued to the bitter end. Lautrec she hoped to reach through the downfall of his sister; but to achieve Bourbon's ruin she sought the aid of her worthy chancellor, who cheered her with the prospect of speedily and thoroughly accomplishing it.

The estrangement between Louise and her son had been but of short duration. Habit, and idleness, and the indifference natural to him, together with the belief in her great administrative ability, soon brought him again under the sway of her pernicious influence, and led to his participation in her unworthy schemes for vengeance on the man who had rejected her love and her proffered hand.

While Paris was in the state of tumult and revolt mentioned above, the Parliament had before them a question for decision respecting a gift made by the king to his mother, of the estates he had seized, of Anne de Beaujeu, Dowager Duchesse de Bourbon, daughter of Louis XI. Bourbon opposed the legal confirmation of this gift by the Parliament, and the judges had entertained his opposition. They also continually delayed their decision, and showed no inclination to assist the king in despoiling his cousin in his mother's favour.

The death of the Duchesse Anne occurred in November, 1522, and these estates, with other possessions and much wealth besides, she left by will to her son-in-law, Duc Charles de Bourbon, at the same time confirming her daughter's testament of the preceding year, by which she had made a donation to her husband of her portion of their joint inheritance.

The first affront to the constable — the depriving him of the command of the vanguard — was followed up, after Lautrec's affair, by that of withholding payment of the pensions or salaries attached to the offices he held in the state. His revenues were so large that this deprivation was a matter of no moment to him. He deigned to take no further notice of it than to treat the sum withheld as a contribution to the public treasury.

Finding that Bourbon was not ambitious of wedding the king's mother, Duprat was of opinion that she might lay claim to his estates, her mother having been of the Bourbon family, and either by a never-ending *procès*, that should deprive him of their revenues, or, assisted by himself, and — if possible to find him — some other equally righteous judge, obtain a decree in her favour, and thus bring utter ruin on this haughty prince of the blood, this last of the great vassals of the crown, who within his vast dominions presumptuously lived in royal state surpassing that of his sovereign.

Duprat had for some time been diligently examining the titles and deeds by which the royal lands were held, the fiefs feminine and the fiefs masculine, comprising the estates of Charles de

Bourbon. He believed that an oversight he had discovered, in the contract conveying Suzanne de Beaujeu's portion of the Bourbon domain to her husband, might be made available for giving colour to the claim preferred by the Duchesse d' Angoulême. At the same time he was fully aware that there were circumstances connected with the signing of that marriage contract which rendered the oversight alluded to null.

Duprat, it appears, had a private pique of his own to avenge. Bourbon had declined to cede to him one of his estates in Auvergne, to which he had taken a fancy, and which he probably now hoped to obtain from the king or his mother as a reward for his services when they entered into possession of the Bourbon inheritance. Forthwith he drew up a memorial informing the duke of the informality in his marriage contract, and of the claim of the Duchesse Louise d' Angoulême, the daughter of a sister of Pierre de Beaujeu, Duc de Bourbon, his wife's father, therefore her cousin and her heiress.

It is asserted that Louise of Savoy still clung, with most strange infatuation, to the hope as well as desire of yet bringing the recalcitrant prince to her feet. His disinclination to a marriage with her would be overcome, she flattered herself, by the step she had taken. His love of grandeur and princely surroundings was supposed to be so deeply rooted a passion that, as he had once married for an increase of wealth, he would now marry to retain it.

Friends in the Parliament, through the agency of Duprat, were to be urged to impress on him that his cause was a hopeless one, and that if brought before them might already be considered lost. From the wealthiest he would then become almost the poorest prince in Christendom. There was, however, a way of avoiding this disaster, and of arriving at a happy settlement of all differences and rival claims — a marriage with the Duchesse d'Angoulême, more than once before indirectly suggested. With her sanction the offer of her hand was now formally made to him. He disdainfully rejected it. "He could never consent," he said, "to make an immodest woman his wife." Her pretensions to be his late wife's heiress he treated with ridicule.

Bourbon seems to have been on terms of friendly intimacy with the young queen — a circumstance much in his favour — paying court where more neglect than respect was generally shown. Also with Marguerite, though not her lover, as some pretend; thus condemning her, while endeavouring to prove that she was one of the most virtuous — as probably she was — of those very rare exceptions to the general depravity of the court.

The queen favoured the idea of a marriage with Bourbon for her sister, Madame Renée, who was now thirteen, the marriage to take place two years later. The wishes of Queen Claude in that or any other matter had no influence whatever with Francis. But Bourbon, acting upon it immediately after he had declined the proffered hand of Louise, made a formal demand for Renée. The king refused, though assuring him, very significantly, that the refusal came from the young lady herself, who had said—as of course was suggested to her, if said at all—that she "could not marry a prince who was on the point of losing his domains."

When the claim to his estates was first put forward Anne de Beaujeu still lived, and, during the few months preceding her death, energetically employed such small authority as in the present reign she still retained, in defence of her son-in-law's rights; counselling him on her deathbed to oppose the pretensions of the infamous Louise and her son, and if driven to extremities to ally himself with the emperor.

As soon as her death occurred, her estates were seized in the king's name and transferred to his mother; the validity of that gift, as well as of her claim to other of the Bourbon possessions, being now under consideration by the Parliament. The king, though countenancing his mother's iniquity, affected to make himself no party to these latter proceedings. It was his mother's private *procès;* but Bourbon could of course no longer doubt that both were determined to ruin him. He dissembled his resentment, repaired to his Château of Moulins, and remained there for a few months in great retirement.

During this time the judges deputed to inquire into the proofs making for or against the claim of Louise arrived at Moulins. The cordial and hospitable reception they met with, and the readiness shown to facilitate their object, impressed them so favourably that they were less disposed than before to be urged by their unprincipled president, Duprat, into doing an act of evident injustice. On their return they remonstrated with the chancellor, who, amazed at their presumption, committed them to prison.

Bourbon is said to have been dignified rather than austere. He possessed great power in attaching to him those who came within the sphere of his influence. His dependents were devoted to him, and his troops, when led by him, full of enthusiasm. Yet he maintained strict discipline, having the very rare faculty of making himself beloved and at the same time feared.

Yet Francis, as a further affront—most disastrously, as it proved, for himself—preferred to give the command of the 40,000 men he sent to recover Milan to the favourite companion of his libertine revels, the incompetent Admiral Bonnivet.

M. Michelet in his "History of France," after speaking of Francis I. as a "splendid automaton," "a stage hero," etc., asks, "Was he legitimate?"

and replies to this question, "Who can tell?" But it appears that Charles de Bourbon once hinted that he was not. Exasperated by the persistent pursuit of a woman he held in aversion, he referred to what were generally termed her "gallantries," naming, as a former chief favourite, "the handsome miller of Cognac," of whom Francis I. was the very counterpart. "This remarkable resemblance was pointed out by Bourbon" (Crowe).

So extreme, indeed, was the immorality of the Court of France of that day, of which the king and his mother were such startlingly gross examples, that no acts of profligacy with which they may be charged can be wholly attributed to the tongue of slander, and but seldom even partly so. There, however, seems to be no proof that a *liaison*, as asserted by some French writers, had existed between Charles de Bourbon as a mere youth and the then Comtesse d' Angoulême.

They are even said to have exchanged rings as an eventual promise of marriage. But disparity of age, and the fact of his having been left an orphan in early boyhood, from which time he was brought up — and trained in a manner wholly opposed to that in which Francis d' Angoulême was reared and ruined by his mother — as the future son-in-law of the Duc and Duchesse de Bourbon — whose dislike to the intriguing widow of Cognac equalled that of Anne of Brittany — alike disprove it. When the old duke died, the young Comte de Montpensier inherited his title and part of his estates. The rest had been settled on Suzanne. The acquiescence of the king was necessary for their marriage and the reunion of the estates. Louis XII. highly approved the arrangement. His consent was willingly given, and the marriage solemnised in 1504, Suzanne being in her fourteenth year, while Charles had just entered his fifteenth.

The contract, prepared by the most learned lawyers of the day, was signed by the king, the princes, the officers of the crown, the archbishop, and fifteen bishops. By this union Charles was declared sole heir of the House of Bourbon, the bride and bridegroom being required to make a reciprocal donation of all other possessions or rights of whatsoever nature. All possibility of future dispute, it was thought, was provided against.

What Duprat relied on was that Suzanne de Beaujeu at that time wanted two or three months of being of the legal age of fourteen to be able to sign such a contract for herself. This was not an oversight on the part of the lawyers. They knew, and of course Duprat also knew, that in marriages contracted in France the presence of the king covered any defect in the civil conditions of the contract, as did that of the dignitaries of the Church any omission in ecclesiastical ones.

The Comtesse d'Angoulême, we are told, was "irritated beyond measure. Had she been earlier informed of this marriage, she might have raised obstacles to prevent it. She resolved on revenge, but meanwhile strove to conquer her love." This is too absurd to believe. She may have wished to secure the boy duke for her daughter Marguerite, then twelve years old; one could then understand her vexation at his marriage.

It is far more probable that, as another account states, it was ten years later — when he appeared at court on the occasion of the marriage of Claude de France and Francis d'Angoulême — that Bourbon had the misfortune to inspire that unsought passionate love in the breast of the depraved-minded Louise of Savoy. Bourbon was then in his twenty-fourth year — a handsome man of dignified bearing, carrying off the palm, even from the all-accomplished Francis, for skill and dexterity in the tournaments and other martial games during the prolonged festivities of that singular mourning wedding — since which period he had been an object of jealousy to the son, and was now the victim of the persecuting love of the mother.

CHAPTER XV.

The Great Bourbon *Procès*. — Bourbon and Charles V. — A Wealthy Bride Offered. — Ill-deserved Treatment. — The Lieutenant-General. — Not Such a Simpleton. — Under the Seal of Confession. — An Importunate Spy. — An Insolent Subject. — The Bourbon Plot. — The Capital in Danger. — A Horrifying Announcement. — A Too Lenient Parliament. — A Stratagem of Madame Louise. — Mental Agony. — A Gloomy Procession. — A Message of Mercy. — Letters of Remission.

ALL Europe was awaiting with anxious interest the result of the great Bourbon *procès* — the spoliation by the king and his mother of a powerful and valourous prince of the blood; second by birth but first by merit, and holding the high office of Constable of France. The 1st of August was appointed for the decision of the Parliament in this matter; when, to the angry amazement of the chancellor, the judges declared themselves, after a short conference, *sans compétence*, and referred the whole question to the consideration of the Council of State.

Indignant at the affront put upon them as a judicial body by the committal to prison of two of their members for representations respecting this *procès* displeasing to the chancellor Duprat, they adopted this method of rejecting the grave responsibility thrown on them of pronouncing judgment in an affair of so much importance, on the merits of which they were not free to express an unbiassed opinion.

Those historians who speak most disparagingly of Bourbon — disregarding the extreme provocation he received — assert that "frenetic pride," a haughty disposition, and some ulterior ambitious views on the crown itself, alone suggested his traitorous projects. While in retirement, they tell us, he deliberately offered his sword to Charles V., and swore to serve him against all opponents; leaving to him the stipulations for a similar alliance with the English king. His conditions, they say, were that the emperor should give him one of his sisters, Eleanor or Catherine, in marriage, with a dowry of 100,000 crowns, and enter into other arrangements of a military character for the capture of the king and dismemberment of France.

On the other hand, it is stated that the emperor narrowly watched the proceedings of Francis I. and Madame Louise, and saw with pleasure Bourbon's imprudent enemies driving him to despair. Through his Flemish emissaries he expressed much sympathy with him, and, while thus increasing the natural irritability of wounded pride, vaguely insinuated, that his ancestral domains being taken from him, he should seek others elsewhere; that for a fortune lost a fortune might be gained, and opportunity occur for vengeance.

The emperor then offered him the Princess Eleanor in marriage, the young widow of Portugal's great king, Dom Manuel, with a fortune of upwards of a million crowns, and much wealth besides. Bourbon, on his part, by his influence within his own domains, was to facilitate the emperor's recovery of Burgundy; to introduce an army of lansquenets into Languedoc, and also aid Henry VIII. in recovering his lost possessions in France.

To expect justice from the Council of State were vain indeed, as Bourbon well knew. Yet, to hasten on the *procès*, he repaired once more to Paris. His projects, or the projects proposed to him, had by some means partly transpired, and when Bourbon was paying his respects one day to the queen, the king unexpectedly entered.

" Ah!" said Francis, abruptly; " so you are going to marry."

" No, sire."

" But I know it. I am sure of it. I know of your communications with the emperor!" he exclaimed, his temper rising. " Bear well in mind what I tell you, and beware!"

" Your majesty menaces me!" replied Bourbon, calmly. " I have not deserved this treatment."

He then left the queen's apartment, and was followed by several of the nobility, who had witnessed with displeasure this display of the king's ill-humour.* Francis was disposed, it appears, to prevent Bourbon's departure; but his own great unpopularity, and the agitation then prevailing in Paris, restrained him, lest consequences other than he desired should flow from it. No command had been given to the constable in the army about to march on Lombardy. But Francis, persuaded by one of Bourbon's friends that he had really treated him too harshly, considering that he was standing on the brink of ruin by the threatened confiscation of his estates, named him lieutenant-general of the kingdom conjointly with Madame Louise, who again was appointed regent during his absence.

The relations existing between Bourbon and Louise made such a nomination an insult, rather than a mark of still existing respect for and confidence in him. Could the king dream that a marriage between them was still possible! It is supposed that he did, and would have been glad that thus the Bourbon *procès* should have ended. Francis, notwithstanding, thought it more prudent that the lieutenant-general — who does not appear to have accepted the appointment — should accompany him to Italy than remain in France.

He was then at Moulins, ill, or, as some writers say, feigning illness. He had partly yielded to the emperor's overtures, with the view, apparently,

---

* "Correspondence of Sir Thomas Boleyn," quoted by Michelet and H. Martin.

of bringing the king to make terms with him from dread of an invasion of Burgundy, and thus obtaining the restitution of his estates, which as an act of justice he could hardly look for. Otherwise he would scarcely have declined to accept the Order of the Golden Fleece, the insignia of which were immediately forwarded to him, and thus have evaded swearing allegiance to Charles V. He failed, also, to comply with the vain request of Henry VIII., who, before forwarding a certain sum agreed on between him and the emperor for the equipment of troops, would have exacted from Bourbon a solemn acknowledgment of him as king of France and England, and his rightful sovereign.*

English troops had landed at Calais to march on Picardy, and a Spanish army was entering France by the Pyrenees — as arranged by Henry and Charles — when Francis, not heeding the attacks on his frontiers, in his eagerness again to invade Italy, set out to take the command of the army at Lyons, stopping at Fontainebleau for a few days' diversion, while the troops marched in from the provinces. On his way he visited Moulins with the intention of making sure of Bourbon by taking him with him to Italy.

---

* Henry had greatly noticed Bourbon at the tournaments of the Field of the Cloth of Gold, and is reported to have said that "if he were *his* subject he should not long keep his head on his shoulders " — " so haughty was his mien."

He found him ill and keeping his bed. To console him, he assured him that he need be under no apprehension of losing his office of constable, and also promised that whatever the decision might be respecting his estates — whether adjudged to the crown as royal fiefs, or to his mother as her inheritance — they should all be restored to him. Bourbon knew too well what the king's promises were worth, and by what influences he was guided, to be such a simpleton — Brantôme says — as to put any faith in his word.

The king had been overtaken *en route* by a messenger from the regent, with the information that the grand seneschal of Normandy, the Sire de Brézé, had reported that two gentlemen of that province had "made known to a priest, under the seal of confession," that a great personage of royal blood, whose name was not mentioned, had conspired against the state with the emperor and the King of England; and that these gentlemen had been urged to join the conspiracy, and facilitate the entry of English troops into Normandy. The regent was at Blois. The priest was to be compelled to name these two gentlemen. The Sires de Matignon and d'Arzonges at once surrendered. The chancellor received their depositions, in which they denounced the constable Charles de Bourbon. Madame la Régente forwarded the news in all haste to her son.

Without referring to this particular communication—well aware, probably, of its worthlessness—the king, with an affectation of frankness and trust, said that "he had been warned of the emperor's schemes to induce him to enter his service." Bourbon acknowledged that overtures had been made to him which he had not encouraged, and had reserved mentioning them for an opportunity of personal communication with the king. But when rather urgently pressed by Francis to accompany him to Lyons, he pleaded his illness as an excuse, suspecting some snare. His physician, however, gave an assurance of his patient being able to make the journey in a litter in the course of a few days. Francis, apparently satisfied, took his departure, leaving at Moulins one of the gentlemen of his suite, Perrot de Wartz, ostensibly that he might inform him of Bourbon's progress towards recovery, but really to keep a strict watch on his movements.

To free himself from this importunate spy, Bourbon, whose illness may have been partly feigned, set out a few days after for Lyons, travelling slowly as far as La Palisse. On arriving there, he declared that he was unable to proceed any further, and desired De Wartz at once to hasten to Lyons to inform the king of his relapse. Profiting by his absence, he immediately turned back, recrossed the Allier, and reached his fortress of Chantelle on the borders of Bourbonnais and Auvergne.

Thence he despatched his confidential agent, the Bishop of Autun, with a letter to the king, proffering him loyal service and fidelity to the end of his life, provided he were pleased at once to restore the possessions he had inherited on the decease of the late Duc Pierre de Bourbon, and immediately to put an end to the *procès*. The bishop was taken prisoner on his journey by the king's uncle, the "Bastard of Savoy," commanding a detachment of troops sent to besiege Bourbon in Chantelle on hearing of his flight from Moulins. His papers were seized and sent to the king, the bishop being detained as a suspected agent in the negotiation with Charles V.

When Francis read Bourbon's letter, he gave way to one of his paroxysms of wrath. That this insolent subject should dare to speak of reserves and conditions, and to make terms as the price of his fidelity; that he should presume to treat with him as an equal! — the enormity of such a crime exceeded that of rebellion.

As soon as the king's angry effervescence had in some degree expended itself, the order for Bourbon's arrest was repeated; a price set on his head; and several companies of soldiers marched on Bourbonnais, hoping to surround him. However, the constable, probably well informed of what was passing at Lyons, where Jean de Poitiers and other of his confidants were arrested, had left Chantelle during the night with the whole of the gentlemen of his household some hours before the arrival of the " Bastard," and reached Herment, a small town of Auvergne, in safety. There he took leave of his companions, naming Franche-Comté as their place of meeting. Accompanied only by the Seigneur de Pompérant, in the disguise of an archer, Bourbon adopting that of his servant, he traversed Dauphiny and Savoy, eluding with but little difficulty the not over-zealous pursuit of the troops that were scouring the country in quest of him. On the ninth day after leaving Chantelle, he arrived at Sainte Claude, in the emperor's dominions of Franche-Comté.

Sixty of his friends, who had also contrived to escape the vigilance of pursuers, were there assembled; but many others, less fortunate or less favoured, had been detected and arrested, while nineteen of the number actually made prisoners had *en route* successfully taken flight.

Arrests at Lyons, on suspicion of complicity in what was called the "Bourbon Plot," were very numerous — persons of all conditions being included in it, on the vaguest grounds, or on none at all. The most deeply compromised, or supposed to be, was Saint Vallier, captain of the two hundred gentlemen of the king's household, who admitted that he knew of Bourbon being in communication with the emperor, but also declared that he had endeavoured to dissuade him from being led into any rash enterprise. The Duc de

Vendôme and other Bourbon princes declared themselves strangers to any plot in which the head of their family was concerned.

The trial of the conspirators was assigned to the Parliament of Paris. The Parisians were then in some alarm for the safety of the capital, the English army, under the command of the Duke of Suffolk, having advanced within twelve or thirteen leagues of Paris. They, however, advanced no further, news of the emperor's troops having been unsuccessful in Champagne inducing them to withdraw and return to Artois. But slight damage was done, and no advantage was gained by them.

The king remained at Lyons, occupied in arresting plotters and conspirators, and sending them to Paris for trial and judgment. But in order to reassure the Parisians and bid them be of good courage, also to kindle the anger of the judges and induce severity in their sentences on the criminals then anxiously awaiting their doom, Francis despatched to Paris a favourite courtier, the Chevalier Chabot de Brion, a rather boastful, swaggering young gentleman, with a stirring message to the Parliament and a soothing one to the burghers. The chevalier informed the Parliament that "the rebel prince had intended to seize the sacred person of their king and to deliver him into the hands of the King of England, and "—further iniquity—"proposed to make mince-meat of the royal children." This horrifying announcement appears to have excited more mirth than indignation.

With reference to the possible invasion of the capital, he begged that the citizens would dismiss from their minds all uneasiness. He assured them of the king's love and thoughtfulness for them. "He has sent me here," he said, "to defend you." The spokesman of the assembled burghers replied to this presumptuous youth with the polite rebuff that, although the Seigneur de Brion was doubtless a worthy gentleman and high in the favour of his sovereign, yet his presence in the capital was not of itself sufficient to give confidence to the citizens and allay the fears of so populous and important a city as Paris.

While the armies of the confederates were invading France, Bourbon remained inactive in Franche-Comté. Still unwilling to take the irrevocable step, he deputed his sister, the Duchesse de Lorraine, to endeavour once more to come to an arrangement with Francis; and some sort of vague promise was given to hear what Bourbon could say in his defence if he would come to him. But this was too evasive to be at all satisfactory. Bourbon could not trust him.

Meanwhile the Parliament was dealing with the conspirators far too leniently to please the king and his mother. Against ten only of the large number of persons accused could they find that any complicity was proved, and that on grounds so slight that a fine or short term of imprisonment was the severest sentence the judges could be induced to inflict.

Francis, in his irritation at the obstinacy of the Parliament in thus refusing to make justice subservient to his desire for vengeance, ordered a certain number of the magistrates of Dijon, Rouen, Toulouse, and Bordeaux to repair to Paris for the fuller investigation of the proceedings. They, however, merely confirmed the sentences of the Parliament of Paris, "finding no cause for their revision."

Yet, besides the formal sentence of death passed in default of appearance (*par contumace*) on those who had escaped, there was one solitary unfortunate convicted of *lèse majesté*, and condemned to lose his head. This was Jean de Poitiers, Seigneur de Saint Vallier, of the younger branch of the ducal House of Aquitaine. Francis professed to be exceedingly inveterate towards him, declaring that he had with difficulty refrained from killing him with his own hand, with so much horror did he regard the crime of an officer of his household conspiring against his crown.

Nevertheless, the judges, it appears, disbelieved the story of this futile conspiracy attributed to Bourbon, and so strangely made known by a priest, to whom it was said to be revealed under the seal of confession. They regarded it as a stratagem of Madame Louise and her chancellor further to incite the king against Bourbon and prevent any possibility of negotiation between them. The king therefore obtained Saint Vallier's condemnation by the Parliament only on condition that the sentence of death should be commuted, or a pardon granted on the scaffold; so that Francis conceded, at the entreaty of Saint Vallier's daughter, the celebrated Diane de Poitiers, nothing but what had already been promised, "of which she was probably then aware" (Michelet).

But Saint Vallier himself was not aware of the arrangement. His punishment certainly far exceeded what was due to his offence — that of having counselled Bourbon to refrain from connecting himself with the emperor, instead of denouncing his friend as a traitor. He knew that he was condemned to die — to lose his head on the scaffold. But such a death in those days of revolting cruelty, of disgusting barbarity — more especially if the offence in any way concerned his sacred majesty — was generally preceded by quartering or tearing to pieces by four horses, and other horrors that sicken humanity to mention.

Saint Vallier's terror of the death that awaited him was so intense that, during the night preceding his intended execution, his hair became perfectly white. Anxiety and grief had also so changed his countenance, given him so aged an appearance, that his guards were startled and terrified when, on daylight appearing, they saw a man whom they did not recognize; their first impression being that the prisoner had escaped, and that another person had taken his place.

Mere personal fear, in all probability, had not induced this mental agony. Saint Vallier bore a noble name, on which dishonour was brought by his death on the scaffold as a traitor to his country and king. He had a young daughter, the wife of the man to whom the strange priest had revealed the secrets of the confessional, who was one of the most beautiful women of her day. What sorrow, what disgrace, what lifelong unhappiness he has brought on her!

The winter of 1523-1524 was one of exceptional severity, and misery, poverty, and disease prevailed in that wretched old Paris. Snow trampled into black mud filled the turnings and windings of its network of narrow streets, and lodged a foot deep in the fore-courts of the walled-in hôtels of the nobility. The regent and her court were at Blois; the queen, then suffering in her health, was at Amboise with Madame Renée and her ladies; while the king, attended by several of his courtiers and favourites, and accompanied by Madame la Comtesse and her suite, was at Lyons.

All is movement, gaiety, and animation there. In Paris a different scene presents itself. It is the 17th of February — a murky morning, with cold, drizzling rain, a leaden sky, and semi-darkness. A gloomy procession enters the Place de Grève — a man bowed down apparently by age or illness, surrounded by guards, and supported by two priests. He ascends the scaffold, and, at the moment that he meekly bows his head to receive the fatal blow, the priest, who knows who is approaching, seizes the uplifted arm of the executioner, as though already he heard the sound of horses' hoofs, and arrests the fall of the hatchet. For the rider is a few seconds behind his time; and but for the prompt action of the priest, "the message of mercy" would have arrived a few seconds too late.

But he comes — he comes! A herald from the king. He seems to have been riding for his very life.

"*Grâce! grâce!*" he exclaims, as he holds up a letter, which is delivered to the priest, while the few spectators of the dreary scene applaud their gracious monarch's clemency.

"Life is spared! — granted by the king," Saint Vallier is told, "at the entreaty of the beautiful Diane." But Saint Vallier does not share the exultation with which those around him welcome the joyful news. He seems scarcely to comprehend it, and bends his head as though he would invite the executioner to delay no longer the fatal stroke. Then suddenly raising himself, he utters an imprecation on the libertine king, and vows that he will slay him! But the king's "message of mercy" does not set him free. Francis has not had the magnanimity to pardon. He has spared Saint Vallier's life; but only to transfer him from the scaffold to a living tomb.

Happily, however, the father's fears are unfounded. The small concession ostensibly made to Diane's urgent prayer has not been purchased at a price that would make life, even with restoration to freedom and honour, hateful to him. Thus reassured, his mind relieved of a bitter pang, he can resign himself to the doom his sovereign has awarded him.*

The "letters of remission" run thus: "That the Seigneur de Saint Vallier be imprisoned for the rest of his life within four walls, where daylight shall be admitted and food supplied to him only through a small grated window." It appears that he either escaped or was liberated some two or three years later, and some writers assert that he was living at his Château of Pisançon in 1539, where he made a will, though they do not give the date of his death (Servan, notes to "*Guerres des Français*").

*The evil repute in which Francis I. was generally held is attested by the "*Journal d'un Bourgeois de Paris*," 1524. Many aspersions, probably wholly unfounded, have been cast on the character of the celebrated Diane de Poitiers, on the faith of a doubtful correspondence attributed to her and Francis.

CHAPTER XVI.

Sufferings of the Troops.— Bonnivet Wounded.— The Chevalier Bayard.— Death of the Chevalier.— A True Knight — Great and Good.— Driven Out of Italy.— Marseilles Besieged.— Three Needy Monarchs.— A March into Picardy and Back. — The Spoils of Mexico and Peru.— War Resumed in Italy. — Death of Queen Claude.—A Compliment to the Queen. — Funeral of Queen Claude.— "Plague-stricken Milan!"— Antonio da Leyva.— The Sentiment of Honour.— Georges Freundsburg.— Honour to Whom Honour is Due.— The Battle of Pavia.— A Delicate Sense of Honour. — Francis a Prisoner.

WING to delays occasioned by the flight of Bourbon, the arrest of his partisans and their prosecution, a change became necessary in the plan of the proposed Italian campaign. The king, in fact, was obliged to resign himself to remaining in France, and giving up the command-in-chief for this year to his *alter ego* Bonnivet, charged to reconquer Italy. The winter set in very early and with extreme rigour. The sufferings of the famished troops, shoeless and half-naked, were terrible — their ranks being daily thinned by want and disease, and the harassing system of warfare with which the old general Prospero Colonna exhausted and disheartened them.

The Swiss still continued to aid in fighting the battles of Europe, in spite of the difficulty of obtaining their pay from the sovereigns they served — but revenging themselves by pillage, or by desertion when their services were most needed. On this occasion, they forsook both armies and marched back to their mountains, in defiance of all efforts to retain them.

After a series of misfortunes and many mistakes — Bonnivet leading his troops into perilous positions, but wanting military talent to extricate them — a musket shot in the shoulder, fortunately for the remnant of his army, disabled their incompetent commander. The Chevalier Bayard, destined to lead forlorn hopes, and to be called to posts of danger, was implored at this critical moment to save what remained of the miserable and menaced French army.

"Save it, if possible, Messire de Bayard!" exclaimed Bonnivet, as he was borne beyond the range of the enemy's guns, for the dressing of his wound.

"Late though it be," replied Bayard, "I will save it, if it costs me my life." Vandenesse, Bayard's companion-in-arms, made the same vow, and, placing themselves at the head of their men, sustained, with desperate courage, the shock of the enemy's troops, thus gaining time for their countrymen to make good their retreat, covered by a small detachment under the Comte de Saint Pol.

But the Chevalier Bayard, the chevalier *par excellence*, the knight "without fear and without reproach," was mortally wounded (30th of April, 1524). Feeling that he had received his death-blow, he requested to be assisted to dismount and placed under a tree, with "his face towards the enemy, never," as he said, "having turned his back to them." Fixing his eyes on the guard of his sword, held upwards to serve as a cross, he made his confession — no priest being at hand — to one of his attendants. Then, desiring that they would leave him and look to their own safety, he addressed his prayer to God, and with calmness and serenity awaited the approach of death.

Bourbon — in pursuit of Bonnivet, a man he detested and who was the cause of much of the ill-will the king had displayed towards him — was passing the spot where the dying chevalier lay. Reining up his horse, he expressed much concern and sympathy at finding the noble-minded, gallant Bayard in so sad a condition. But, with failing breath, he answered: "Pity me not; I die as a man of honour. It is I who should pity you, to find you serving against your prince, your country, and your oath." Bourbon is said to have passed on without reply.* Bayard's friend, the brave Vandenesse, was also killed by a shot from an arquebuse.

---

* Martin du Bellay.

The Marquis da Pescara, who, with Bourbon, commanded the imperial army, on hearing that Bayard was dangerously wounded, and could not be moved from the spot he had been placed in, ordered a tent to be pitched there, and sent his surgeon to attend him. But the chevalier's hours were numbered. He died in the course of the day, wept and regretted by those who had caused his death, "his last acts being characterised by the same heroic and Christian simplicity as had distinguished him through life."

His body, by Pescara's direction, was embalmed and sent to his family in Dauphiny. As the *cortége* traversed the dominions of the Duke of Savoy, by his orders royal honours were paid to Bayard in every town. On arriving at Dauphiny, the whole population, from the Alps to Grenoble, accompanied the body to its resting-place. A month of strict mourning was observed throughout the province — all *fêtes* and amusements by general consent being abstained from.

Bayard's noble and generous treatment — rare in those days — of the prisoners whom the chances of war had thrown into his hands, had gained him admirers and friends among rival and opposing nations as well as in France. "His life was but a series of brilliant achievements and virtuous actions. Always victorious in the tournaments and single combats, daring in surprises, ably conducting expeditions more important, he was the most distinguished of warriors. Gentle, unaffected, unassuming in society, tender and respectful lover, sincere friend, and true chevalier, humane and liberal, he was the best of men. One cannot read without emotion, admiration, and pleasure, of all he did for humanity, for glory, and for gallantry,— his beneficence, while heightening his other virtues, adding a touching interest to the greatness of his military reputation." (Servan.)

The ideal hero of the old chivalric romances seems to have never in reality been more nearly approached than in the person of the noble Chevalier Bayard, with whom chivalry may be said to have ended.*

The complete evacuation of Italy followed the death of Bayard,— Admiral Bonnivet, whose wounds do not appear to have been very serious, leading back the shattered remains of his army into France. In the rear of that miserable army — whose ranks grew thinner and thinner as, worn out by fatigue and disease, the unfortunate soldiers dropped down on their homeward march, strewing the roads with the dying and the dead —

---

* The narrative of his heroic deeds (" *Gestes du bon Chevalier* "), an anonymous work dedicated to the three estates of the realm by a contemporary writer — attached friend or dependent — who adopts the pseudonym of " *Loyal Serviteur*," is perhaps the most interesting and trustworthy of the many works that have been written in praise of " the noblest man in France," whom both contemporaries and posterity have agreed to name "*Le chevalier sans peur et sans réproche.*"

was a weary-footed multitude of the wretched inhabitants of the towns of Lombardy, who had either been driven out with the French, or, being utterly ruined, in their desperation had followed the devastators of their homes to seek a refuge in their country, and possibly a means of livelihood.

Bonnivet was a favourite of Madame Louise as well as of her son. A gracious reception therefore awaited him, notwithstanding the errors he had committed, the loss of three-fourths of his army, and his ignominious flight from Milan. But another favourite, Chabot de Brion, had been more successful in aiding the Marseillais to defend their city, which had been attacked by the imperialist troops on the land side. They were speedily compelled to raise the siege and decamp, while the French fleet had beaten off the Spanish admiral's ships destined to aid the besieging army by a blockade of the port.

The emperor had named Bourbon lieutenant-general of the imperial armies. The command was, however, shared with the Spanish general Pescara, an arrangement which led to jealousy and disagreement. Bourbon, on heading his division of the forces, had intended to march on Lyons and his own domains in Bourbonnais, etc., where he expected to be received with open arms. But the emperor, believing that Bourbon would then avail himself of the opportunity of making terms with Francis and sacrifice imperial interests to his own, ordered an attack to be first made on Marseilles.

Charles was very anxious to obtain possession of that port. It would have been as convenient to him to have his Calais by which to enter France on the south, as it was to Henry VIII. to possess that facility in the north. Bourbon, though not pleased with the order that frustrated his own plans, was yet little disposed, when once the attack was made, to raise the siege and evacuate Provence. The idea of retreating before Francis enraged him. He therefore proposed a renewal of the attack on the following day, which was overruled by Pescara.

The military authorities state that Francis should then have made peace. The army of Marseilles had been raised by means of the most onerous taxes, the most shameful exactions, and cessation from war was necessary for the prosperity of the country. Commerce was almost at a standstill. Men were taken from their occupations, their families left unprovided for, and famine and disease were general. Henry and Charles were as much in want of money for the support of their armies and the carrying out of their schemes of conquest as Francis himself.

But, elated by his success at Marseilles, the king determined to carry his conquering arms once more into Italy, and in person to avenge the reverses of Lautrec and Bonnivet, and the death of the brave Chevalier Bayard.

Clement VII. (Giulio de' Medici), who, to the disgust of Wolsey, had succeeded Adrian VI., proposed his mediation, with a view to a general peace. Like his predecessors, he would have preferred to keep the French out of Italy. But Wolsey, whose hopes of reigning in Rome had been rudely cast down by the election of Clement, a man in the prime of life, evinced much lukewarmness when peace was proposed; being unwilling to facilitate a project emanating from his successful competitor. He resented the little zeal the emperor had displayed on his behalf, after the many assurances he had given him of his firm support in the conclave.

Again, then, he inclined towards the French alliance, and, though not venturing immediately to recur to it, yet meditated gradually bringing over his royal master to his views. Henry VIII. may be said to have virtually withdrawn from the coalition against France after Suffolk's fruitless march into Picardy and back again. His attention was now more particularly occupied with the movements of the Scotch, and in taking measures to repel their invasions.

The emperor, on his part, was too eagerly intent on conquest to give any serious heed to Clement's peaceful views, though scarcely knowing whither to turn for the funds needed for that object. Yet Mexico was then pouring her riches into Spain; not, however, into the Spanish king's treasury. That remained empty, while many a noble Hidalgo, who with a very great name — or, one should rather say, many very great names, and nothing but his sword for the upholding of their dignity — two or three years later, having joined the conquering expeditions of Pizarro, suddenly became the possessor of millions many times told — "rich beyond the dreams of avarice."

Men of the humblest condition who had had any part in those adventures were able to make ease and idleness their sole occupation for the rest of their lives. Ill-gotten wealth, indeed, obtained by crimes and atrocities at the very mention of which the blood curdles. The emperor king's share of the booty was the smallest. The first fruits of the spoils of Mexico, sent to him by Cortés, fell into the hands of a French corsair, and it was not until the reign of Charles's successor, Philip II., when the conquest of Peru was more complete, that the monarchs of Spain greatly profited by the enormous influx of the precious metals — the proceeds of rapine, cruelty, and bloodshed.

The consequences of this sudden and immoderate increase of wealth were very disastrous for Spain. Her commercial prosperity declined. Contempt for labour became a national vice, and Spain, who had looked to conquer the sceptre of the world with her gold as well as her arms, was destined to see that fatal and criminal gold pass by degrees out of her superbly idle hands into the laborious ones of other nations. "After having depopulated America, Spain, before the end of the sixteenth century, began to be dispeopled and ruined herself" (H. Martin).

It was towards the middle of October when Francis I., contrary to the advice of his most experienced officers, La Trémouille, La Palice, and others, resolved on resuming the war in Italy. They were rather weary of this everlasting ultramontane warring; but to take the field so late in the year they regarded as little better than madness. Vainly, however, did they remind the king of the great suffering in the late campaign, which must necessarily be again endured by the troops, with the probable loss of life that would ensue from exposure to the rigours of a winter passed under tents. But Francis preferred the advice of the young generals who had been engaged at Marseilles. Especially he relied on the counsels of the able commander who had just lost him an army and "his heritage."

Bonnivet's voice was decidedly for war. But so unpopular was he with the troops that the detachment he was to lead in this new expedition, by threats of punishment could alone be induced to serve under him. His favour with Francis, however, had rather increased than abated; for Bonnivet, knowing his sovereign's admiration of beauty, had described to him in such glowing terms the marvellous loveliness of a young Milanese lady, the Signora Clarissa, that his ardent desire to see her was the real motive of the hasty resolve of a winter campaign in Italy. The resolve was worthy of a "chevalier king." To rescue lovely damsels from real or fancied dangers was one of the imperative duties of chivalry.

But although this royal libertine could cross the Alps in pursuit of his pleasures, he was unable or unwilling to tear himself from the fascinations and depravity of the life he led at Lyons to visit his dying young wife. The amiable and gentle Queen Claude, after several months of suffering, had recently died at the Château de Blois, in her twenty-fifth year. She had habitually lived in great retirement, much occupied with the education of her young sister Renée, and with her children — three sons and two daughters, the eldest then seven years of age. The king's mother had usurped her place as queen, as by her overbearing will and restless ambition she had also usurped the government of the country, whether formally invested with authority as regent or not.

The king's affections were chiefly bestowed, such as they were, on his mother and sister. Claude had no part in them, and exercised no wifely influence over him. What tenderness or affection he had in reserve then belonged more or

less to the Comtesse de Châteaubriand, his chief
mistress, whose wiles and graces made her a formidable rival to Madame Louise, who, for a long
time, vainly strove to detach the king from her.

The court tacitly accepted the countess as
maîtresse-en-titre, though not openly avowed by
the king. She too, it appears, was not desirous
of bearing that honourable title. The fears of her
husband on her first appearance at court were, it
may be probably inferred from their subsequent
reunion, set at rest by that omission; while her
brutal brothers, whatever advancement they may
have owed to her influence, certainly preferred to
believe it due to their own superlative merits.
That there was no declared *maîtresse-en-titre* in
the lifetime of the queen was, however, said to be
a compliment that Francis felt compelled to pay
to the virtue of his wife, and to the sentiment of
veneration in which she was held by the public.

But very different was the feeling of the public
towards their profligate king. Never at any time
approaching the enthusiasm and affection which
M. Ranke is almost alone in asserting that Francis
inspired, it became more bitterly antagonistic than
before when his heartlessness and utter want of
respect to the memory of the pious daughter of
the much-revered Louis XII. was generally known.

Queen Claude was temporarily entombed at
Blois. Her funeral at St. Denis, together with
that of the infant daughter who died in 1517, did

Castle of Blois.
Photo-etching from a photograph.

not take place until two years after, when the ceremony was performed with great pomp and state, the carriers of salt attending in full force.* The superstition of the time sent many afflicted pilgrims to the tomb of "the good Queen Claude," and frequent miraculous cures were attributed to her.

As nothing could shake the king's resolution to march at once on Milan, opposition gave way before his persistency, lest prudent counsels should be stigmatised as cowardly unwillingness to face danger with him. The French army was now 45,000 strong, having been augmented by 15,000 Swiss, of whose proneness to desert in a body at any moment the humour seized them Francis had been vainly reminded. With the king at their head, they passed the Alps at Mont Cenis, and marched direct on Milan.

But with all their diligence to anticipate the imperialists, — who, being obliged to take the longer route by Monaco and Fiscol, were with the same object making forced marches, — as a detachment of the French, under the Marquis de Saluzzo, entered the city by one gate, the imperialists, commanded by the Viceroy of Naples, Lannoy, appeared at the other. The latter would have had the inhabitants oppose an armed resistance to the

---

* This was in virtue of their singular privilege, of ancient date, of carrying the bodies of deceased royalty as far as the first cross of St. Denis, when they gave up their burden to the monks of the abbey.

entry of the French. But so terrible had been the ravages of the plague that the once populous capital had become one vast desert. Exhausted, ruined, overwhelmed by the miseries of war, of which their country was unceasingly the battle-ground, deep dejection had settled on the languid survivors of the sad catastrophe, and rendered them incapable of a courageous resolution (Servan). Whether the lovely Miss Clarissa had fallen a victim to the terrible epidemic with which Milan had been visited we are not informed. It is to be hoped that she escaped both the plague and the "chevalier king's" attentions.

Possession of the plague-stricken capital, of which the French were left the undisturbed masters, did not imply possession of the duchy; to accomplish which many more important conquests were yet to be made than that of a depopulated city whose feeble surviving inhabitants had neither energy nor desire to defend themselves. Lannoy had retired to Lodi to await expected reinforcements. The strongly fortified city of Pavia, with a garrison of 6,000 men, was occupied by the famous Spanish general, Antonio da Leyva — so skilful a leader, so pitilessly cruel a conqueror.

The French had encamped themselves very advantageously in and near the château and park of Mirabella, where Francis assembled a military council, composed of officers experienced and prudent, with others as brave, undoubtedly, but young, rash, and without judgment, to decide whether Lodi or Pavia should first be attacked.

Charles V. rarely, if ever, it appears, commanded in person. At the period in question, he was in Spain ill of a quartan ague, and so utterly destitute of funds that the pay of his army (which, wide as his dominion was, and wider still his vast ambition to make it, did not amount to more than 16,000 men) was many months in arrear, destitute also of ammunition, provisions, clothing, and every necessary for its efficient equipment. When Henry VIII. was applied to for the contribution which he had promised to pay monthly towards carrying on the war against France, he not only refused it, but demanded repayment of the sum already advanced.

The various peoples Charles ruled over were alike unwilling to burden themselves with the expense of his wars, and his authority was so restricted that he was unable to follow the example of Francis I. and invent and levy taxes at his own good pleasure. With difficulty, then, were the miserable troops shut up in Lodi and Pavia restrained by their officers from open mutiny. Of little effect were the splendid hopes held out of much booty, if no pay, in store for them, and slight the impression made by harangues to inspire them with the sentiment of honour and with endurance for honour's sake. To afford them some slight relief, Lannoy mortgaged the revenues of Naples, and

Leyva determined on taking the sacred vessels of the Church, and the shrines of the saints, which were melted down and converted into a sort of money, to satisfy the urgent needs of the moment.

The siege of Pavia began on the 20th of October. Francis, who is said to have known nothing of the science of war as conducted by the experienced captains of those days, rejected the counsels of those who recommended Lodi as the point of attack, while explaining to him the probable advantages and almost certain victory he might thus secure. Bonnivet's advice and opinion were opposed to theirs, and, being seconded by that of several of the young nobility, of whom the corps of gendarmerie was composed, it prevailed with the king.

Three months elapsed, and, though various plans of assault had been tried, no progress was made; Leyva being determined on the most obstinate resistance, animating his troops by his example, and sharing in all the fatigue and hardships he called on them to endure. Bourbon, meanwhile, disposed of the valuable jewels he still possessed, and, being further assisted with money and valuables by the Duke of Savoy — who had withdrawn from his alliance with France — instead of remaining inactive in Lodi, passed into Austria and raised an army of 12,000 lansquenets and 500 cavalry on his own account, with which he rejoined Pescara, at Lodi.

These lansquenets — German infantry — were headed by the famous Georges Freundsberg, a man of gigantic stature, great strength, and exceeding valour, said to be an excellent citizen, enthusiastic patriot, and most zealous Lutheran. He had embraced with ardour the opportunity of joining the war in Italy, with the hope of it leading in some way to the humiliation of the papacy, of which he was the inveterate enemy. His great ambition was to lay his own sacrilegious hands on his holiness. For the purpose of strangling him, he had a strong chain made of pure gold, because, as he said, "Honour to every one to whom honour is due." But, as Freundsberg had a son shut up in the besieged city of Pavia, and four hundred of his countrymen were there, also, the hope of rescuing them may have induced him to join in this expedition as much or more than the desired honour of strangling the Pope with a gold chain.

The imperial army, now reinforced, marched to the relief of Pavia. Francis had weakened his forces by sending detachments on a fruitless expedition to Naples and elsewhere. The troops he had with him were wearied and jaded by nearly four months of continual alarms, sorties of the enemy, and daily skirmishes, in which the advantage was almost always on the side of the imperialists. To take Pavia, Françis must now fight a battle. A council of war was held. The king was advised to raise the siege, avoid the battle, and retire with his weary troops to Binosco.

But the counsels of prudence, as Servan remarks,* were not always the most agreeable to the royal ears. The young generals were enraged at the humiliating suggestion to retreat, while Bonnivet urged on the king the dishonour cast on the patriotic French army, the shame that must attach to him by retiring before the traitor Bourbon.

Clement VII. had secretly made peace with Francis, and now wrote to him offering the same advice as La Trémouille and the older generals. But the king had had the folly publicly to vaunt and make known far and wide that "he would take Pavia or perish under her walls." "Unfortunately," writes Robertson † (one would almost fancy in irony), "Francis's notions of honour were delicate to an excess that bordered on what was romantic, and, rather than expose himself to the slightest imputations, he chose to forego all the advantages that were the certain consequences of a retreat." He, in fact, accepted battle, and, greater calamity still, Bonnivet was charged with the disposition of the troops and general arrangements of the army on that famous, but fatal, day.

The French waited in their entrenchments the advance of the imperial army (February 24, 1525). The details of this battle will not, of course, be

* "*Guerres en Italie.*"
† "Life of Charles V."

looked for in these pages. They are given in full in Servan's "*Guerres des Français en Italie*," and in Guicciardini's "Memoirs;" also, more or less minutely, by Martin du Bellay, Fleuranges, and other military writers, and historians generally.

The actual battle, begun early in the day, really lasted but an hour (Servan). The frightful massacre that followed — in which the Spaniards especially, like birds of prey athirst for blood, tortured, mangled, with shouts of savage glee, every poor wretch that fell into their hands — ceased not while a glimpse of daylight remained, and companions occupied in the same murderous work could be distinguished from their foes. Not less than 10,000 victims were thus sacrificed to the "chevalier king's" "delicate sense of honour."

Among them were the flower of the French nobility, who, while endeavouring to protect Francis from capture or from death, fell fighting by his side. Those who were not cut down by the imperialist troops — the young King of Navarre, Fleuranges, Chabot de Brion, Anne de Montmorency, and others — were taken prisoners with the king. It is said that Francis had his horse shot under him, and that he then fought desperately on foot. Other accounts state that the horse stumbled, threw him into a ditch, and rolled over him, and that two soldiers released him from the pressure of the horse, but quarrelled over the sharing of his finery — jewelled orders, etc.

Pompérant, the companion of the constable's flight from Chantelle, coming up, recognised the king, and suggested his surrender to Bourbon,— a proposal he naturally rejected. The viceroy Lannoy was then sent for. To him Francis gave up his sword; the viceroy on his knee receiving it, and returning his own in exchange to the royal captive. Francis escaped with two very slight wounds — mere scratches on the forehead and hand.

Several generals of distinction fell in this battle. The unfortunate Bonnivet was slain. Bourbon would seem to have been anxious that this enemy should fall by his hand. When, however, he beheld his dead and mangled body, he was affected, and exclaimed, "Ah, wretched man! you have caused not only my ruin, but the ruin of France."

But no sorrowful feeling came over him when he heard that Francis was a prisoner. A smile then suddenly animated his usually serious countenance, and, with a sort of boyish glee, he threw up his marshal's baton in the air and caught it again, but without uttering a word. His great satisfaction with what had occurred was, however, too evident, from the almost involuntary act that had given expression to it, to need words to make it clearer.

CHAPTER XVII.

Tout est perdu fors l'honneur. — Honour but Partly Satisfied. — Appeal to Charles's Generosity. — Meeting of Bourbon and Francis. — Bribing the Guard. — Escape of Henri d'Albret. — Alas! What a Hypocrite He Was! — Edifying Remarks. — To Arms! To Arms! — Embarrassing Requests. — An Alliance with Portugal. — The Spirit of Moderation. — A Cry of Indignation. — The Chevalier King Wavers. — Counter-propositions. — A Pledge of Reconciliation. — The Holy Italian League. — An Ungenerous Proceeding. — The Interesting Captive. — Meeting of Charles and Francis. — Marguerite's Diplomacy. — An Heroic Sacrifice. — Burgundy Ceded; Honour Saved. — The Armies of the Empire. — The Monarch's Return. — Not Long in Suspense.

"MADAME, *tout est perdu fors l'honneur.*" Sublimely laconic and energetic announcement, which the Jesuit historian, *le père* Daniel (in his "*Histoire de France*," published towards the end of the seventeenth century), first ventured to give to the world as the sole contents of the epistle of Francis I. to his mother after the defeat of Pavia. Certainly he names his authority — the Spaniard Da Vera, author of a life of Charles V. But the Jesuit father was not led astray by faith in Da Vera's veracity. He knew that the statement was false, but accepted it on the same principle as led later writers to follow his example — "*Se non è vero è bene trovato.*"

It was striking — " Madame, all is lost save honour ! "

One can imagine the "chevalier king," had he hastily but written these words — almost rivalling in celebrity the famous " *Veni, vidi, vici* " — handing with dignified air his missive to an attendant, who folds and secures it, as royal missives were then wont to be secured, with a thin gold and crimson cord and tassels; then placing it in a small pouch together with the king's safe-conduct through France, delivers it to the well-armed messenger.

To have added even the words which in the original epistle follow — " *honneur, et la vie, qui est sauvé*" — would have detracted in some degree from the sublimity of the message. For what was life compared with honour? As regarded the lives of others, evidently nothing at all to Francis I., as bore witness the thousands deliberately doomed to death that he might strive to fulfil the vain boast that he would take Pavia. He did not take it, and knew that he could not. Honour was therefore only partly satisfied by the attempt to do so; for, failing in his attempt, he had vowed that he would perish under the walls of that city.

Many of the young nobility who had encouraged his foolhardy resolve really did so — being smitten with deep remorse on beholding the plain on which the gory battle was fought, covered with the limbs and mangled headless bodies of the hapless victims of their criminal folly. Turning wildly on their pursuers, they rushed on their pikes, seeking by their own death to make some atonement for the horrible tortures and loss of life they had been the cause of inflicting on others. Francis I. should have done likewise.

The Spanish officer, Penalosa, deputed by Lannoy to convey the news of the king's defeat to the emperor, was also the bearer of a letter from Francis, appealing to Charles's generosity. Being eager to learn his decision respecting him, he gave the messenger permission to cross France, and charged him with his letter to the regent, who was at Lyons.* Very humble indeed, for a king of France, was the appeal to the emperor; very diffuse, very humiliating; deprecating imprisonment,

---

* Francis's letter to his mother was as follows: " Madame, — Pour vous avertir comment se porte le ressort de mon infortune, de toutes choses ne m'est demouré que l'honneur et la vie qui est sauve, et pour ce qu'en notre adversité cette nouvelle vous fera quelque peu de réconfort, j'ai prié qu'on me laissât vous écrire ces lettres, ce qu'on m'a agréablement accordé. Vous suppliant de ne vouloir prendre l'extrémité de vous-même en usant de votre accoutumée prudence, car j'ai espoir en la fin que Dieu ne m'abandonnera point; vous recommandant vos petits enfants et les miens; vous suppliant faire donner sûr passage pour l'aller et retour en Espagne à ce porteur qui va vers l'empereur pour savoir comme il faudra que je sois traité. Et sur ce très humblement me recommende à votre bonne grace. FRANCOIS." — " Lettres d'État de Granvelle."

and urging on him that, instead of having in his hands a useless captive, he might render a king his slave forever (*rendre un roi à jamais votre esclave*).

It was in Lannoy's camp that Bourbon and Francis met once more. Naturally, both were compelled to impose considerable restraint on themselves. The former, concealing his satisfaction at his great revenge, advanced towards his sovereign and respectfully kissed his hand, which the latter tolerated only by an effort, repressing his rising indignation at the approach of the rebel prince.

Until Charles's good pleasure could be known Francis was removed to the citadel of Pizzighitone, where again Bourbon was admitted to the presence of the king, who, forgetting, apparently, that he was far the more blameworthy of the two, thus addressed him: "Are you indeed so very proud of your victory, knowing that they whom you have oppressed, vanquished, and dispersed are your near kinsmen?"

"Sire," replied Bourbon, "have I not been driven to this? Otherwise, how willingly would I have abstained from it!"

Francis seems to have derived some sort of satisfaction from this reply, as he is said to have retired with Bourbon into an embrasure and conversed with him for some time, apart from others who were present. This may have suggested Lannoy's idea that Bourbon and Pescara might be brought to connive for their own advantage in the escape of the royal captive. For Bourbon and Pescara both considered that Francis was their prisoner far more than the emperor's, — they having found the funds for raising the reinforcements, and with them fighting the battle which, without such aid, would not have ended in victory.

Two prisoners had successfully bribed their guards very soon after their capture. One was the King of Navarre, confined in the fortress of Pavia, and who had offered 100,000 crowns for his ransom. Pescara refused it. He then resorted to other means for obtaining his liberty. Some anxiety was one day felt at his remaining unusually late in bed; but there was an unwillingness to disturb him. Yet when evening drew on, and his majesty, with closed curtains, was still supposed, from his heavy snoring, to be sleeping, it was thought right to ascertain if he were ill. The captain of the guard entered and respectfully drew aside the drapery, when, instead of Henri d'Albret, there — still pretending to sleep — lay his servant, who had had permission to attend on the king and to go in and out of the fortress. Being of similar height and figure, the servant's clothes had effectually disguised the master, who had passed through the *corps de garde* unrecognised — favoured by the duskiness of a winter afternoon and the gold-dust that had dimmed the eyes of the guards. Horses were waiting for him outside the fortress, and when the discovery was made he was well on his way to Piedmont. One naturally asks, what became of this faithful servant? but with his fate History has not condescended to concern herself.

The escape of a prisoner of so much importance to the emperor as the King of Navarre, whose dominions he wanted, might well occasion Lannoy's anxious fears for the safety of the still more important royal personage under his own care. For Charles was in no haste to reply to the humble petition of the captive king, but had privately written to Lannoy — who was greatly in his confidence — "As you have taken the King of France for me, I beg of you to keep him safely."

Charles was more elated with this victory, gained on his birthday, than was expected. From its decisiveness he believed himself already master of Europe; that Christendom was conquered, if not by, yet for, him; and that to lay low the power of the infidel — his great ambition — must be his next exploit. But while his inward satisfaction was known to be great, it was not in his character to give way to any enthusiastic demonstration of it. When the news arrived in Madrid, his first act was to retire to his chapel to offer up thanks to God for the success of his arms — after the impious custom of making a God of mercy an accomplice in the murderous exploits of war. Charles, like an excellent Christian, forbade bonfires, bell-ringing, and all public rejoicings. "Such exultation," he said, "was indecent then. It was a war between Christians, and the glory of the victory must be ascribed to God alone; while for himself, he regarded it only as affording him an opportunity of proving his affection towards his friends, his clemency towards his enemies, and of restoring peace to Europe." (Alas! what a hypocrite he was!) " But when he had triumphed over the Grand Turk, sounds of mirth and gladness should resound throughout Christendom."

Courtiers, grandees of Spain, the whole of the *corps diplomatique*, thronged the presence-chamber — vying with each other in the eager expression of their congratulations. But the solemn young monarch, who possessed a large measure of what has been termed a "royal virtue," — the power of greatly dissembling, — gravely rebuked every allusion to the captive king by expressions of sympathy with him, of pity for his mischance, and by many edifying remarks on the ups and downs of life, the instability of human grandeur, and the reverses of fortune from which the greatest of monarchs were not exempt, — a striking example of which was afforded in the sad misfortune that had befallen the King of France.[*]

Some noble and generous act of clemency towards his prisoner must surely have been looked for by those who listened to his words, or were the

---

[*] Robertson; H. Martin; "State Papers."

recipients of his written sentiments. But Charles had no intention of parting with his prize without an adequate return. How to secure the greatest advantage from his unexpected good fortune was therefore a subject for mature reflection.

Great, however, was the consternation in France when news arrived of the sanguinary battle of Pavia, the capture of the king, and the massacre of the army and the flower of the French nobility. A cry of distress was raised throughout the land, the people vehemently accusing the regent, the chancellor, and the king himself, with having brought this great calamity and trouble on the nation. The country was supposed to be in danger of invasion, and the general cry was "To arms!" to defend the territory. But the whole blame of what had happened was unjustly thrown by the regent on the Duc d'Alençon, who had reached Lyons with the few troops of the small detachment he had commanded, and with whom he was accused of cowardly flying from the battle-field, instead of leading them on to be massacred with the rest.

Madame Louise at this crisis, if no less unscrupulous than usual, yet displayed considerable ability in the energetic measures she adopted, and great sagacity in the choice of men to carry them out, for remedying the evils she had brought on her son and on France. She was compelled to lay aside much of her haughty manner, and to submit with good grace to the reproaches of the Parliament, who in council decided that "not a foot of French territory should be ceded to the emperor, even should they be compelled to leave the king in his power;" and to this decision she was obliged to submit, or at least to appear to do so.

But she wrote pressingly to Charles, urging him to treat his prisoner well, and made overtures to Henry VIII. — through Wolsey, of course — in very flattering terms, which pleased both king and cardinal, and impelled the latter to find some pretext for inducing Henry to break with Charles and resume friendly relations with France. Public rejoicings were made in England in celebration of Charles's great victory, and a special envoy despatched to the Spanish court to congratulate him. The envoy, however, was charged to inform the emperor that Henry, as his ally, expected to participate in the fruits of the victory. He requested, therefore, that Guyenne might be invaded with a force sufficient to give him possession of it, in accordance with the terms of the treaty of Bruges, "by which Charles had bound himself to aid Henry to recover his kingdom of France."

As though desirous of giving an amusing turn to his demands, he required that the "usurper of his kingdom" might be transferred to him for safe keeping in England. As a special mark of his confidence, he also announced that he was prepared to send the emperor's *fiancée*, the Princess Mary, either to Spain or the Netherlands, to be educated as the emperor might desire, until the time fixed for their marriage.

These were extremely embarrassing requests, whose object was doubtless sufficiently clear to the emperor, as the hand of Wolsey was conspicuous in them. As to his *fiancée*, Charles seems to have regarded his betrothal to Mary as no more binding on him than his numerous other betrothals. Henry was probably aware that the emperor had very recently sent his ambassador to Lisbon formally to ask of Dom Joan the hand of his sister, the Princess Isabella of Portugal. This princess possessed an immense fortune, which to the needy monarch of so many kingdoms — restrained by poverty in his vast ambition to rule over many more — must have been an attraction greater than Isabella's reputed beauty. A further advantage was that a marriage with her involved the possibility of enforcing at a later date some remote claim on the crown of Portugal. The solemnisation of this marriage was awaiting the settlement of the political difficulty with France and the release of the king.

After a delay of nearly three months, during which Charles had long and frequently deliberated on the matter with his advisers, the conditions of Francis's liberation were made known to him by the Comte de Reux in the emperor's name. But, as though further to humiliate him, Bourbon and Lannoy were appointed his plenipotentiaries to discuss those conditions with him.

The Bishop of Ozma is said to have strongly urged Charles to adopt the more generous course of restoring Francis to liberty without any conditions whatever, trusting solely to his gratitude for the result. But Charles had no generosity, and no faith, probably, in his rival's gratitude. He therefore preferred the advice of the Duke of Alba, which (as reported by Guicciardini) was "to profit to the utmost by the calamity that had fallen on Francis, that the French monarchy might be irretrievably ruined."

The document, of which De Reux was the bearer, was read by him to the regent in council at Lyons, as he passed through that city on his way to the king. It began by asserting that in strict legality the emperor might claim the whole of the kingdom of France; but desiring to act in a spirit of moderation, he waived that claim of ancient date, and required: 1st. That the king should ally himself with him against the Turks, and furnish 20,000 men for the expedition, the emperor being the head of it; 2dly. The betrothal of the dauphin to the Infanta of Spain, the emperor's neice; 3dly. Restitution of the duchy of Burgundy, with all other countries, cities, and lordships possessed by Duke Charles of Burgundy at the time of his death; 4thly. The cession of Provence to the Duc de Bourbon, the emperor's future brother-in-law, with restitution of all his ancestral domains whatsoever, to be, with the addition of Provence, erected into a kingdom exempt from all subjection to the crown of France; 5thly. Restitution to the King of England * of all that justly belonged to him, the King of France charging himself with the indemnity promised by the emperor to the King of England; 6thly. The annulment of the proceedings against Bourbon and his friends; and, finally, the renunciation of all the pretensions of France to Naples, Milan, or any other territory in Italy.

The council responded to the emperor's monstrous pretensions by a cry of indignation; and Francis, after De Reux had read the rigorous conditions he was required to submit to, exclaimed in the vehemence of his rage that he would rather spend his life in prison than purchase liberty on such terms.

Francis, a short time before, had written a letter to the same effect addressed to foreign courts, the French nobility, and the Parliaments of the kingdom. This letter made so good an impression that, together with the emperor's pro-

---

* Charles did not then know that Henry proposed to withdraw from his alliance and enter into a treaty with France. This he did immediately after the emperor had made known his claims on the captive king, towards whose release he promised his aid — but selling his good offices at a very high price.

posed dismemberment of France as the price of his captive's liberty, it caused a general revulsion of feeling in the king's favour. Forgetting the invectives so recently lavished both on Francis and the regent, and the charges brought against him of ruining the nation for the carrying on of his fruitless wars, and his no less expensive amours, the one thought now seemed to be, what was to be done to obtain this injured monarch's release. " If it were a question of money, his ransom to any amount should instantly be forthcoming, and to protect the frontiers and repel invaders all France was ready to arm."

But the king soon wavered in his chivalric resolve to live and die in captivity. His longing to return to his accustomed libertine life prompted him, after the first paroxysm of rage had subsided, to draw up a series of counter-propositions in reply to the emperor's conditions. The concessions he professed himself ready to make were even more humiliating than those required of him. Burgundy was the great difficulty; rather because the Burgundians were prepared to resist being handed over to Charles as subjects of Spain, than from any unwillingness on the part of Francis to give them up, if the sacrifice would open his prison doors.

He proposed, then, that Eleanor, the Dowager-Queen of Spain, should be given in marriage to him instead of to Bourbon, and Burgundy be considered her dowry; the emperor's second son succeeding to the duchy should Eleanor leave no male issue. He renounced all his claims on Italy, Milan excepted, reserving those only for the benefit of Eleanor's possible heirs. He abandoned the suzerainty of Artois and Flanders, and consented to buy back Picardy.

Very recently he had contrived secretly to despatch a messenger with his seal and a letter to Solyman II., asking aid to obtain his release. Yet he promised to furnish, as required by the emperor, 20,000 men to attack him. Charles de Bourbon was to be reinstated; and to compensate him for the loss of Eleanor, was to be offered the hand of a French princess — Madame Renée, probably. As if this was not enough, Francis placed the whole of the fleet and army of France at the emperor's disposition, to assist in any enterprise in which he might desire their co-operation; also, to join him himself, or send him one of his sons (Henri Martin).

An ambassador from Madame Louise and the council of regency arrived in Spain at about the same time as the messenger from Pizzighitone. He, too, was the bearer of counter-propositions; but far less unreserved than those of the king. The regent, however, had, with extreme want of delicacy, and, for a woman of her acknowledged diplomatic ability, want of tact, offered the emperor, as a pledge of reconciliation, the hand of her daughter Marguerite, the recently widowed Duchesse d'Alençon.

But two or three weeks had elapsed since the death of her husband, bowed down by excessive grief and shame at the overwhelming reproaches heaped on him by his wife and mother-in-law. The latter accused him of not preventing the capture of "her Cæsar, her lord, her love;" the former drove him from her presence with horror, for not releasing the adored brother from his captors, or at least attempting it, though in the effort he had sacrificed his own worthless life. Yet it does not appear that he was able to either save or assist this precious son and adored brother. Poor Alençon was also stigmatised by the *sobriquet* of the "deserter of Pavia," which he took so much to heart that he survived his return to France scarcely two months. By Alençon's death, Charles de Bourbon became first prince of the blood.

It was the custom of Charles V. to take much time to reflect on and mature his projects before arriving at a decision; sometimes, indeed, he reflected so long that the opportunity of executing them had passed away. It was fortunate for France that it was so; for while he remained inactive in Spain, instead of following up the victory of Pavia by an immediate invasion of France, as Bourbon and Pescara were expecting, the regent had had time secretly to join the league against him with the Pope, the Venetian and other Italian states, and Henry of England.

Francis, meanwhile, had been removed to Spain at his own request; the poverty of the emperor's resources being evident in the fact of Francis being obliged to send for his own galleys to convey him to Barcelona, and to furnish vessels for the Spanish troops that escorted him as a prisoner.

He was lodged in the fortress of Xativa under the strictest surveillance. Thence he sent Montmorency, who had obtained his liberty on payment of a heavy ransom, to express his great desire to confer with the emperor, not only respecting terms of peace and his own liberation, but with reference to the establishing and confirming of Italy in subservience to him, before the Italian potentates had time to unite in opposing it.

By this sacrifice of the Italian states, with whom his mother had just entered into an alliance on his behalf, Francis hoped to recover his liberty. This was the 2d of July. By Charles's order, the king was transferred to the Alcazar of Madrid, still closely guarded by General Alarcon. The emperor was at Toledo, where he continued to reside for some weeks after pretending that his presence was necessary at the Cortes assembled there.

It was certainly most ungenerous, if not absolutely cruel, to calculate, as the emperor evidently did, on ultimately subduing his captive and wresting an unqualified assent to his preposterous conditions by the effect produced on his mind by prolonged incarceration in a gloomy fortress, and his weariness and impatience of confinement. On the other hand, Francis did not bear captivity in a manly and chivalric spirit. This hero of romance, cast down and in trouble, then appeared what he really was, as M. Michelet remarks, "a Poitevin gentleman of very poor stuff."

The libertine is become a devotee from despair. He begins to fast; abstains from meat, of which he informs his mother and sister, who are moved beyond measure. His sister forbids him to fast, and sends him the Epistles of Saint Paul ("the daily bread of the reformers") as spiritual food, urging him not to refuse it. "Some recluse," she says, "has confided to a holy man that if the king will read Saint Paul he shall find deliverance." But his languishing spirit seeks consolation in putting his misfortunes and amours into feeble rhymes, worthy of Saint Gelais or other of the many poetasters of the day.*

In the high-flown language of a model chevalier he addresses sonnets and rondeaux to the unknown mistress of his imagination — the lady of his heart, *par excellence*. His occupations excite the curiosity of the ladies of Madrid, and when they learn that he is chiefly employed in fasting,

---

* Some pleasing poetry has been attributed to Francis I., but it is doubtful that he was its author.

praying for restoration to the society of lovely woman, and pouring out his sighing soul in verse, their sympathy is at once awakened. Fancy surrounds him with a halo of romance, and fair *señoras* on their way to matins, as they cast a pitying glance towards the frowning tower of the Alcazar, breathe an earnest prayer for the speedy release of the captive king.

The great interest the Spanish ladies took in the fate of the king must have been, for awhile, no slight consolation to him.* But poetry and the sympathy of the fair sex could not sustain his languishing spirit for ever. Melancholy began to mark him for her own, and Charles was informed by the physicians he had sent to attend his captive, that it was he, not they, who could restore the failing health of their patient.

Alarmed by the hint that he might possibly lose the ransom he exacted by over-persistence in wearing out his prisoner, the emperor hastened to Madrid. Francis had been seven months in captivity when Charles, for the first time, visited him.

---

* Francis is said to have been much gratified, when taken prisoner at Pavia, at the eagerness displayed by the soldiers to share in what was taken from him, rather to preserve as a relic than with reference to its intrinsic value. His vanity, too, was flattered by their admiration of his swordsmanship. His armour was sent to the emperor, who gave it to his brother — reserving only the sword for himself. Nearly three centuries later, both sword and armour were taken by Napoleon from Madrid and Vienna and transferred to the Musée of Paris.

He addressed him with an appearance of great cordiality, was profuse in expressions of regard and good-will, promised that negotiations should be speedily resumed, and, as he hoped, soon satisfactorily brought to a close. A safe-conduct was also granted to his sister, sent by the regent to console her brother.

She was provided, also, with full powers to negotiate. Madame Louise—whose offer of her daughter to the emperor had not even been noticed by him—fancied it would be a means of giving Marguerite the opportunity of exercising her great powers of fascination on Charles, and thus facilitate Francis's restoration to liberty.

The Spanish nobles seem to have been greatly charmed by Marguerite's engaging manners, her liveliness, her witty conversation, and the attachment she displayed towards her brother. They paid assiduous court to her, but Charles, while paying her marked respect, was not induced by her wiles to abate aught of his demands, or to admit her claim to negotiate. With reference to her brother's proposal to marry his sister Eleanor, he told her she was promised already to Duc Charles de Bourbon, a promise from which, except by consent of that prince, he could not free himself. His other conditions he had referred to his ministers for discussion.

Marguerite was made the agent, probably an unwilling one, of her mother's treachery. She revealed to Charles the secret of the Holy League (the Pope being at the head of it) that was forming against him for the emancipation of Italy from the yoke of the empire. But, from another quarter, it had already been made known to him. The object of the regent, consequently, was not furthered by her baseness, and Charles being freed from all alarm on the score of the king's health, was as little disposed as before to yield on the great question at issue — the cession of Burgundy.

Francis, therefore, proposed to thwart the views of his enemy by a heroic sacrifice — his abdication in favour of the dauphin, with his mother or sister as regent. He, however, reserved to himself the right of resuming the crown he professed to resign, should he recover his liberty. But, as had often happened before, having formed a great resolution, Francis shrank from carrying it out. "It remained, therefore, a mere velleity" (H. Martin). His sister, who, according to his first impulse, should have been the bearer of this important document to Paris, was suddenly compelled to hasten her departure. Being suspected, during her three months' residence in Madrid, of political intrigue and of planning the king's escape, an order, of which she was privately informed, was issued for her arrest the moment her safe-conduct should expire. The Maréchal de Montmorency was then leaving Spain, and, accompanied by him, Marguerite made the journey with a speed most unusual in those days, reaching the French frontier only an hour or two before the expiration of her pass.

Burgundy seemed then on the point of being given up to the emperor by command of the regent, she and Francis embarrassing each other by independently issuing orders and counter-orders concerning it. But, worn out at last, by this never-ending contention, Francis yields. Summoning his mother's ambassadors to his presence, he has recourse to the doubtful expedient of swearing to them, in order to save his honour, that what he is about to promise he will never perform; that his renunciation of Burgundy shall be considered null and of no effect, being a promise made under constraint.

The French plenipotentiaries then, by his direction, announce to the emperor's ministers that the king cedes the coveted duchy to their imperial master in full sovereignty. Charles believes he has triumphed, and this second victory he has the satisfaction of knowing is entirely his own.

It was agreed that the treaty should be ratified by the regent at the first frontier town, the hostages for its fulfilment to be either twelve French gentlemen or the king's two eldest sons, Francis undertaking to return to his prison if within four months the ratifications with the states of Burgundy were not exchanged, and the duchy finally transferred to the great-grandson of Charles the Bold.

The king was to marry Eleanor, she preferring the King of France with diminished territories to the Duc de Bourbon with no territory at all. To compensate the duke for the loss of the lady's hand, his ancestral possessions, and the kingdom promised him (for Charles, having obtained Burgundy, no longer urged Bourbon's claims), he was to have the probable investiture of the duchy of Milan, ceded by Francis, and — *vice* Pescara, deceased — the post of lieutenant-general of the armies of the empire. These armies consisted of as many of the rabble of all countries as he might be able to collect together and find funds to support.

As though he scarcely trusted Francis — and his sagacity must have been greatly at fault to trust him — or was unwilling to part with his captive, the emperor detained him nearly two months after the signing of the treaty. But during that time they frequently appeared in public together, apparently on the most amicable terms. Sometimes they were accompanied by the bride-elect, but the marriage was deferred until the bond was fulfilled.

At last, on the 18th of March, 1526 — the emperor being about to set out for Seville to marry the Princess Isabella — Lannoy conducted the king to Fontarabia. A small vessel was moored in the middle of the river Bidassoa, the limit of the two kingdoms, where Marshal Lautrec exchanged the dauphin and his brother Henry — the twelve gentlemen not being forthcoming — for the King of France. The king kissed and blessed his poor weeping children, who were conveyed to the Spanish shore, while their heroic father, with Lautrec, made for the opposite one. There an Arab horse awaited him, which he quickly mounted, exclaiming with joyful voice as he raised his hat, as if again to salute la belle France, " I am once again king!" (*Me voici roi derechef!*") He then galloped off at full speed to St. Jean de Luz, and thence to Bayonne without drawing rein.

Madame la Régente, with a train of young beauties in her suite, the Duchess d'Alençon, the fair Comtesse de Châteaubriand, and the rest of the ladies and gentlemen of the Court, awaited at Bayonne their monarch's return.

But following quickly on his arrival appeared the officer deputed by Lannoy to bear back the ratification of the Treaty of Madrid, which, as stipulated, was to take place on the king's arrival in the first frontier town he stopped at. Francis, however, informed him that "as he could not alienate his subjects without their consent, he must ascertain what were the wishes of the Burgundians before he could give effect to the cession of their duchy."

At all events, the emperor was not kept long in suspense as to the value of the concessions he had wrung from the captive king.

CHAPTER XVIII.

His Native Air Prescribed.— More Betrothals Proposed. — Increased Dissipation. — Mademoiselle d'Heilly.— A Numerous Family.— A Wayward Girl of Many Moods.— The Jewels Returned.— The Countess's Revenge.— The New *Maîtresse-en-titre*.— The Peasants' War.— A Cure for Lutheranism. — A Gallican Holy Office. — The Bishop and His Disciple. — The Hermit of Vitry. — Louis de Berquin.— Marriage of Marguerite. — A Restraint on Court Gaiety.

FRANCIS was not at all anxious to face his good people of Paris after his long-enforced absence from France; and much disappointment was caused by it. The king and his court having made a short sojourn at Bordeaux, where jousts and tournaments celebrated his return, repaired to Cognac; the pretext being that, after thirteen months of rigourous confinement in a foreign prison, his native air (Cognac was his birthplace) was prescribed by his physician as necessary for the restoration of his health.

He, however, took no sort of interest in the affairs of his kingdom, which seemed scarcely at all to concern him; and having thanked the Sultan Solyman — whose reply to the king's appeal arrived only after his release — for his friendly expression of sympathy with him, and generous offer of the aid of his powerful armies and vast treasures, he relapsed into his former licentious course of life.

Under the idea that the marriage of Francis with the emperor's sister might be considered as broken off, another princess was offered to him, as seal and pledge of the eternity of a reconciliation with England. This was the Princess Mary, the former *fiancée* of the dauphin and the once-destined bride of Charles V. Once again her hand was free; but Francis evinced no inclination to take this little girl of ten or eleven years for his wife. He pleaded that he might yet be called on to fulfil his engagement to Eleanor.

It was then suggested that Mary should be betrothed to Francis's second son, Henri, the godson of Henry VIII. But the proposal of a matrimonial alliance with France was so unpopular with the English people, that it was thought expedient to leave the question open for future consideration — the more so as the young prince whose betrothal was proposed was then a prisoner in Spain. Francis was, however, profuse of thanks to Henry VIII. for the part he had taken in securing his release, which seems to have amounted to nothing more than that, being jealous of the emperor's increasing power in Europe, he joined the league against him. For this service he was paid — or perhaps, according to the custom of the period, he received only the promise of payment —

a sum so large that "in itself it amounted to a right royal ransom."

The king's increased dissipation was but too clearly apparent even to his courtiers, his ministers, his generals, and was but too well turned to account by his mercenary and avaricious flatterers, whose interest it was that the country should be ill-governed — and the monarch weak, proud, despotic, a slave to his passions — and the people wretched. Of such men was the chancellor, Duprat, who, together with the regent — no longer bearing the title, yet relinquishing none of the authority of the office — ruled France despotically.

While Francis was absent, his mother very considerately had trained a new mistress for him. She was resolved on destroying the influence which the Comtesse de Châteaubriand had so long retained over him, and which so often had thwarted her own projects; but now, as she hoped, was by absence greatly weakened. The king had warmly greeted the fair countess; and gazing on her with admiration, declared that "no such lovely lady had met his gaze since he had parted from her."

The wily Louise, on hearing this compliment, turned smilingly towards a young lady who, seated a little behind her, seemed rather to avoid than court observation, and bade her come nearer. It was the custom for the young ladies-in-waiting of Madame Louise to seat themselves around her on cushions or carpets spread on the floor for their use. A tall, slight, elegant girl, of fair, roseate complexion, with deep blue eyes, and bright auburn hair, rose from her cushion, and seated herself, as bidden, beside the king's mother. Her demeanour was sedate and modest. She seemed not to notice, and was therefore in no way embarrassed by the bold, libertine gaze the king fixed on her; which indeed was only usual with him whenever any fresh, youthful face met his view.

But the young lady's beauty appeared to make no deep impression on him. He turned again to the countess and resumed his conversation with her. The countenance of Anne de Pisseleu, called Mademoiselle d'Heilly, was not strictly beautiful, and when in repose was noticeable only for its expression of calmness and placidity, of which there was little in her character. She had been unusually well educated; though her father, Guillaume de Pisseleu, Seigneur d'Heilly, having been three times married, is said to have had a family of thirty children to provide for — Anne being a daughter of the second wife.

Demure as she looked, Mademoiselle d'Heilly was full of life and spirits. The vivacity of her conversation and her singular power of lively repartee were wonderful in one so young — for she was but eighteen. When it was her mood to be animated, she was beautiful also; her airs and graces, her wiles and caprices, the changing expression of her intelligent countenance, even her violent gusts of temper which often subsided into mirth and laughter, became her exceedingly. Her form was perfectly symmetrical, and the gracefulness of her movements added to her other attractions.

This fair young damsel, who was to enslave the king for the rest of his life, had been recommended by a friend to the notice of Madame Louise. She was portionless, she had twenty-nine brothers and sisters (surely all were not living), but she was wonderfully talented, read Latin and Greek, and possessed all the accomplishments of the time. Madame Louise was moved to pity, and received Mademoiselle d'Heilly into her band of "maids of honour." Soon she detected qualities in her *protégée* that made her a suitable agent in the carrying out of the project she had long had so much at heart. This wayward girl of many moods had fascinations which she believed would outweigh those of the countess; besides, she was ten years younger.

There appear to have been no scruples on the part of Anne de Pisseleu to adopt the part her benefactress assigned her. It was, as all know, successful; though there was nothing surprising in Francis falling into the snare. He was, doubtless, greatly surprised, when he saw the quiet, modest girl, whose tameness a few hours before had deprived her of the honour of a second glance from him, surrounded by a circle (a sadly narrowed one since Pavia) of youthful courtiers, who hung on her words, laughed at her freaks, courted her smiles, and — when she rather confounded them with the extent of her learning, which, with a sort of gay triumph she was fond of displaying — pronounced her "the most charming and beautiful of learned ladies, and the most learned of the beautiful."

The susceptible Francis listened with admiring wonder. His inflammable heart at once took fire, and was laid at this fascinating damsel's feet. But, further surprise, she received the monarch's advances with a well-assumed air of saucy imperiousness that might have daunted a lover who had not the advantage of being a king, and have even sent back Francis a suppliant for pardon to the neglected and saddened countess. But Françoise de Foix is now aware that her ten years' reign is ended. For Louise of Savoy, herself — an act worthy of her — has with her own hand presented to her son the well-trained mistress she has destined to be the countess's successor.

Many scenes of storm and sunshine, of hope and despair, are said to have occurred between the king and Madame de Châteaubriand; for she did not readily yield to the loss of her influence over him, but added to the triumph of her rival and her enemy by fruitless efforts to regain it. When, however, the approaching marriage of Mademoiselle d'Heilly with the Duc d'Étampes was announced, she perceived that the time had arrived to withdraw from the court.

She was required to return the costly jewels which the king had given her, that they might serve as a marriage present for the adornment of the bride of the new noble duke.* As so much munificence and lavish expenditure on his favourites have been ascribed to Francis I., it is difficult to believe that so paltry a demand emanated from him, unless urged on him by his mother. However, the countess is said to have been so indignant that she revenged herself by having the stones removed from their setting and the gold melted down as an ingot, in which state she gave back those mementoes of the king's regard and affection.

Madame de Châteaubriand then returned to

* A promise to reinstate him in his family possessions had induced Jean de Brosse, Comte de Penthièvre, to consent to marry the king's mistress. On his mother's side he was a grandson of Philippe de Comines. His father had left France with the constable, Charles de Bourbon, and was killed at Pavia. He was one of the nineteen gentlemen whom the Parliament condemned to death after their escape. All his property was confiscated. To the son's application for the restitution of a part, if not the whole of it, this marriage was proposed to him as a condition for acceding to his prayer. The king confirmed his title of Comte de Penthièvre, gave him the collar of the Order of Saint Michel, made him Governor of Brittany, and created him Duc d'Étampes to serve as a new title for his mistress. Of course she was the wife of De Brosse only in name; but she so far acknowledged him as a husband that she received and kept his salary as governor.

Brittany. According to Brantôme, her husband, on her arrival, locked her up in a dark cell in his château, and, after keeping her there for six months, had a vein opened in both her arms and feet, and allowed her to bleed to death.*

The court having now an acknowledged *maîtresse-en-titre*, became, under her lively influence, more dissipated than ever. Dancing and *comédies chantantes* were beginning to be far more in favour than hitherto — the duchess being especially fond of both, and excelling, it appears, in the dance. For every species of pleasure and pastime this lady's fertile fancy devised, the king found ample leisure; but for his duties he found none, and the affairs of the kingdom fell completely into the hands of Madame Louise and Duprat.

Francis apparently disdained to give heed to any measures conducive to the welfare of his subjects and the prosperity of the country; or festivity and gallantry, hunting-parties, and other amusements drove them entirely out of his mind.

* The above tradition is disproved by the French State Papers, which mention incidentally that " Francis I., having convoked the States of Brittany in 1532 at Vannes, resided while there with the Count and Countess of Châteaubriand. On his departure the king, after bestowing several marks of his favour on the count, presented the countess with the two estates of Rhuis and Socinio." Her death took place in 1537, eleven years after her *liaison* with the king had ended. She frequented the court, too, it appears, from time to time after the death of Madame Louise in 1531.

To the pleasures of the chase he gave himself up immoderately, probably from having been long deprived of a pursuit he was fond of. But while hunting a stag at Saintonge he was thrown from his horse, was taken up unconscious, and for awhile serious consequences were expected to ensue. Francis had had so many falls, so many blows and wounds on the head, besides the slight ones of Pavia, that he seemed to bear a charmed life, so speedily did he recover from all those dangerous mishaps.

The political troubles of the time were complicated by religious fanaticism and persecution. The neighbouring revolution of the peasants of Germany — called the Peasants' War — had so far extended to France that the peasants of Alsace and Suabia had risen *en masse*, and marched direct on Lorraine, pillaging the châteaux and massacring the inhabitants; threatening to enter France, expecting the peasantry to join them, having heard that all the nobility had been killed at the battle of Pavia. The Comte de Guise put an end to the invasion of Lorraine by the most rigourous and unsparing slaughter.

The Parliament had concluded a long list of grievances submitted to the regent by requiring a more rigid punishment of Lutheranism, considering that the leniency and great indulgence shown towards persons affected with that heresy had drawn down Divine vengeance on the nation.

Though not at all zealous for the faith herself, the regent, to gratify the Parliament, without heeding their more justly complained of grievances, requested the opinion of the doctors of Sorbonne on the readiest way of eradicating the Lutheran heresy. They replied, "Let the guilty be compelled to retract or be severely punished, and let none be exempt, whatsoever their rank." She carried her inquiry further, and being then anxious to gain the Pope's favour, prayed him to tell her "what was the best remedy against Lutheranism?" His holiness briefly replied in a word of much meaning — "The Inquisition."

Marguerite's known leaning towards the "new opinions" had more than once called forth expressions of strong disapprobation from the Sorbonne. Without actually naming her, it was made perfectly clear against whom these unfavourable allusions were directed. Under the spiritual direction of Briçonnet, Bishop of Meaux — himself accused of heretical views — Marguerite had become very ardent in the cause of reform, and had endeavoured to influence Francis and Madame Louise in its favour.

"Once she flattered herself that she had almost made converts of them, and brought them to see that making known the truths of God was not heresy." But neither the king nor his mother was likely to seek acquaintance with the truth of God as Marguerite sought it. She desired to find in the pure Gospel doctrine a guide for her conduct, a solace for her troubled mind, oppressed by some secret sorrow, or by remorse for some repented sin.

Yet her efforts are believed to have inclined Francis towards toleration, and induced him to afford protection to men of learning who had either embraced the reformed religion themselves and were persecuted by the Sorbonne, or were partisans of those who had. At all events, no one had yet been burnt at the stake in France as a heretic, when the king set out for Italy. But the results of the fatal campaign of Pavia, following on the constable's revolt, which seemed to threaten the monarchy, drove the regent to seek in the papal alliance the possibility of her son's release, and a means of satisfying both the clergy and the Parliament.

The Roman Inquisition transferred to the French capital, the people would not have tolerated. A Gallican Holy Office was therefore established in Paris and other large cities of the kingdom, composed each of two doctors of the Sorbonne and two parliamentary judges, authorised by a Papal Bull to commit any atrocities that seemed good in the eyes of those cruel and ignorant fanatics. Madame Louise, herself, ordered the arrest of a young man named Jacques Pavanne, a disciple of the Bishop of Meaux. This was an indirect attack on Marguerite. At first, Pavanne retracted, then disavowed his retractation. Again he was seized, and, "persisting in his errors," was burnt on the Place de Grève.

This alarmed the bishop, who, less firm in maintaining his opinions than the youth who had suffered for them, when cited before the judges, disavowed all he had taught, condemned Luther's writings, and was absolved, promising all that was required of him, except the persecution of others. Marguerite, though pitying the bishop's lamentable fall, then changed her confessor.

Soon after, in order to strike terror into wavering minds by a terrible example of the rigour with which this new Inquisition was prepared to punish deserters from the true faith, both clergy and people were summoned by the tolling of the great bell of Notre-Dame to witness the agony of an unfortunate hermit who had lived in the forest of Vitry, and whose crime was that he had preached to the peasantry the doctrines of the heretics of Meaux. He was to be burnt, or, rather, roasted over a slow fire, his flesh torn off with red-hot pincers, with other horrors devised by the demoniacal tribunal that condemned him, the Sorbonne doctors assuring the people that the man they were conducting to the stake was also "doomed by divine wrath to be afterwards cast into the flames of hell."

The provincial tribunals vied with the capital in the horror of their proceedings, inventing tortures disgraceful to humanity, to add to the suffering of a lingering, frightful death; tortures often supported with such unflinching courage that even the wretches employed to inflict them were struck with terror and a feeling of reverential awe by the wonderful endurance of their victims. The pleadings of Marguerite were of little avail. She herself, as well as those she protected, was vehemently menaced by the fanatics, ecclesiastical and judicial, who made no secret of their hatred towards her.

Appeals to her mother were vainly made. The infamous Duprat, who aimed at the papacy, secretly urged the regent not to allow her daughter to obtain an undue ascendancy over her. At the same time, he endeavoured to convince the king — then in captivity, and from whom Marguerite was exerting herself to obtain a formal prohibition of these horrors — "that the newfangled opinions tended to nothing less than the overthrow of monarchy divine and human" (H. Martin).

When Louis de Berquin, the translator and commentator of the writings of Luther, Melancthon, and Erasmus, was brought before his enlightened judges a second time — having once before been released by the king's order — declared a heretic and condemned to death, Francis, still a prisoner at Madrid, wrote, at Marguerite's request, to the inquisitorial commissioner that he would judge of the matter himself. Soon after Francis was free, and, on his arrival at Bayonne, Marguerite obtained from him an order to release both Berquin and the poet Marot, who had rendered the psalms into verse. But so unwilling were the fanatics to give up Berquin, that it was necessary to send an officer of the king's guard to bring him from his cell in the Conciergerie.*

In default of Erasmus himself, his works were condemned and burned; as also those of the reformers Lefèvre d' Étaples, Farel, and others. This irritated the "Father of Letters." He declared that "he would defend and protect those men of excellent learning who were the chief ornament and glory of his reign," and required that the books destroyed should be reprinted.† The release of the captive of Spain had therefore been anxiously looked forward to by the reform-

---

* Berquin was arrested a third time in 1529 and condemned to do penance three times; afterwards to be shut up for life in a cell of the Episcopal prison, without books, pens, paper or ink. Contrary to the advice of friends, who knew that this sentence would be set aside by the king, he appealed against it to the Parliament, by whom he was the next day sentenced to be "burnt, together with his books, on the Place de Grève, and that immediately, before the king or the regent could interfere to rescue him." At once this sentence was carried out — a large crowd assembling to witness it.

† The Swiss reformer Zwingli at this time dedicated his book, "True and False Religion" ("*Vraie et Fausse Religion*"), to Francis I., and sent it to him from Zurich.

ers, with expectations doomed, unfortunately, to disappointment.

The marriage of Marguerite some few months after (January, 1527) was an unfavourable event for the reforming party in France, — her frequent absence from the French Court diminishing much of the effect of her influence on the king. Henri d'Albret was her junior by several years; but political motives imposed this marriage on her, it being to the interest of France to keep up a close alliance with the sovereign of the small kingdom of Navarre. Marguerite had then become rather more serious than was agreeable to the ladies of Madame Louise's circle, or to Madame Louise herself, who often complained that the presence of Madame d' Alençon was a restraint on the gaiety of the court.

CHAPTER XIX.

Anne Boleyn. — Vexing Her Liege Lord. — Amusing the Ambassadors. — Let Him Return to Captivity. — The Modern Regulus. — Great Services Recompensed. — Bourbon's Band of Adventurers. — Vivas for Bourbon. — The Grand Imperial Army. — In Pursuit of Bourbon. — The Doomed City. — Death of Charles de Bourbon. — Fruitless Prayers. — The Sack of Rome.

WHEN the Duchesse d'Alençon married Henry of Navarre, a young English girl, who since the death of Queen Claude had been a member of her household, left France and returned to her family in England, where she was introduced to the court as one of the ladies of Queen Katharine. This young girl was Anne Boleyn, who, if born in 1507 — the most probable date given — was then in her twentieth year. The freshness of youth, fine eyes, an elegant figure, and an abundance of auburn hair, were her chief personal attractions, which, with a lively disposition and the graces of manner she had acquired in France, completely fascinated Henry VIII.

For some time previously he had meditated seeking a reversal of the dispensation obtained from Pope Julian II., enabling him to marry Katharine of Aragon, his brother's widow. After eighteen years of marriage he began to grow weary of her. "She who hitherto had been so serious, had taken," he said, "to laughing, to going out, to kissing her hand to the people who cheered her, and to showing no sympathy with him — and this merely to vex her liege lord" ("State Papers"). Naturally, he became much troubled in mind, a prey to anxiety and a remorseful conscience, lest, by his marriage with Katharine, he had, peradventure, unwittingly done what was unlawful.

When first assailed by these doubts he appears to have been desirous of marrying the Duchesse d' Alençon, whose sisterly devotion in journeying to Spain to console her brother, and to facilitate, if possible, his release, had greatly charmed him. He had serious thoughts of then asking her in marriage, that she might hold herself in readiness at once to fill Katharine's place when vacant. Some correspondence, diplomatically vague, seems to have passed on the subject, but of course no such premature demand for her hand could be seriously entertained, while political motives also made it inexpedient to give any encouragement at that moment to Henry's views for the repudiation of the emperor's aunt.

Francis had, indeed, more than enough on hand of his own arrangements to settle with the emperor, than appeared likely to terminate without having recourse once more to war. Not that he allowed his troubles to interfere with his pleasures. Quite the reverse; for the arrival at Cognac of Lannoy, the Viceroy of Naples, and other ambassadors, charged by the emperor again to demand the execution of the Treaty of Madrid, was but the signal for further festivities. Lannoy, who had done his best to mediate, though with little or no success, between Francis and Charles, was received most graciously, and the embassy in general entertained magnificently. The king amused and detained them, in fact, while he gave his adherence to the Holy League for the expulsion of the emperor from Italy.

Probably that which more exasperated than amused them was the scene got up as a reply to the demand of their imperial master. The notables and prelates of the realm were convoked at Cognac personally to inform the emperor's delegates that "the dismemberment of France was not in the king's power. They would not suffer it; and should he think of commanding it, he would not be obeyed." The deputies of the states of Burgundy were then introduced, and "solemnly declared they would submit to no change in the government of their country. From the time of Clovis," they said, "they had been governed by princes of France, and would continue to be. If Francis I. should abandon them, they were determined then to take up arms to resist any other domination."

Informed of this, Charles, greatly irritated at having been so completely duped by Francis, replied that "if the king had not the power to dispose of his provinces, he at least was able to fulfil his oath and return to captivity. Let him not," he said, "throw on his subjects the odium of his own bad faith. To fulfil his engagements he has but to return to Spain. Let him do so!" Francis's sole response was to read aloud in the presence of Lannoy the terms of the treaty with the Pope and the Italian states, which until that morning he had deferred signing.

Henry VIII. was declared protector of the Holy League. He was to receive a large sum of money after certain stated conquests had been made. He took no active part in it; but in consideration of an annual payment of 50,000 crowns, renounced his pretensions to the throne of France. As soon as Francis had signed this league, Clement VII. absolved him from the oath he had taken to fulfil the stipulations of the Treaty of Madrid.

A Diet of the empire was then assembled at Spire, to which Francis sent an ambassador to explain that "although the King of France would willingly, like Regulus, have returned to captivity and undergone the most cruel torments rather than fail in his word, his subjects and the safety of his country would not permit of this self-sacrifice. He offered, therefore, two million crowns for the retention of Burgundy and the ransom of his sons."

The allusion to the Roman consul Regulus was a singularly unhappy one. The ambassador must have introduced it into his message in irony.

The Holy League, which was to free Italy from a foreign yoke, failed entirely from want of troops, want of money, and in some instances want of will, to accomplish the object in view. The same wants prevented the emperor from effectually opposing this league, for his coffers, like those of his grandsire Maximilian, were always empty; and although his fleets were constantly entering his ports laden with the spoils of the Indies, yet their cost is said to have often exceeded what they returned, at least to the treasury of the state. His army, which for several months had received no pay, was destitute of clothing and also ill-provisioned, refused to march when ordered.

But the disunion of the Italian states, and the failure of Francis to send the aid he had promised in troops and money — for he sought rather to sacrifice them to his interests than to assist them in supporting their own — served the imperial cause almost as well as an army. The Pope and the Venetian states remonstrated. But Francis was too deeply immersed in pleasure to feel any anxiety about the fate of his allies; and his tenderly attached mother would not allow any matters of business likely to be annoying or wearisome to be submitted to him. She preferred to manage them herself.

Bourbon's desperate condition, and the project attributed to him of turning the difficulties of both emperor and king to account and conquering a kingdom for himself independent of· them, was also a means of laying Italy once more prostrate and at the mercy of Charles V.

Charles was desirous of recompensing the great services Bourbon had rendered him, and Pescara dying suddenly (poisoned, it was suspected), he gave him the sole command of an army that existed not. He promised him, too, the sovereignty of Milan, if he could conquer that duchy, and with a very small sum of money and a roving commission sent him forth, somewhat after the manner of a freebooter, to levy such troops as he could, and with them subdue or conquer.

The name of Charles de Bourbon was a power in Italy and the German states amongst those roving bands of mercenaries who hired themselves out to fight for those who paid them best, or, in default of pay, permitted unrestrained plunder. Thousands soon flocked to his standard — Italians, Spaniards, and Germans — the money he had brought with him not sufficing to enroll them all at a crown per head. How were these conquering hosts to be paid — for no further remittance of funds was sent to him — except by plundering the cities that had declared against the emperor?

He had driven out Sforza from Milan, and promised the unfortunate Milanese, who regarded him as a saviour, soon to return to them. Whatever his motives — whether to conquer on his own account, or to break up the league against the emperor — Bourbon assembled his adventurous bands, for the most part old soldiers who had already served under him; courageous, pitiless, but devoted to their chief. He told them that he was as destitute as they were, that he was now a poor cavalier with nothing but his sword to depend on; that he could offer them no pay; that they would have much hardship and privation to endure, but that supporting it bravely he would lead them to victory and wealth. With enthusiasm they shouted " *Vive* Bourbon!" and vowed to follow wherever he led, even "*à tous les diables.*"

The ransom of two or three prisoners at Milan furnished him with the means of distributing a trifle of money amongst those dauntless hordes. In three separate bands — Italian, Spanish, and German — headed by Bourbon, Philibert de Chalons, Prince of Orange (another great commander, of whom Francis had made an implacable enemy), and Georges Freundsberg, they began their march. It was the depth of winter; yet they were full of spirits, observing also from habit a kind of discipline that under the circumstances could hardly have been enforced. Wholly without provisions or other necessaries for the equipment of an army, they subsisted on what the inhabitants of the villages and small towns they passed through, instigated by terror, eagerly supplied them with; their commanders sharing their hardships. The once brilliant and wealthy Charles de Bourbon plodded on on foot like the rest; his sole retinue, one of his soldier band, leading a weary-footed mule, the bearer of all he possessed — his armour.

Terror spread throughout Italy. The principal cities put themselves in a state of defence, for none knew where this grand imperial army, on conquest and plunder bent, would strike its first blow.

Meanwhile, for nearly two months, onward they march, cutting their way through thick forests, fording swollen rivers, traversing with extreme difficulty mountain roads, where the snow already lies thick and is still falling fast. Too often they are without food; too many without clothing to defend their toil-worn bodies from the rigours of the winter, and the best shod at the outset are now shoeless. Courage begins to fail these bands of desperadoes. The stoutest hearts and strongest frames succumb to starvation, disappointed hopes, and misery, and sinking on the ground seem resigned to die.

Others are more disposed to mutiny, to menace their commander-in-chief, even to whisper the word "cowardice." For several cities they had approached on their route — Placentia, Bologna, and others — Bourbon had seen fit to retreat from, finding them too well guarded, too well prepared to resist the attack of ill-disciplined troops wanting artillery and other necessaries for successful warfare.

But although adverse fate had made him almost as desperate as the men who followed his fortunes, Bourbon was generous and humane. He possessed also a sort of eloquence that greatly swayed the soldiery, and gave him considerable power over them. Addressing them on the present occasion, he soothed their anger, revived their courage, and by promises (terrible promises, certainly) of great booty to compensate their sufferings, called on them still to endure. As usual, they responded by vivas and oaths of fidelity.

In great alarm for the safety of Florence and Rome, Clement VII., after heaping reproaches on the libertine King of France, concluded a truce with Lannoy for a period of eight months — the head of the league being thus withdrawn from it. In all haste messengers were despatched in various directions in pursuit of Bourbon and his wild band, to stay their march, in consequence of the suspension of arms. It was too late. Already his troops were ravaging the papal territories, and seemed to be on their way to Florence.

Hearing of a truce, the men began to rave and threaten; and Lannoy, who sought Bourbon in his camp, dared not approach it. Disregarding the message he brought, the line of march was suddenly changed, and the cry was no longer " To

Florence!" but "To Rome!" On the 5th of May, Bourbon encamped before that doomed city; the men, as they came in sight of it, loudly singing in praise of their leader as he pointed to its palaces and churches. Having posted his troops behind St. Peter's, he sent a trumpet demanding permission to enter the city and purchase provisions.

On the morning of the 6th the attack began, the army being divided into three brigades. The mists of daybreak concealed their advance from the Romans until they had nearly approached the moat that surrounded the ancient city walls. Then each brigade rushed to the assault, shouting the refrain of a song they had composed in Bourbon's honour —

> "*Silence à vous, César, Annibal et Scipion!*
> *Vive la gloire de Bourbon!*"

The first two assaults were repulsed with vigour. The third was lead by Bourbon himself. He was clad in complete armour, over which he wore a casaque of silver tissue, that his troops, recognising him foremost in the fight, might be inspired with fiercer courage. He had beheld with dismay the repulse of the first two brigades; they now returned to the charge to support the third. Leaping from his horse, he seized a scaling ladder, planted it against the walls, and was ascending it.

Louise of Savoy, Duchesse d'Angoulême.
Photo-etching from painting in the
Chateau de Beauregarde.

But at that moment a shot fired from the ramparts near San-Spirito laid him low.

Some accounts say that Bourbon died immediately, shot through the heart, and that the Prince of Orange, who succeeded him in the chief command, threw a cloak over him to conceal his death from the soldiery, and prevent the consternation and confusion that would have immediately ensued. Another statement is that Bourbon, feeling that he was wounded, was assisted to descend, and carried into a neighbouring chapel. The Thracian Gate being afterwards taken, he was conveyed into the Church of San-Sisto, where a priest was found to confess him. He desired to be taken to Milan, though some fancied he meant Rome, as he died murmuring "À Rome! à Rome!"*

Thus died Charles de Bourbon, the victim of the intrigues, the infamous arts, the persecution of a shameless woman of unbridled passions — the evil genius of France. "Spain, whom he served too well, neglected him; France, whom he betrayed, pitied him, and cast all her hatred and horror of his revolt on the Duchesse d'Angoulême who had driven him to it" (Servan).

But the death of Bourbon did not save Rome.

---

* The sculptor Cellini claims to have fired the shot that proved fatal to Bourbon. He gives an account of the siege and sack of Rome in his memoirs, and, as usual with him, states that his part in it was a conspicuous one.

The soldiers were soon aware that their general was killed. Their rage was furious. They vowed to avenge his death. "Bourbon! Bourbon! blood! blood! carnage! revenge!" they screeched in the madness of their wrath. The assault was renewed, and speedily these brigand bands were in possession of the Holy City.

Clement VII., on their approach, excommunicated Bourbon and the whole of his army, and during the combat was offering up fruitless prayers for victory at the altar of St. Peter's, though he had neglected to take the most ordinary precaution to prevent defeat or to secure the safety of the city. When the shrieks and lamentations of the unfortunate people met his ear, and he knew that Rome was taken by a barbarous and pitiless enemy, Italians as well as Spaniards and Germans, he fled to the castle of St. Angelo.

The sack of Rome is one of the most terrible events of warfare that history records. No quarter was given. All were slain without regard to age or sex. The most horrible tortures were inflicted to extort money or to compel their unhappy victims to declare where treasure was concealed. Drunk with fury, they committed excesses which the mind recoils from dwelling upon, while the pen depicts them. Churches and palaces were plundered, and Rome remained for some months in the possession of these brutal drunken hordes, wholly deaf to the voice of humanity. Their commander was powerless to restrain them, and it was well for Bourbon that he did not live to witness the unspeakable horrors inflicted by the ruffian bands he had let loose on the Holy City.

CHAPTER XX.

Relieved from a Difficulty. — Clement VII. a Prisoner. — War for the Release of the Pope. — The Pope's Ransom. — Clement Escapes in Disguise. — The Divorce and Absolution. — Burgundy or Captivity. — Royal Condescension! — A Bold and Startling Opinion. — Magnanimous Frenchmen! — The Challenge and the Reply. — The Chevalier King Holds Back. — Marriage of Madame Renée. — Madame Renée's Bridal Dress. — Edifying and Effective. — An Accomplished Pupil. — The French Fleet in the Levant. — Loss of a Faithful Ally. — Heretics and Infidels. — Two Wily Female Diplomatists. — The Ladies' Peace. — New Coinage for the Ransom. — Mutual Precautions. — The Spanish Bride. — Fall of Florence.

THAT Rome had fallen; that the Pope was a prisoner — besieged in the Castle of St. Angelo, to which untenable fortress, with strange fatuity, he had fled for safety — was unlooked-for news that gratified Charles V. no less than it surprised him. The death of Bourbon, to whom he owed victories towards which he had supplied neither money nor men, also relieved him from much difficulty — that of suitably rewarding the man who had declined to become his courtier; who yet served him with his sword while intent on avenging his own great wrongs and creating a future for himself, independent of both emperor and king.

Great, however, as his satisfaction may have been at an event so favourable to his political views, Charles felt compelled by the indignation expressed throughout Europe at the horrors of the sack of Rome — surpassing all that history relates of the atrocities of Alaric and his Visigoths, and in which Spaniards had been the most conspicuous for the savage brutality of their crimes — to hasten publicly to disclaim all knowledge of Bourbon's intention of assaulting the Holy City.

His queen had just given birth to an heir to the Spanish crown, and for the celebration of this auspicious event preparations on a grand scale had been ordered. They were now countermanded, and general festivity gave place to general mourning. Religious processions paraded the streets, carrying the relics and shrines of the most popular saints. The churches were thronged, and day and night prayers were offered up throughout Spain for the release of God's vicegerent.

Yet the Pope was the prisoner of an army that fought under the imperial banner, and whose commander-in-chief held the city in the emperor's name.* The Pope's ransom was fixed by the army at 400,000 ducats, though an order from

---

* Freundsberg did not enter Rome with his lansquenets. Their mutinous conduct while on their march so enraged him that a fit of apoplexy ensued, which proved fatal.

Charles, one might suppose, would have set him free at once. It was believed, however, that the desperadoes cantonned in Rome would have wholly disregarded his order, and probably have committed further outrages. The odium of his detention nevertheless rested on the emperor.

Henry VIII. and Francis I. announced their intention of releasing the pontiff by force of arms, — Henry engaging to contribute a large proportion of the sum required for the pay and equipment of the army, which was to be raised in France, and commanded by Maréchal Lautrec. Preparations for resuming the war were speedily begun. Charles, in consequence, relaxed a little towards Francis, offering to accept the terms he had himself proposed when a captive. But Francis, now free, would listen to no such arrangement.

More than a twelvemonth had elapsed from the time of the king's liberation ere he entered his capital. He then thought it right to visit the chapel of Ste. Calez — the saint to whom he had especially addressed his prayers in captivity. Her shrine, with those of other holy saints and martyrs, had been on the altar during the whole period of his absence, in order to ensure that success which, it appears, it was not their good pleasure to grant him. The shrines were now replaced in their niches, the saints' good offices having once more been entreated for the future. "The king and his court then returned to St. Germain-en-Laye, where they remained some time, — Francis going to Paris at night only, masked, and in disguise."

The army designed for the liberation of the Pope made several conquests in Italy, Maréchal Lautrec, as he steadily advanced towards the Papal states, taking and ravaging many towns to avenge former defeats of the French. Charles, fearing therefore that the Pope would be freed by main force, proposed to release him on payment of 250,000 ducats to the imperial troops; his two nephews being delivered into the charge of the imperial generals as hostages until the whole of the ransom — now increased to 500,000 — should be fully paid. Several other stipulations were added, to all of which Clement assented, without any intention of fulfilling them. He had supported with little dignity the inconveniences of captivity, to which his own folly had doomed him, and as soon as provisions failed surrendered the castle and all its treasures.

He now determined not to put himself into the power of the Spaniards, but rather to carry out a plan he had carefully arranged for his flight, which he effected on the 9th of December, the evening previous to that appointed for completing the arrangements with the imperialists for his liberation. His disguise was a blouse, a long false beard, and a tattered slouched hat, which partly concealed his head and face. He had a basket on his arm, and an empty sack on his back. No suspicion being excited, he passed the sentinels unchallenged, supposed to be one of the domestics of the major-domo of the papal palace. Travelling all night — a conveyance having been in waiting for him — he was safely housed in the dilapidated, old episcopal palace of Orvieto before his escape was discovered.

Some few days after, the Pope received at Orvieto the unwelcome visit of an English envoy, deputed by Henry VIII. to request that the dispensation from his former marriage, which his holiness had promised before his captivity to forward to the king, might now be entrusted to him; his highness's grace being set on marrying Madame Anne Boleyn. "Clement was much perplexed by this ill-timed demand. He admitted the promise, but pleaded recent events as a valid excuse for its non-fulfilment; while from the dread he was then in of the resentment of the Spaniards, and also because of the charge received from the emperor to do nothing prejudicial to the queen, he must beg at least," he said, "for delay."

But Knight vehemently protested against any further delay. "Had not his holiness already informed his royal master that he would comply with his desire? Now he strove to evade it. How, then, could he expect his word to be trusted to in future? Thus closely pressed, a promise was at last wrung from the Pope — "though it cut him to the heart " — to send the divorce to Henry, but on condition that it should not be acted upon until after he, Clement, was fully restored to liberty.

Some months later Clement made his peace with Charles V. One of the secret articles of this treaty stipulated that the Pope should give absolution to all the soldiers who had taken part in the excesses committed in Rome; the emperor desiring to make use of this horde of demons in his "holy war" against the infidel, Solyman II., who had invaded Hungary and threatened Vienna. " In an age so fertile in instances of striking immorality," writes M. Henri Martin, "there was perhaps none more scandalous than this papal absolution, covering every crime that hell itself could have dreamt of." Charles V. confirmed the leaders in their command, and made no scruple of taking every advantage of the sacrilegious victory they had obtained for him.

Meanwhile, negotiation with no satisfactory result had been continued between Francis I. and the emperor. The latter still demanded Burgundy or the king's return to captivity. Francis was willing to yield on all points except Burgundy and a Spanish prison, but repeated his offer of two million crowns to redeem the duchy and to ransom his sons. He proposed, also, to renew his engagement to Eleanor, whose dowry was a million crowns, which dowry was not to be paid, so that nominally the ransom offered amounted to three millions.

The Duchesse d' Étampes, whose favour and influence were daily increasing, seemed likely to develop, under an air of gaiety and thoughtlessness, into a formidable political intriguer. She already exacted as much homage as though she were Queen of France; and the power over the king she secretly exerted was immense, while openly she affected to receive the monarch's attentions with extremest diffidence and reserve. The prospect of a new queen at the Court of France in no way dismayed her. " If the king married Eleanor it would not affect her position; and if his marriage was a political necessity, she would be the last of his advisers to oppose it."

Francis had, however, become weary of this long-pending negotiation with the emperor. He wanted money for his wars, for his pleasures, and one must at least give him credit for desiring to ransom his sons; the more so as Charles had cynically informed him that the climate of Spain did not seem to agree with the dauphin.

The Pope had absolved Francis from his oath. He would now be absolved by his people — just because it was his *bon plaisir* that their voice should be with him on this occasion. Yet he forbore to assemble the States General in which the people would have had a voice, but convoked a "bed of justice," or assembly of notables, for the 12th of December in Paris.

Francis appeared in person, and while deprecating the idea of any body of men in the state attempting to limit his authority, condescended to explain to them his position towards Charles V. "He spoke of the indignities he had endured in captivity, and of his object in assembling his trusty councillors, his faithful subjects and vassals — his need, in fact, of subsidies. If the emperor accepted peace, he would promptly require two millions of gold crowns for the ransom of the young princes, his hostages. If he declared for war, he would still want the same sum for the expenses of his armies; unless the friends, as he considered them, whose advice he now asked should be of opinion that honour demanded his return to Spain."

Of course their answer was not doubtful; he ran no risk by consulting them. Yet there was one voice against him. Bishop Poncher, of the diocese of Paris, was of opinion that the king was under an obligation to return to Spain, and that, in the event of his doing so, some limits should be placed to the authority of the regent. The boldness of this advice or opinion startled and alarmed the assembly,* who were then dismissed to take into consideration the best means for satisfying the king's needs, and to assemble again on the 30th.

* It was considered high treason, and some days after the bishop was seized and put in prison, where eventually he died.

On this second occasion Cardinal Bourbon, in the name of the clergy, offered 300,000 gold crowns as their contribution towards the two millions, on these conditions : That the king should endeavour to obtain the Pope's release ; that he should exterminate the Lutheran heresy, and that he should preserve the immunities of the Church. The Duc de Vendôme on the part of the nobility, the President de Selve for the Parliaments, and the provost of the merchants for the city of Paris, declared their readiness to provide the ransom of the young princes.

Amidst great enthusiasm Francis was declared absolved from his oath, the Treaty of Madrid null and void, and his loyal subjects prepared, as they assured him, to die rather than allow his return to imprisonment.

Francis was but little accustomed to have his wants so promptly supplied and with such earnest expressions of satisfaction.

"Magnanimous Frenchmen!" he exclaimed, much elated, "I will live then in your midst, as you tell me my presence is necessary among you." To which he added the gracious assurance that "he would always take their advice in good part," though he did not promise that he would follow it.

By way of rejoinder to these proceedings, the emperor put the plenipotentiaries of both Henry and Francis under arrest. The two kings responded by challenging him — "Clarencieux," king-at-arms, and "Guyenne," the French king's herald, conveying the challenges to Burgos, where Charles, in full audience, received those important personages.

To the English king-at-arms he spoke very calmly, and with an affected indifference that seemed to say his challenge was scarcely worth notice. But towards the French herald he assumed a very different tone. The prudent, phlegmatic Charles lost all command of his temper. His indignation was boundless, and bitter invectives and uncomplimentary epithets were unsparingly heaped on Francis — his prisoner, as he termed him — whose presumption in addressing such a declaration to him utterly amazed him.

The herald, being unwilling to repeat the emperor's message to the king, feigned to have forgotten the chief part of it. The emperor renewed it for the king's edification. "He had acted," he said, "in a cowardly manner, wickedly, maliciously, and, if he averred to the contrary, he would maintain it personally against him." "Guyenne" returned to Charles with a written challenge, in which he was told he "lied in the throat," and a place of meeting was demanded. It appears that a delay of some months occurred before this challenge reached Charles, when, instead of naming the place for their rendezvous and returning it by "Guyenne," he sent it by his own herald, "Burgundy."

The place he appointed was the river Bidassoa, the particular spot — some island, probably — to be selected by gentlemen chosen by the combatants respectively. Charles demanded Francis's reply within forty days; failing which, the delay of the combat must rest with him.

Europe looked on amused while the heralds of the emperor and the King of France (Henry VIII. seems to have withdrawn from the contest) were travelling to and fro with challenges, defiant messages, and furious demands that the lists be appointed. The result of this combat, when first announced, was anxiously awaited. But months passed on, and no combat took place. Charles cooled down, and idle taunts and recriminations abated the keenness of resentment. Yet, strangely enough, it was the "chevalier king" who occasioned the delays and raised up the obstacles that prevented so famous a rencounter. The prudent and politic Charles was far more in earnest than he.

But in spite of the horrors of wars that were ended, and the preparations for those to come, France, through the length and breadth of the land, was looking joyously forward to much festivity. Madame Renée, the younger daughter of Louis XII., after her many betrothals, was about to marry the young Duke of Ferrara, Herculano d' Este, son of the Duke Alfonso and Lucretia Borgia. Renée, who had just entered her eighteenth year, was a lively, piquante brunette, greatly resembling her mother, Anne of Brittany, as well in character (having a decided will of her own) as personally, which in after years was proved by her fearless protection of the reformers, and the very great interest she took in art and letters.

Her marriage is described by that dilligent *chroniqueur*— "*Le Bourgeois de Paris*"—as a very stately ceremony, and an event of deep interest to all. It was attended by the barons of Brittany, their wives and daughters, and the principal ladies and gentlemen of that duchy, also by the princes, princesses, and grand seigneurs of France. The Cardinal Archbishop of Sens, Duprat, chancellor of finance, married the happy pair "at the door of the Ste. Chapelle, and low mass was afterwards chanted by the treasurer (bishop) of the chapel."

Madame Renée, following the example of her sister, the late Queen Claude, endeavoured to retain in vogue the graceful fashions introduced by Anne of Brittany. The costumes of the ladies generally, varying, of course, in colour and material, were similar, on this occasion, to that of the bride, who wore an under-dress of rich white Lyons satin, over it a long training skirt, open in front, of Venetian silver brocade, with bodice and hanging sleeves bordered with jewels, and confined at the waist by a silver *cordelière* with tassels of silver intermingled with jewels. Her hat was of white velvet with narrow brim, edged with pearls and diamonds, a small white plume and long veil of Italian tissue falling low at the back. A band of jewels round her throat, and Italian gloves fringed and jewelled, completed the young duchess's *toilette*. Doubtless the dress of the bridegroom was no less elegant than the bride's. For we know that the gentlemen of that day vied with the ladies in the richness of their attire, their velvets, satins, laces, plumes, and jewels.

The bride's return to the palace was made the occasion of a popular ovation, illuminations, fireworks, etc. The "Bourgeois" speaks of it as "*un grand triomphe.*" A sumptuous banquet in the great hall of St. Louis was followed by a state ball, while still further to honour and to sanctify the happy event, "two Turks, brought from Rhodes by the grand master, were baptised on the marriage day." The ceremony of regenerating these infidel dogs proved a no less edifying than effective and impressive solemnity, the chevaliers of the Order of Rhodes attending in full array as sponsors.

For several weeks, the court was a continued scene of gaiety and festivity, jousts and tournaments, hunting-parties, masques, banquets, and balls succeeded each other without intermission, banishing all unwelcome thoughts that might otherwise have troubled the king. Burgundy, the emperor and his challenges, the Pope at Orvieto, the prayer of Lautrec for money to pay his troops, the poor little princes in Spain pining for home, all were forgotten by Francis, immersed in a daily round of pleasures.

Gayest among the revellers was the young Duchesse d'Étampes, giving little heed to her royal lover, and none at all to those passing caprices, those sudden fits of admiration, with which other *belles* inspired him, and which, at times, seemed to threaten the continuance of her reign. But she exercised so singularly fascinating an influence over him, that she could recall him a captive at her feet at her will. His infidelities gave her no pain, for she had no affection whatever for him.

She was ambitious of political power, yet preferred to exert it indirectly by artfully suggesting her views to the king, as if in mere playfulness, and by skilfully flattering his self-love, in which she was an adept, leading him to believe those views were his own, and all her political wisdom derived from him. Madame Louise had reason to be proud of her pupil. It would almost seem that she was especially trained to succeed her.

Courtly festivities and general rejoicings at last came to an end, and the young Duke and Duchess of Ferrara left France for Italy.

The fortune of war, meanwhile, had turned in

favour of Maréchal Lautrec, whose former exploits had been but a series of disasters. After the escape of the Pope from St. Angelo, Lautrec marched with his army on Naples, took several towns, and nearly completed the conquest of the kingdom, the city alone holding out. To prevent supplies reaching the garrison, the port was blockaded by Genoese vessels commanded by Philippino Doria, nephew of the famous Andrea Doria. The Spanish galleys attacked them, were beaten off, and the viceroy and the Prince of Orange taken prisoners. Andrea was expected with nineteen vessels to complete the blockade, which would have assured the conquest of Naples to France.

But that strange fatality that always attended the interference of the king lost him both Genoa and Naples. The former had just been restored to France by Doria, the Genoese requesting to be governed by their own laws and ancient usages. This the king refused, proposing also to transfer from Genoa to Savona the right to receive the duty on salt. At the same time, he sent an insulting message to Doria, and his dismissal as "admiral in the Levant." Doria had considered the viceroy and general, taken by his nephew in his own vessels, as his prisoners, not the king's. Francis was indignant, sent the Comte de Barbezieux to supersede him, and to arrest him if he could.

Doria had formed a squadron of twelve vessels wholly equipped by himself. With them were a few galleys — "Francis's fleet in the Levant." These latter Doria delivered to his successor, who neither could nor dared attempt to arrest him. The vessels blockading Naples were withdrawn, the garrison immediately revictualled, and the long-coveted conquest of that kingdom was lost to France. The Genoese, finding that one source of commercial profit was to be withdrawn from them, and the removal of other branches of trade also threatened, declared themselves free, called on their countryman, Doria, to defend them, and offered him the title of Doge.

Their request he complied with; the title they would confer on him he declined. The only result, therefore, of the king's ill-timed petulance was the loss of Naples and Genoa, and the services of a faithful ally, much attached to France, yet a zealous patriot. Further reverses occurred in the north of Italy. The plague spread to the French camp. Maréchal Lautrec died of it, and three-fourths of his army. Général de Saint-Pol was surprised by the Spaniards at Londriano, taken prisoner, and nearly the whole of his small army mercilessly massacred. These events, together with the defection of the Pope, the head of the league, at last convinced Francis that he could not reestablish himself in Italy. He began, therefore, to be disgusted with war. The laurel crown had no longer charms for him. Freedom from war's anxieties, leisure for the pursuit of pleasure and the encouragement of letters and *les beaux arts* were now, to his fancy, all that made life desirable.

Peace! then — peace with honour if possible — but peace at all events and at any price!

The embarrassments of Charles V. made peace with France and Italy almost a necessity also with him. He had both heretics and infidels to combat, and, with the blessing of heaven and the holy saints, as he hoped, to conquer; though neither the one nor the other seemed to fear his menaces.

Those sovereign princes of Germany and imperial cities that had embraced the reformed religion were preparing to take up arms in defence of their faith against both the emperor and the German Catholic states. At a second Diet held at Spire in April, 1529, they had protested against a decree of the emperor, then announced, enacting that severest pains and penalties, and in some cases death, should be inflicted on those obstinate heretics who continued to profess Lutheranism or other heretical doctrine. After this solemn protest the princes and deputies of the cities withdrew from the Diet.*

The infidels were, perhaps, more formidable opponents than the heretics, who required only to be allowed to worship God in peace after their

---

* From this time the Lutherans and other reformers were called Protestants.

own manner. Solyman the Magnificent had overrun Hungary, driven out the Austrians, and received the homage, as his vassal, of its elected king, John Zapoly. At the head of his overwhelming and conquering hosts, with whom were joined his Christian tributaries, and in whose camp was a secret agent of the King of France, Solyman was preparing to march on Vienna.

In this dilemma a truce was signed at Hampton Court by Henry VIII. with Margaret of Austria, Governess of the Netherlands, on the part of Charles V. and Bishop Jean du Bellay for Francis I. This truce led to a general peace. As no amicable arrangement of their differences seemed possible between the emperor and the king, and as their plenipotentiaries were also unable to come to one for them, the discussion and settlement of the conditions of peace were confided to two wily female diplomatists — Margaret of Austria and Louise of Savoy.

These ladies met at Cambray, armed with full powers from their respective sovereigns. Two adjoining houses were prepared for their reception, and a communication opened between them, in order that no prying eyes might watch their going in or coming out or take note of the length of their conferences. No person whatever was admitted to them, lest suggestion or comment should embarrass them, or impose restraint on the fulness of their interchange of thought and opinion. The Treaty of Madrid was taken as the basis of the new agreement, and a sort of modification of it was signed by Mesdames Margaret and Louise on the 5th of August.

The Treaty of Cambray, called *la Paix des Dames* — the Ladies' Peace — was considered even more disgraceful than that of Madrid, and the reproach and dishonour of the reign of Francis I. His intention, however, was to execute as much only of the treaty as was convenient to him; and while sacrificing all his allies after compromising them, he made secret promises to defend them. Especially to the Florentines, who were contending for their freedom against emperor and Pope, he promised to send aid as soon as he had ransomed his sons. To excuse the baseness of his submission to the emperor in the eyes of the people, he complained vehemently before the Parliament of the pressure put upon him by Charles to extort over and above the ransom of the children in ready money a part of their patrimony. But his promise to reinstate Bourbon's heirs and the Prince of Orange in their possessions remained almost wholly unfulfilled.

Not until the 1st of July, 1530, did the exchange of the hostages for their ransom take place, though fixed for the 10th of March. It had occurred to the chancellor Duprat that by coining new money with a hundredth part of alloy more than that in general use, a gain of 40,000 crowns on the two millions might be effected — of course, under the delusion that the fraud would pass undiscovered. The Spaniards, however, were rigidly severe respecting the purity of their own coin, and, besides, had probably some suspicion of the intended deterioration of this new French money.

At all events, the masters of the Spanish mint were sent to Bayonne to test, conjointly with the chiefs of the French mint, the coin offered in payment of the ransom. A deficiency in value was proved to the extent above named, which Duprat was compelled to make good. This dishonourable transaction created in the Spaniards a feeling of great distrust of the French, and after the money had been counted and tested, and locked up in forty-eight cases bearing the double seal of the masters of the French and Spanish mints, the grandmaster and marshal of France, Anne de Montmorency, was required to supervise its conveyance to the French shore of the Bidassoa.

In the middle of that stream a small vessel was anchored, where, as when Francis was released, the exchange was to be made. On the Spanish side the constable of Castile with the two young princes awaited the arrival of the ransom — the Portuguese queen with her retinue being with them, and temporarily lodged in the neighbourhood. A very strict lookout seems to have been kept up on the Spanish shore as the treasure and its convoy approached. The movements of a small detachment of troops that followed the grand marshal appeared to the Spanish officer so suspicious, that he fancied some conspiracy was on foot to seize the princes when they came to the river's edge, and to withhold the ransom.

A panic seized him. He ordered the princes and the people that were with him to mount. and, though night was drawing on, galloped off with the precious charge confided to him into the interior — the queen following in her litter. A delay of nearly four months was thus occasioned. At last, when precautions sufficiently humiliating on both sides had been taken against a surprise, the exchange was effected in mid-stream on the 1st of July.

Queen Eleanor afterwards crossed the river in a boat, — several boats following with her retinue. The king was there to receive her, to whom she curtseyed most profoundly, he bowing almost to the ground in the same ceremonious manner. She was dressed in the Spanish costume, and wore many jewels. "Her earrings were diamonds as large as walnuts." The king married her without any delay, and almost privately, at the small chapel of the Convent of de Verrières. He then conducted her to Bordeaux, where, on her entry, the exceeding magnificence of her dress, the splendour of her jewels, and her hat with a plume and feathered edge like the king's, created considerable sensation.

The disgraceful treaty of Cambray, a triumph for Charles V., covered Francis I. with opprobrium. With it terminated the political career of Louise of Savoy. It would almost seem that she herself, on reflecting on her work, had been stung by remorse for the disgrace she had contributed to inflict on France and her son. No prominent part appears to have again been taken by her in public affairs, and in little more than a year after the fatal treaty was signed she died at Grez, a village in Orléans. Immense sums, abstracted from the revenues of the state, were found in her coffers after her death.

Italy now lay prostrate, existing by sufferance, at the feet of Charles V. Yet heretics and infidels then gave him so much occupation in Germany that he was compelled to abate a little of his rigour towards the rebellious Italian states; lest by setting his foot too heavily on the necks of their princes, he should move them to turn again and unite in a struggle for liberty more effectual than before.

Republican Florence alone felt the full weight of his, as well as the Pope's resentment. She had driven out the degenerate Medici, and only on condition that she consented again to submit to their despotic yoke, to receive them as her hereditary rulers, would the emperor listen to any proposals for peace. As many as the plague had spared of those brigand bands he had absolved of their crimes, Clement sent forth to besiege and ravage the city of his birth, and wantonly to afflict its inhabitants.

After treason, rather than force, had subdued them, and the terms of their capitulation were violated, many Florentine citizens fled their country. Many more were sent to the scaffold. Michael Angelo, who had assisted in the defence of the city, was, indeed, pardoned. A man of his genius and ability was not easily replaced, and Clement had need of him. Thus fell the republic of Florence, to wear again, after her heroic struggle for freedom, the chains and fetters forged by the Medici!

END OF VOL. I.

www.ingramcontent.com/pod-product-compliance
Lightning Source LLC
Chambersburg PA
CBHW030215170426
43201CB00006B/90